A Pocketful of Prose

Contemporary
Short Fiction

| A Pocketful of Prose | Contemporary Short Fiction |

David Madden

Louisiana State University

THOMSON

™

WADSWORTH

Australia • Canada • Mexico • Singapore • Spain
United Kingdom • United States

THOMSON
♦
™
WADSWORTH

A Pocketful of Prose: Contemporary Short Fiction
David Madden

Publisher: *Michael Rosenberg*
Acquisitions Editor: *Aron Keesbury*
Development Editor: *Marita Sermolins*
Editorial Assistant: *Cheryl Forman*
Marketing Manager: *Carrie Brandon*
Marketing Assistant: *Dawn Giovanniello*
Associate Marketing Communications
    Manager: *Patrick Rooney*
Production Assistant: *Jen Kostka*

Associate Production Project Manager:
    Karen Stocz
Manufacturing Manager: *Marcia Locke*
Permissions Editor: *Stephanie Lee*
Compositor: *Cadmus Professional
    Communications*
Text Designer: *Jeanne Calabrese*
Cover Designer: *Paula Goldstein*
Printer: *West Group*

Thomson Higher Education
25 Thomson Place
Boston, MA 02210-1202
USA

Asia (including India)
Thomson Learning
5 Shenton Way
#01-01 UIC Building
Singapore 068808

Australia/New Zealand
Thomson Learning Australia
102 Dodds Street
Southbank, Victoria 3006
Australia

Canada
Thomson Nelson
1120 Birchmount Road
Toronto, Ontario M1K 5G4
Canada

UK/Europe/Middle East/Africa
Thomson Learning
High Holborn House
50–51 Bedford Road
London WC1R 4LR
United Kingdom

Latin America
Thomson Learning
Seneca, 53
Colonia Polanco
11560 Mexico
D.F. Mexico

Spain (including Portugal)
Thomson Paraninfo
Calle Magallanes, 25
28015 Madrid, Spain

For more information about our products,
contact us at:
**Thomson Learning Academic Resource
Center
1-800-423-0563**

For permission to use material from this
text or product, submit a request online at
http://www.thomsonrights.com.
Any additional questions about
permissions can be submitted by email
to **thomsonrights@thomson.com**

Student Edition: ISBN 1-4130-1561-1
Instructor's Edition: ISBN 1-4130-1912-9

Credits appear on pages 339-341, which
constitute a continuation of the copyright page.

Contents

Preface

THIS VOLUME OF THE POCKETFUL OF
PROSE collection includes twenty-five contemporary stories by
well-known and emerging writers; all have appeared in a wide variety of popular, mass circulation and literary, small circulation
magazines in a single year, 1990. Some of the authors will be recognized as well-known, others are newer to publication. The topics of the stories are as varied as the styles used to present them, but
they all give voice to contemporary experiences and issues.

When we first began developing this volume, the goal was to
represent a variety of authors, publications, styles, and subjects,
while showcasing some of the finest fiction published in 1990. It
was also important to represent writers of different ethnic back-
grounds, ages, experience, and gender. In the final analysis, we
have accomplished each of these goals. The authors (men,
women, minorities, old and young) deal with both present day
and enduring personal problems and public issues, using a variety of styles and techniques.

Note to the Instructor

The stories in this volume can be used in a variety of approaches
to teaching fiction. Instructors using the more traditional artistic approach, which claims that a study of the techniques of fiction prepares students to respond most fully to all the elements
of whatever fiction they may read in the future, will find a variety

of fresh examples and illustrations of these techniques. Instructors who prefer the political approach, which teaches readers to be aware of the way the rhetorical strategies of writers tend to modify or reinforce, and control or change, the political attitudes and behavior of readers, will discover a rich resource of material for discussion.

Both the traditional artistic approach and the newer political approach assert that, without help, most students are ill-prepared to respond fully enough to the most important effects of fiction. As a result of content alone, this volume can be seen as primarily serving the political approach, while the companion *Vintage* volumes primarily serve the artistic approach. However, proponents of each approach are adept enough in their strategies to allow all volumes to serve either purpose.

To what extent the writers themselves, and their readers, are influenced by the revision-of-the-curriculum controversy may become apparent as the study of these stories progresses.

Acknowledgments

In the selection of these stories and the writing of the Introduction, I had the benefit of Peggy Bach's imaginative critical insights.

I would like to thank the reviewers of this text, Robert Esch, of the *University of Texas at El Paso;* Jon G. Bentley of *Albuquerque Technical-Vocational Institute;* and Alma Nugent of *Villa Julie College* who contributed constructive comments in the early stages of the development of this text. We extend a special thanks to those who sent magazines and gave permission for use of the magazines' title lettering in this text. Thanks to Michael Pollin and Ellen Ryder of *Harper's;* Becky Fogle of *McCall's;* Reginald Gibbons of *Tri-Quarterly,* Steve Hill and Cathy S. Jewell of *Antaeus;* Jody A. Benjamin of *Granta;* Rowan Gaither of *The Paris Review;* Eileen Schnurr of *Mademoiselle;* Peter Stitt of *The Gettysburg Review;* Eleanor Sullivan and Russell Atwood of *Ellery Queen's Magazine;* Carolyn Heney and Harry Levine of *Lear's;* Charles H. Rowell of *Callaloo;* Sallie Bingham and Frederick Smock of *American Voice;* Alice K. Turner, Mark Healy, Marcia Terrones and Camy D. Gould of

Playboy; Staige D. Blackford of *Virginia Quarterly;* Richard Burgin of *Boulevard;* Lois Rosenthal of *Story;* Scott L. Towner and Sheila Williams of *Isaac Asimov's Science Fiction Magazine;* Gordon Lish of *The Quarterly;* James McKinley of *New Letters;* Robley Wilson, Jr. of *North American Review;* Caroline Marshall of *PEN;* Jessica Dineen of *Ploughshares;* Jill Frisch and Joy Weiner of *The New Yorker;* Will Blythe and Eric Perret of *Esquire* and T. R. Hummer of *New England Quarterly.*

Special thanks also go to William Abrahams, editor of *The Prize Stories, O. Henry Awards* and Katrina Kenison, editor of *The Best American Short Stories.*

At Wadsworth, my Publisher, Michael Rosenberg, my Acquisitions Editor, Aron Keesbury, and my Developmental Editor, Marita Sermolins, shared my vision of this text and supported m desire to try new approaches to the creation of textbooks. They helped shape the collection from start to finish. Thanks also the Production Project Manager, Karen Stocz, and Designer, Jeanne Calabrese, whose talents made it possible to meet the design and production challenges of the text.

Baton Rouge   *David Madden*

August 1991   *Lousiana State University*

Introduction

Reading Contemporary Short Stories in the 1990's

Features of the contemporary literary scene have determined the criteria for selecting these stories. One intention of this anthology is to satisfy the demand for stories that present the problems facing individuals and society. To secure fiction as current as possible, stories were chosen from issues of magazines published in a single year, 1990. Future editions of this *Contemporary* volume will also draw on the most recent works possible.

The subjects and themes of these stories are both universal and topical. A variety of writers are represented: half are women and several are ethnic writers. They employ both traditional and contemporary techniques. Stories from both commercial, mass circulation magazines and literary, small circulation quarterlies are included.

Stories and articles in magazines tend to deal with the latest contemporary personal and social issues. That concern is readily apparent in each story in this collection. Many of them focus upon personal problems within the context of social issues; even when the author focuses upon social issues, personal conflict is the crucible.

Most of the writers in this anthology published for the first time in the 1980's, some as far back as the late 1960's. It may be illuminating to keep in mind that most, if not all, of the authors of these stories studied writing in university workshops, taught by other writers who are also products of the university creative writing courses that began to appear in greater and greater numbers in the early 1950's. We may imagine them in creative writing workshops exploring with great deliberation the various traditional and innovative techniques of writing fiction (along, perhaps, with those of poetry, playwriting, screenwriting, the personal essay, and the "new journalism"). So as readers of their work, you will perceive their use of techniques they learned in writing workshops. Most of these writers also studied in college the various changing critical approaches to literature, within the dynamic contexts of the political and social controversies that have developed during the past three decades.

Contemporary Issues in Short Stories from Current Magazines

One of the advantages of discussing and writing about very recently published stories by relatively new writers is that, except for reviews, nothing has yet been written about them. That allows greater possibilities for fresh insights. In-class analysis of the more readily accessible magazine and newspaper reviews of anthologies and of collections of stories by individual writers (including some of the writers and stories in this volume) may prove useful. Examining and questioning the claims and assumptions of reviewers may prepare you for your own writing about these stories.

For instance, here are passages from Robert R. Harris' review of Tim O'Brien's *The Things They Carried* in the *New York Times Book Review:* "This is a collection of stories about American soldiers in Vietnam. . . . All of the stories deal with a single platoon. . . . A few are unremittingly brutal; a couple are flawed two-page sketches. . . . Mr. O'Brien strives to get beyond literal descriptions of what these men went through and what they felt. He makes sense of the unreality of the war . . . by probing his memory of the terror and fearlessly confronting the way he has dealt with it as both soldier and fiction writer. In doing all this, he not only crystallizes the Vietnam experience for us, he exposes the nature of all war stories. . . . And by subjecting his memory and imagination to such harsh scrutiny, he seems to have reached a reconciliation, to have made his peace. . . ." After you have read O'Brien's "Field Trip," ask yourself whether any of the above generalizations illuminate the story.

A certain excitement and immediacy infuse the discussion of fiction chosen very recently from the current magazines that make up a literary scene as shifting and ever-changing as individuals and society themselves. In that spirit, included here is a story that simultaneously appeared in regular newspapers around the country and was heard, in a dramatic reading by an actor, over the National Public Radio network, Allen Wier's "Texas Wedding Party."

This collection of stories—among the best of 1990—may guide you as you read stories in magazines from now on. The mass circulation magazines (with circulations as high as three million) appeal mostly to men (*Playboy* and *Esquire*) or mostly to women (*McCall's* and *Mademoiselle*) or to the general reader (*Harper's* and *The New Yorker*). Writers often come suddenly into prominence. The first published stories of Alice Schell and Anya Achtenberg are reprinted here; in 1990 several stories appeared in different kinds of magazines by each of these writers: Rick Bass, Susan Straight, Richard Bausch, Lynna Williams, and E. S. Goldman (who started late in life). But one or two writers in this volume may fade from view or even disappear within a few years.

And that is true of magazines. Although most of the magazines in which these stories appeared have been around for more than 50 years—*The North American Review*, for instance, is in its 175th year—some of the newer literary quarterlies may have suspended publication by the time you read this sentence. At this moment, several indicate that they are changing owners or formats.

The mass circulation magazines consist of fiction, articles, regular columns of advice in various areas of the lives of their readership, and lush ads for a wide variety of products and services, along with letters from readers. The editors' assumption about their readers is that they want a variety of material that takes a similar approach each issue. To lure the reader who is moving through this microcosm, teasers, illustrations, and ads enhance the stories. "I was a meat eater; she was a vegan ecoterroist. Did we have a future?" is the teaser above the title "Carnal

Knowledge" in *Playboy*. A full page illustration of the face of an attractive young blond woman appears opposite. As the reader turns the pages, another teaser, a quotation from the story, appears inset on the page to lure the reader through pages of large and small ads.

By contrast, the editors of literary quarterlies assume that their readers are predisposed to read literature, without enhancements, except for ads announcing more literature. You may imagine how these considerations help to determine the choices writers, editors, and readers make.

To add a dimension to discussion of the personal and social issues raised in these stories (and the techniques used in them) you may want to look through current issues of the magazines from which the stories in this anthology were taken.

To keep track of some of the better stories published each year, you may also want to consult the following annual anthologies that guided the process of considering which writers to include here (editions during the past decade, concentrating on the past three years, were considered): *O. Henry Prize Stories* (started in 1918), edited by William Abrahams; *The Best American Short Stories* (started in 1915), edited by Shannon Ravenel from 1978 to 1990, and co-edited by a different short story writer each year; *The Pushcart Prize: Best of the Small Presses* (started in 1975), edited by Bill Henderson. Because many people still find the category "Southern fiction" useful, *New Stories from the South* (started in 1985), edited by Shannon Ravenel, was consulted. It is quite likely that some of the stories in this volume will appear in one or more of the annuals listed above.

These stories deal with contemporary personal problems and social issues, such as relations between sister and brother ("Brother"); relations between children and parents ("Freedom, A Theory of," "The Leap," "Electric City," "Family Supper"); adoption ("The Mother Who Never Was"); illness ("Kat"); death ("Such Occasions"); love ("Fires"); childhood ("Personal Testimony"); religion ("I Am Here to Tell You It Can Be Done" "Good Works"); jazz ("Lush Life"); the present illuminated by the past ("Texas Wedding Party"); racial conflict ("Trains at Night," "Two Useful Visits"); child abuse

("Slamming on Pig's Misery," "Dragon's Seed"); quality of life among the elderly ("Good Works"); violent crime ("The Man Who Knew Belle Starr"); nuclear crisis ("Desert Blues"); the homeless ("Cold Ground"); life in the ghetto ("Two Days Gone"); animal abuse ("Carnal Knowledge"); ecology ("Bears Discover Fire"). Of course, these stories deal with far more than these topics.

These stories may be seen to support the claim that a major purpose of fiction is to help us understand our roles as children, men and women, husbands and wives, parents, grandparents, and to understand our character, personality, and emotional problems. In the process of coming to understand ourselves, we understand others, because our problems reflect the problems of others within the larger social and political context. And understanding those contexts helps us to understand ourselves. For instance, "I Am Here to Tell You It Can Be Done" and "Personal Testimony" deal with ways institutional religion affects individuals within the family or larger social context.

As you discuss these stories from perspectives that one may call, in the broadest sense of the word, "political," you may want to speculate on this question: In so far as the most worthwhile fiction *reflects* (and interprets and sometimes takes a stand on) aspects of society, does (or should) it also *affect* society? And if so, how? Comparatively, how do the various types of fiction—so-called commercial and literary—*reflect* and *affect* society?

Elements and Techniques of Contemporary Fiction

The artistic approach to the study of fiction focuses upon techniques; the "political" or social approach examines techniques in different ways, sometimes to show how writers, especially in the past, have insidiously, though not necessarily consciously, controlled reader responses to promote results of questionable value to mankind at various stages in history. Setting aside, for the moment, these two polar approaches, it might be helpful if we take a look at some of the more technical features of the kinds of stories that, given the objectives previously described, have been chosen for inclusion in this anthology.

Setting: Always an important consideration in fiction, setting is used in some contemporary stories in new ways. While region continues to be important—most of the major regions of the United States, the South, New England, the West, and urban and rural areas are represented here, along with Canadian, Korean, Japanese, and Mexican settings—nature as a metaphorical expression of the spirits and psyches of the characters pervades several stories.

For instance, compare the use of *fire* in Richard Ford's "Electric City" with Rick Bass's use of it in "Fires." "The summer of that year was a time of forest fires," the narrator of Ford's story tells us. Smoke hangs over this story of the slow disintegration of a Western family. In the end, when the father goes off to fight it, the fire becomes almost a traditional symbol. A few pages into the story, Bass's narrator tells us, "The fires' haze never settled in our valley but would hang just above us, on the days it was there, turning all the sunlight a beautiful, smoky blue and making things when seen across the valley—a barn in another pasture, or a fence line—seem much farther away than they really were. It made things seem softer, too." He juxtaposes that image to this one: "There was a long zippered scar on the inside of Glenda's knee that started just above her ankle. . . ." The fire and its smoke become an analog to the phases and aspects of the narrator's relationship with the woman runner, but the two are never directly linked. This deliberately nebulous, but deeply suggestive, use of setting, and of other kinds of key images, is characteristic of many current stories, whether they appear in mass circulation or in quarterly magazines.

Story and Plot: Except for "Dragon's Seed" and "Carnal Knowledge" and the two genre stories, "The Man Who Knew Belle Starr" and "Bears Discover Fire," these stories do not depend upon narrative structure for their effect. The emphasis is on conveying through the narrator's first person or third person voice a sense of a particular phase in a character's life, as in "Lush Life," "Two Days Gone," and "Such Occasions."

Conflict: Most of the conflicts depicted in these stories, even in the crime story "The Man Who Knew Belle Starr," are internal, between two conflicting aspects of a character's spirit or psychology.

Sometimes a story delineates more a malaise than a conflict, as does "Such Occasions."

Even when the emphasis is on social problems, as in "Desert Blues" and "Slamming on Pig's Misery," the conflict is not as dramatically posed as in such stories in the past.

Point of View: Well over half the writers in this volume decided to allow one of their main characters to tell the story in the first person. This point of view seems particularly appropriate in a time when writers are moved to examine the causes and describe the circumstances of personal and social problems. The first person narrator says, in effect, "This happened to me and what happened to me may illuminate what is happening or will happen to you." The narrator of "Such Occasions" begins: "Let me tell you what happened to me when my husband died and my husband's brother came to help me pack for my move to Toronto."

In a first person story, whether the narrating character is talking about himself or herself, or about another dominant character, he or she is always the main character, partly because the author strives to leave the deepest impression on the reader through the effect of the voice itself, as in "Cold Ground": "In my sleep I was deaf. People spoke to me and to each other but I heard nothing."

These stories provide several variations on the first person narrative. One of them is a dramatic monologue—the narrator of Mona Simpson's "I Am Here to Tell You It Can Be Done" is speaking to an audience that is present in the story itself. "I want to tell you, don't believe what you've already heard about me. Believe this here alone. I'll tell you far worse than what they know." By comparison, is the woman narrator of Edna O'Brien's "Brother" speaking to herself? Aloud? Or to another person? To whom? And what difference would an answer make?

Few of the third person stories are broadly omniscient; usually one character is favored over the others, as in "Dragon's Seed," and "Trains at Night." Less and less often does the author confine the reader's experience to the perceptions of the main character, as do the authors of "Slamming on Pig's Misery," "Kat," "The Man Who Knew Belle Starr," and "Desert Blues."

Voice and Present Tense: Whether the protagonist narrates in first person or the author narrates in his or her own voice, writers today, influenced perhaps by contemporary poets, develop with close stylistic attention a distinctive voice, conveying a tone, an attitude, an atmosphere. To dramatize the immediacy and urgency of contemporary problems, the author, more often than ever before, couches the story in the present tense, or in a mixture of tenses, as in "Desert Blues," "Brother," and "Two Days Gone." "The last night of church camp, 1963," the narrator of "Personal Testimony" begins, "and I am sitting in the front row of the Junior Mixed-Voice Choir looking out on the crowd in the big sanctuary tent."

The relation of style to point of view is sometimes more carefully controlled in recent fiction. The point of view in "Desert Blues" is third person, limited to the experiences of one character; the style perfectly suits her, especially at this critical point in her life. "Everything was cold and blue all the time. There were no longer any increments or divisions. Diana Barrington was surprised by how much she missed them, lines and frontiers, clocks and dates and the debris of convention that she, a poet, had insisted on divesting herself of. Now there was only the icy blue, Baltic blue agony. She felt as if fierce angular waves rose and broke behind her face." See also "Fires," "Texas Wedding Party," and "Electric City."

Other Techniques and Devices

Comparison and Contrast: Fiction, like most forms of writing, thrives on comparison and contrast to emphasize emotion and meaning. "Two Useful Visits" suggests in its title a deliberate comparison and contrast. The way the narrator of "Fire" describes the landscape and the creatures on it before Glenda comes into his life and the way he describes it after she leaves is a contrast he feels in his very bones. This technique is so basic and vital that each story will offer numerous examples.

Metaphor: There is less reliance now than in decades past on incidental figures of speech. Like contemporary poets, fiction writers today employ metaphors that express deep, ineffable psychological and spiritual states. Louise Erdrich opens "The Leap" with these lines: "My mother is the surviving half of a blindfold trapeze act, not a fact I think about much even now that she is sightless, the result of encroaching and stubborn cataracts." Kazuo Ishiguro opens "Family Supper" with: "Fugu is a fish caught off the Pacific shores of Japan. The fish has held a special significance for me ever since my mother died after eating one."

Symbolism: Few contemporary writers employ symbolism in the traditional way; they rely more on metaphors of a kind described above.

Allusion: Contemporary writers seldom make use of the device of allusion as a way of adding another dimension to their stories. Margaret Atwood's "Kat" employs literary and historical allusions, but mainly to evoke the special literary milieu of her protagonist. Writers today tend to allude to the story's own elements. For example, Richard Ford alludes often to fire in "Electric City."

Irony: Unlike many writers of the past, contemporary writers do not generally design their stories around ironic patterns of action or character. A sense of irony may serve their characters at times, as in "Freedom, a Theory of," but that is quite different from the traditional use of irony prevalent from the 1890's through the 1960's.

Dialogue: As first person narratives seem to serve the purposes of the contemporary writer more often than third person, the increasing dominance of dialogue seems to enhance the first person narrative, as in "Electric City," "Lush Life," "Family Supper," and "Such Occasions." However, it is also true that writers are more willing now to use very little dialogue if pure narrative achieves their purpose more effectively, as in "Texas Wedding Party."

Context and Implication: Until recent years, writers developed a controlled context that enabled them to convey feelings and meanings through implication, especially when using the third person, limited omniscience point of view. The trend now is to create a surface of explicit statements enhanced by a relatively nebulous but suggestive context, as in "Fires."

Genre: Literary writers have, in recent decades, made use of the various traditional and popular genres for more serious purposes. Terry Bisson uses fantasy in "Bears Discover Fire"; Louise Erdrich in "The Leap" and Alberto Alavaro Ríos in "Trains at Night" use allegory; Richard Bausch uses the crime story in combination with the effect of western legend in the present in "The Man Who Knew Belle Starr."

Theme and Meaning: Although first person narrators and characters in third person narratives often consciously make thematic statements, as in "I Am Here to Tell You It Can Be Done" and, with irony, in "Desert Blues," theme and meaning are conveyed rather than overtly stated or clearly expressed in structure and conventional symbolism. That is true even of stories that obviously deal with social issues.

Titles: Some titles are, initially, simply interesting or intriguing, such as "Texas Wedding Party," "Slamming on Pig's Misery" and "Bears Discover Fire." Attention to titles as you begin to read a story and as you finish will illuminate all your other responses to a story; titles gather potency as the story moves along. Start with the key words in titles and assume that they have both literal and secondary meanings and relevance. Consider that a title may be a pun, an allusion to a well-known phrase, or that it may prove to be ironic. Consider "Freedom, A Theory of," "Personal Testimony," "Carnal Knowledge," "Fire," "Cold Ground," and "Such Occasions." For instance, "Field Trip" is an experience all school children share; but the narrator is a veteran who takes his little daughter to see the battlefield in Vietnam, where phrases such as "field of fire" and "field of vision" are implied. That's a start.

Beginnings and Endings: The editors of *The Mississippi Review* are so acutely aware of the inherent potency of beginnings that in 1990 they devoted an entire issue to the openings of stories, good and bad, that were submitted to them within a year's time. Beginnings usually deliver far more than a reader, on first reading, can consciously assimilate; it is very likely, however, that readers absorb everything unconsciously.

Much of a story's effect upon a reader may be traced to the author's control of elements and techniques introduced in the beginning and reiterated, with variations that reflect the development of key elements, in the end. Let's test that theory now, choosing several opening and closing lines as examples.

> From **"Desert Blues"**: "Everything was cold and blue all the time." "There are things blue and things other and how now and finally she is no longer cold."
>
> From **"Fires"**: "Some years the heat comes in April. There is always wind in April, but with luck, there is warmth, too. There is usually a drought, so that the fields are dry. . . ." "Is Glenda still running? It is mid-February. It hurts to remember her. The field across the road lies scorched and black, hidden beneath a cover of snow."
>
> From **"I Am Here to Tell You It Can Be Done"**: "I want to tell you, don't believe what you've already heard about me. Believe this here alone. I'll tell you far worse than what they know." "You've heard my confession. Now I want to learn yours. . . . Now that you know, see if you still want to open yourself and try and believe in somebody like me."
>
> From **"Freedom, A Theory of"**: "The story my father told—before he abandoned my mother and me, before he reappeared years and years later to beat the stuffings out of me—concerned his sister Shirley. . . ." Look at the last page of the story.

The importance of starting effectively is illustrated in the choice of "The Leap" as the opening story of this anthology. The beginning of that story provides a breath-taking leap into contemporary fiction.

About the Editor

Professor of Creative Writing at Louisiana State University since 1968, David Madden is a well-known writer in all the genres in the Pocketful Series.

Two of his eight novels have been nominated for the Pulitzer Prize, *Sharpshooter: A Novel of the Civil War* and *The Suicide's Wife*, which was made into a movie.

The Shadow Knows and *The New Orleans of Possibilities* are his two collections of short stories.

Since 1957, many poems, essays, and stories by David Madden have appeared in magazines ranging from *Redbook* and *Playboy* to *The Kenyon Review* and *The New Republic*.

His plays have been performed at Actor's Studio, Yale Drama School, Ohio University, and Barter Theater, among many others.

He has written numerous books and essays on major American, British, and European writers, including Faulkner, Katherine Anne Porter, Flannery O'Connor, Robert Penn Warren, James M. Cain, Wright Morris, Thomas Wolfe, Nathanael West, Katherine Mansfield, Emily Bronte, James Joyce, Albert Camus, Jules Romains, and Franz Kafka. As founding director of the United States Civil War Center, he has written on Civil War history.

Writers in the five genres have contributed essays to a book to be published in 2006 called *David Madden: A Writer for All Genres*.

Louise Erdrich

Louise Erdrich is the author of *Love Medicine, The Beet Queen, Tracks, Baptism of Desire, Jacklight* (poems), and *The Crown of Columbus* (with her husband, Michael Dorris). Her stories have been reprinted in *The Best American Short Stories.*

The Leap

MY MOTHER IS THE SURVIVING HALF OF A BLINDFOLD TRAPEZE ACT, not a fact I think about much even now that she is sightless, the result of encroaching and stubborn cataracts. She walks slowly through her house here in New Hampshire, lightly touching her way along walls and running her hands over knickknacks, books, the drift of a grown child's belongings and castoffs. She has never upset an object or as much as brushed a magazine onto the floor. She has never lost her balance or bumped into a closet door left carelessly open.

It has occurred to me that the catlike precision of her movements in old age might be the result of her early training, but she shows so little of the drama or flair one might expect from a performer that I tend to forget the Flying Avalons. She has kept no sequined costume, no photographs, no fliers or posters from that part of her youth. I would, in fact, tend to think that all memory of double somersaults and heart stopping catches had left her arms and legs were it not for the fact that sometimes, as I sit sewing in the room of the rebuilt house in which I slept as a child, I hear the crackle, catch a whiff of smoke from the stove downstairs, and suddenly the room goes dark, the stitches burn beneath my fingers, and I am sewing with a needle of hot silver, a thread of fire.

I owe her my existence three times. The first was when she saved herself. In the town square a replica tent pole, cracked and splintered, now stands cast in concrete. It commemorates the disaster that put our town smack on the front page of the Boston and New York tabloids. It is from those old newspapers, now historical records, that I get my information. Not from my mother, Anna of the Flying Avalons, nor from any of her in-laws, nor certainly from the other half of her particular act, Harold Avalon, her first husband. In one news account it says, "The day was mildly overcast, but nothing in the air or temperature gave any hint of the sudden force with which the deadly gale would strike."

I have lived in the West, where you can see the weather coming for miles, and it is true that out here we are at something of a disadvantage. When extremes of temperature collide, a hot and cold front, winds generate instantaneously behind a hill and crash upon you without warning. That, I think, was the likely situation on that day in June. People probably commented on the pleasant air, grateful that no hot sun beat upon the striped tent that stretched over the entire center green. They bought their tickets and surrendered them in anticipation. They sat. They ate caramelized popcorn and roasted peanuts. There was time, before the storm, for three acts. The White Arabians of Ali-Khazar rose on their hind legs and waltzed. The Mysterious Bernie folded himself into a painted cracker tin, and the Lady of the Mists made herself appear and disappear in surprising places. As the clouds gathered outside, unnoticed, the ringmaster cracked his whip, shouted his introduction, and pointed to the ceiling of the tent, where the Flying Avalons were perched.

5   They loved to drop gracefully from nowhere, like two sparkling birds, and blow kisses as they threw off their plumed helmets and high-collared capes. They laughed and flirted

openly as they beat their way up again on the trapeze bars. In the final vignette of their act, they actually would kiss in midair, pausing, almost hovering as they swooped past one another. On the ground, between bows, Harry Avalon would skip quickly to the front rows and point out the smear of my mother's lipstick, just off the edge of his mouth. They made a romantic pair all right, especially in the blindfold sequence.

That afternoon, as the anticipation increased, as Mr. and Mrs. Avalon tied sparkling strips of cloth onto each other's face and as they puckered their lips in mock kisses, lips destined "never again to meet," as one long breathless article put it, the wind rose, miles off, wrapped itself into a cone, and howled. There came a rumble of electrical energy, drowned out by the sudden roll of drums. One detail not mentioned by the press, perhaps unknown—Anna was pregnant at the time, seven months and hardly showing, her stomach muscles were that strong. It seems incredible that she would work high above the ground when any fall could be so dangerous, but the explanation—I know from watching her go blind—is that my mother lives comfortably in extreme elements. She is one with the constant dark now, just as the air was her home, familiar to her, safe, before the storm that afternoon.

From opposite ends of the tent they waved, blind and smiling, to the crowd below. The ringmaster removed his hat and called for silence, so that the two above could concentrate. They rubbed their hands in chalky powder, then Harry launched himself and swung, once, twice, in huge calibrated beats across space. He hung from his knees and on the third swing stretched wide his arms, held his hands out to receive his pregnant wife as she dove from her shining bar.

It was while the two were in midair, their hands about to meet, that lightning struck the main pole and sizzled down the guy wires, filling the air with a blue radiance that Harry Avalon must certainly have seen through the cloth of his blindfold as the tent buckled and the edifice toppled him forward, the swing continuing and not returning in its sweep, and Harry going down, down into the crowd with his last thought, perhaps, just a prickle of surprise at his empty hands.

My mother once said that I'd be amazed at how many things a person can do within the act of falling. Perhaps, at the time, she was teaching me to dive off a board at the town pool, for I associate the idea with midair somersaults. But I also think she meant that even in that awful doomed second one could think, for she certainly did. When her hands did not meet her husband's, my mother tore her blindfold away. As he swept past her on the wrong side, she could have grasped his ankle, the toe-end of his tights, and gone down clutching him. Instead, she changed direction. Her body twisted toward a heavy wire and she managed to hang on to the braided metal, still hot from the lightning strike. Her palms were burned so terribly that once healed they bore no lines, only the blank scar tissue of a quieter future. She was lowered, gently, to the sawdust ring just underneath the dome of the canvas roof, which did not entirely settle but was held up on one end and jabbed through, torn, and still on fire in places from the giant spark, though rain and men's jackets soon put that out.

10   Three people died, but except for her hands my mother was not seriously harmed until an overeager rescuer broke her arm in extricating her and also, in the process, collapsed a portion of the tent bearing a huge buckle that knocked her unconscious. She was taken to the town hospital, and there she must have hemorrhaged, for they kept her, confined to her bed, a month and a half before her baby was born without life.

Harry Avalon had wanted to be buried in the circus cemetery next to the original Avalon, his uncle, so she sent him back with his brothers. The child, however, is buried around the corner, beyond this house and just down the highway. Sometimes I used to walk there just to sit. She was a girl, but I rarely thought of her as a sister or even as a separate person really. I suppose you could call it the egocentrism of a child, of all young children, but I considered her a less finished version of myself.

When the snow falls, throwing shadows among the stones, I can easily pick hers out from the road, for it is bigger than the others and in the shape of a lamb at rest, its legs curled beneath. The carved lamb looms larger as the years pass, though it is probably only my eyes, the vision shifting, as what is close to me blurs and distances sharpen. In odd moments, I think it is the edge drawing near, the edge of everything, the unseen horizon we do not really speak of in the eastern woods. And it also seems to me, although this is probably an idle fantasy, that the statue is growing more sharply etched, as if, instead of weathering itself into a porous mass, it is hardening on the hillside with each snowfall, perfecting itself.

It was during her confinement in the hospital that my mother met my father. He was called in to look at the set of her arm, which was complicated. He stayed, sitting at her bedside, for he was something of an armchair traveler and had spent his war quietly, at an air force training grounds, where he became a specialist in arms and legs broken during parachute training exercises. Anna Avalon had been to many of the places he longed to visit—Venice, Rome, Mexico, all through France and Spain. She had no family of her own and was taken in by the Avalons, trained to perform from a very young age. They toured Europe before the war, then based themselves in New York. She was illiterate.

It was in the hospital that she finally learned to read and write, as a way of overcoming the boredom and depression of those weeks, and it was my father who insisted on teaching her. In return for stories of her adventures, he graded her first exercises. He bought her her first book, and over her bold letters, which the pale guides of the penmanship pads could not contain, they fell in love.

I wonder if my father calculated the exchange he offered: one form of flight for another. For after that, and for as long as I can remember, my mother has never been without a book. Until now, that is, and it remains the greatest difficulty of her blindness. Since my father's recent death, there is no one to read to her, which is why I returned, in fact, from my failed life where the land is flat. I came home to read to my mother, to read out loud, to read long into the dark if I must, to read all night.

Once my father and mother married, they moved onto the old farm he had inherited but didn't care much for. Though he'd been thinking of moving to a larger city, he settled down and broadened his practice in this valley. It still seems odd to me, when they could have gone anywhere else, that they chose to stay in the town where the disaster had occurred, and which my father in the first place had found so constricting. It was my mother who insisted upon it, after her child did not survive. And then, too, she loved the sagging farmhouse with its scrap of what was left of a vast acreage of woods and hidden hay fields that stretched to the game park.

I owe my existence, the second time then, to the two of them and the hospital that brought them together. That is the debt we take for granted since none of us asks for life. It is only once we have it that we hang on so dearly.

I was seven the year the house caught fire, probably from standing ash. It can rekindle, and my father, forgetful around the house and perpetually exhausted from night hours on call, often emptied what he thought were ashes from cold stoves into wooden or cardboard containers. The fire could have started from a flaming box, or perhaps a build up of creosote inside the chimney was the culprit. It started right around the stove, and the heart of the house was gutted. The baby-sitter, fallen asleep in my father's den on the first floor, woke to find the stairway to my upstairs room cut off by flames. She used the phone, then ran outside to stand beneath my window.

When my parents arrived, the town volunteers had drawn water from the fire pond and were spraying the outside of the house, preparing to go inside after me, not knowing at the time that there was only one staircase and that it was lost. On the other side of the house, the superannuated extension ladder broke in half. Perhaps the clatter of it falling against the walls woke me, for I'd been asleep up to that point.

20   As soon as I awakened, in the small room that I now use for sewing, I smelled the smoke. I followed things by the letter then, was good at memorizing instructions, and so I did exactly what was taught in the second-grade home fire drill. I got up, I touched the back of my door before opening it. Finding it hot, I left it closed and stuffed my rolled-up rug beneath the crack. I did not hide under my bed or crawl into my closet. I put on my flannel robe, and then I sat down to wait.

Outside, my mother stood below my dark window and saw clearly that there was no rescue. Flames had pierced one side wall, and the glare of the fire lighted the massive limbs and trunk of the vigorous old elm that had probably been planted the year the house was built, a hundred years ago at least. No leaf touched the wall, and just one thin branch scraped the roof. From below, it looked as though even a squirrel would have had trouble jumping from the tree onto the house, for the breadth of that small branch was no bigger than my mother's wrist.

Standing there, beside Father, who was preparing to rush back around to the front of the house, my mother asked him to unzip her dress. When he wouldn't be bothered, she made him understand. He couldn't make his hands work, so she finally tore it off and stood there in her pearls and stockings. She directed one of the men to lean the broken half of the extension ladder up against the trunk of the tree. In surprise, he complied. She ascended. She vanished. Then she could be seen among the leafless branches of last November as she made her way up and, along her stomach, inched the length of a bough that curved above the branch that brushed the roof.

Once there, swaying, she stood and balanced. There were plenty of people in the crowd and many who still remember, or think they do, my mother's leap through the ice-dark air toward that thinnest extension, and how she broke the branch falling so that it cracked in her hands, cracked louder than the flames as if she was vaulted with it toward the edge of the roof, and how it hurtled down end over end without her, and their eyes went up, again, to see where she had flown.

I didn't see her leap through the air, only heard the sudden thump and looked out my window. She was hanging by the backs of her heels from the new gutter we had put in that year, and she was smiling. I was not surprised to see her, she was so matter-of-fact. She tapped on the window. I remember how she did it, too. It was the friendliest tap, a bit tentative, as if she was afraid she had arrived too early at a friend's house. Then she gestured at the latch, and when I opened the window she told me to raise it wider and prop it up with the stick so it wouldn't crush her fingers. She swung down, caught the ledge, and crawled through the opening. Once she was in my room, I realized she had on only underclothing, a bra of the heavy stitched cotton women used to wear and step-in, lace-trimmed drawers. I remember feeling light-headed, of course, terribly relieved, and then embarrassed for her to be seen by the crowd undressed.

25   I was still embarrassed as we flew out the window, toward earth, me in her lap, her toes pointed as we skimmed toward the painted target of the fire fighter's net.

I know that she's right. I knew it even then. As you fall there is time to think. Curled as I was, against her stomach, I was not startled by the cries of the crowd or the looming faces. The wind roared and beat its hot breath at our back, the flames whistled. I slowly wondered what would happen if we missed the circle or bounced out of it. Then I wrapped my hands around my mother's hands. I felt the brush of her lips and heard the beat of her heart in my ears, loud as thunder, long as the roll of drums.

Tim O'Brien

Tim O'Brien is the author of *Going After Cacciato, If I Die In a Combat Zone, Box Me Up and Ship Me Home, Northern Lights,* and *The Things They Carried.* His stories have been included in *Prize Stories: The O. Henry Awards* and *The Best American Short Stories.*

Field Trip

TWENTY YEARS AFTER LEAVING VIET-
NAM, I returned with my daughter Kathleen. There we visited the
site of Kiowa's death, that place where he had disappeared under
mud and water, folded in with the war when the field exploded,
and where I now looked for signs of forgiveness or personal
grace or whatever else the land might offer. The field was still
there, though not as I remembered it. Much smaller, I thought,
and not nearly so menacing. And in the bright sunlight it
was hard to picture what had happened on this ground some 20
years ago. Except for a few marshy spots along the river, everything was bone-dry. No ghosts—just a flat, grassy field. The place
was at peace. There were yellow butterflies. There was a breeze
and a wide blue sky. Along the river two old farmers stood in
ankle-deep water repairing the same narrow dike where we had
laid out Kiowa's body after pulling him from the muck. Things
were quiet. At one point, I remember, one of the farmers looked

up and shaded his eyes, staring across the field at us; then after a time he wiped his forehead and went back to work.

I stood with my arms folded, feeling the grip of sentiment and time. Amazing, I thought. Twenty years.

Behind me, in the jeep, Kathleen sat waiting with a government interpreter, and now and then I could hear the two of them talking in soft voices. They were already fast friends. Neither of them, I think, understood what all this was about, why I'd insisted that we search out this spot. It had been a hard two-hour ride from Quang Ngai City, bumpy dirt roads and a hot August sun, ending up at an empty field on the edge of nowhere.

I took out my camera, snapped a couple of pictures, then stood gazing out at the field. After a time Kathleen got out of the jeep and came to stand beside me.

"You know what I think?" she said. "I think this place stinks. It smells like . . . God, I don't even *know* what. It smells rotten."

"It sure does. I know that."

"So when can we go?"

"Pretty soon," I said.

She started to say something, but then hesitated. Frowning, she squinted out at the field for a second or so, then shrugged and walked back to the jeep.

KATHLEEN HAD JUST TURNED TEN, and this trip was a kind of birthday present, showing her the world, offering a small piece of her father's history. For the most part she'd held up well—far better than I—and over the first two weeks she'd trooped along without complaint as we hit the obligatory tourist stops. Ho Chi Minh's mausoleum in Hanoi. A model farm outside Saigon. The tunnels at Cu Chi. The monuments and government offices and orphanages. Through most of this Kathleen had seemed to enjoy the foreignness of it all, the exotic food and animals, and even during those periods of boredom and discomfort she'd kept up a good-humored tolerance. At the same time, however, she'd seemed a bit puzzled. The war was as remote to her as cavemen and dinosaurs.

One morning in Saigon she'd asked what it was all about. "This whole war," she said, "why was everybody so mad at everybody else?"

I shook my head. "They weren't mad, exactly. Some people wanted one thing, other people wanted another thing."

"What did *you* want?"

"Nothing," I said. "To stay alive."

15   "That's all?"

"Yes."

Kathleen sighed. "Well, I don't get it. I mean, how come you were even here in the first place?"

"I don't know," I said. "Because I had to be."

"But *why*?"

20   I tried to find something to tell her, but finally I shrugged and said, "It's a mystery, I guess. I don't know."

For the rest of the day she was very quiet. That night, though, just before bedtime, Kathleen put her hand on my shoulder and said, "You know something? Sometimes you're pretty weird, aren't you?"

"Well, no," I said.

"You are *too*." She pulled her hand away and frowned at me. "Like coming over here. Some dumb thing happens a long time ago and you can't ever forget it."

"And that's bad?"

25   "No," she said quietly. "That's weird."

IN THE SECOND WEEK OF AUGUST, near the end of our stay, I'd arranged for the side trip up to Quang Ngai. The tourist stuff was fine, but from the start I'd wanted to take my daughter to the places I'd seen as a soldier. I wanted to show her the Vietnam that kept me awake at night—a shady trail outside the village of My Khe, a filthy old pigsty on the Batangan Peninsula. Our time was short, however, and choices had to be made. In the end I decided to take her to this piece of ground where my friend Kiowa had died. It seemed appropriate. And, besides, I had business here.

Now, looking out at the field, I wondered if it was all a mistake. Everything was too ordinary. A quiet sunny day, and the field was not the field I remembered. I pictured Kiowa's face, the way he used to smile, but all I felt was the awkwardness of remembering.

Behind me, Kathleen let out a little giggle. The interpreter was showing her magic tricks.

Things change.

30 There were birds and butterflies, the soft rustlings of rural anywhere. Below, in the earth, the relics of our presence were no doubt still there, the canteens and bandoliers and mess kits. This little field, I thought, had swallowed so much. My best friend. My pride. My belief in myself as a man of some small dignity and courage. Still, it was hard to find any real emotion. It simply wasn't there. After that long night in the rain, I'd seemed to grow cold inside, all the illusions gone, all the old ambitions and hopes for myself sucked away into the mud. Over the years that coldness had never entirely disappeared. There were times in my life when I couldn't feel much, not sadness or pity or passion, and somehow I blamed this place for what I had become, and I blamed it for taking away the person I had once been. For 20 years this field had embodied all the waste that was Vietnam, all the vulgarity and horror.

Now it was just what it was. Flat and dreary and unremarkable. I walked up toward the river, trying to pick out specific landmarks, but all I recognized was a small rise where Jimmy Cross had set up his command post that night. Nothing else. For a while I watched the two old farmers working under the hot sun. I took a few more photographs, waved at the farmers, then turned and moved back to the jeep.

Kathleen gave me a little nod.

"Well," she said, "I hope you're having fun."

"Sure."

35 "Can we go now?"

"In a minute," I said. "Just relax."

At the back of the jeep I found the small cloth bundle I'd carried over from the States.

Kathleen's eyes narrowed. "What's that?"

"Stuff," I told her.

40   She glanced at the bundle again, then hopped out of the jeep and followed me back to the field. We walked past Jimmy Cross's command post, past the spot where Kiowa had gone under, down to where the field dipped into the marshland along the river. I took off my shoes and socks.

"Okay," Kathleen said, "what's going on?"

"A quick swim."

"Where?"

"Right here," I said. "Stay put."

45   She watched me unwrap the cloth bundle. Inside was Kiowa's old hunting hatchet.

I stripped down to my underwear, took off my wristwatch, and waded in. The water was warm against my feet. Instantly, I recognized the soft, fat feel of the bottom. The water here was eight inches deep.

Kathleen seemed nervous. She squinted at me, her hands fluttering. "Listen, this is stupid," she said, "you can't even hardly get *wet*. How can you *swim* out there?"

"I'll manage."

"But it's not . . . I mean, God it's not even *water*, it's like mush or something."

50   She pinched her nose and watched me wade out to where the water reached my knees. Roughly here, I decided, was where Mitchell Sanders had found Kiowa's rucksack when we went back to dig him out. I eased myself down, squatting at first, then sitting. There was again that sense of recognition. The water rose to midchest, a deep greenish brown, almost hot. Small water bugs skipped along the surface. Right here, I thought. Leaning forward, I reached in with the hatchet and wedged it handle-first into the soft bottom, letting it slide away, the blade's own weight taking it under. Tiny bubbles broke along the surface.

I tried to think of something decent to say, something meaningful and right, but nothing came to me.

I looked down into the field.

"Well," I finally managed. "There it is."

My voice surprised me. It had a rough, chalky sound, full of things I did not know were there. I wanted to tell Kiowa that he'd

been a great friend, the very best, but all I could do was slap
hands with the water.

55   The sun made me squint. Twenty years. A lot like yesterday,
a lot like never. In a way, maybe, I'd gone under with Kiowa, and
now after two decades I'd finally worked my way out. A hot afternoon, a bright August sun, and the war was over. For a few
moments I could not bring myself to move. Like waking from a
summer nap, feeling lazy and sluggish, the world collecting itself
around me. Fifty meters up the field one of the old farmers
stood watching from along the dike. The man's face was dark and
solemn. As we stared at each other, neither of us moving, I felt
something go shut in my heart while something else swung open.
Briefly, I wondered if the old man might walk over to exchange
a few war stories, but instead he picked up a shovel, raised it over
his head and held it there for a time, grimly, like a flag. Then he
brought the shovel down and said something to his friend and
began digging into the hard, dry ground.

I stood up and waded out of the water.

"What a mess," Kathleen said. "All that gunk on your skin,
you look like. . . . Wait'll I tell Mommy, she'll probably make you
sleep in the garage."

"You're right," I said. "Don't tell her."

I pulled on my shoes, took my daughter's hand and led her
across the field toward the jeep. Soft heat waves shimmied up out
of the earth.

60   When we reached the jeep, Kathleen turned and glanced out
at the field. "That old man," she said, "is he mad at you or
something?"

"I hope not."

"He looks mad."

"No," I said. "All that's finished."

E. S. Goldman

E. S. Goldman's first published story appeared in 1988 in *The Atlantic*; several more appeared there in 1990; his stories have also been reprinted in *The Best American Short Stories*. He has published *Big Chocolate Cookies*, *Earthly Justice*, and *Going Back to Sea*.

Good Works

I

THE ADS IN THE SCHOOL PAPERS AND SUMMER-THEATER PROGRAMS and church-bazaar fliers aren't from stores in the mall, they're from Henryot's or The Pharm or Beth's or me. When two high-school girls come in with those big notebooks (they always travel in pairs to sell ads; it's such a, you know, like an *awful* experience asking strangers for money) I can tell it's an ad as soon as they walk in the door.

If it isn't an ad it's raffle tickets or they want merchandise for an auction. They think we get merchandise free. They talk about sales and profits as if they were the same. They don't know anything. They know what I knew at their age.

I always used to ask their names. I used to think, Do I know her mother? Is her mother a customer? What circulation do

I get? I let them know in a polite way it was blackmail. Before I gave in I asked why they didn't go to the mall and ask those big jeans outfits they give all their business to, those mix-and-match tycoons listed on the stock exchange. I got back the kind of S.A.T. 850 look that tells the Japanese they're going to inherit the world. Sometimes they enlightened me, "There's nobody to talk to at those places. It's a big deal. They have to get an okay from Oklahoma."

So they nickel-and-dime the local merchants to death.

5   I was always aggravated by it until Mahlon Weber said, "Forget it. What does it amount to? Make believe you had to take a couple hundred dollars a year more in markdowns. Dole it out with a big smile as if you enjoyed it. They'll tell their mothers how nice you are."

Fair enough. Mahlon was a real-estate man but he knew more about stores than anybody else. When my husband was killed in the head-on on that damn Route 6 and I had the insurance money, I thought of opening a shop and asked Mahlon for a location. I mentioned the new strip of shops they were building in back of the printing plant.

"Forget it. Not one of those people will be in business in five years. They can't make *a living* in rooms that small, Eleanor, only jewelers can make a living in three hundred square feet on Cape Cod except in a mall. Work for somebody for a year and find out some things. Then come and see me if you still want to do it." And I did.

That was eighteen years ago. I still don't do anything important without first having coffee with Mahlon Weber.

It was my first year in business and I was still in my grudging mode about ads when a frail little black man wearing a clerical collar came in. I knew as soon as he walked in the door he wanted some kind of contribution and I knew I not only was going to give it to him but I wanted to. I was on his side. We didn't see many black people shopping gift stores at my end of the Cape. We see more now, mostly professionals—lawyers and doctors who know their way around. Portuguese people are part of the scene here like everybody else, but that's not black. A few resort areas

on the Vineyard and around Bass River and Hyannis have substantial black clientele. They just don't come to this part of the
Cape, or they hurdle it and go to Provincetown. I don't know the
details. I don't try to save the world. I just open my door.

10   I can't tell you how simpatico I felt for this little guy before
he even opened his mouth. It was as hot an afternoon in August
as we ever get. Everybody was at the beach, we had only a couple
of elderly nonswimmers poking through the stock, and here
comes this little ancestrally black preacher in a big collar he
could have entered from the bottom, a Capone-brim black felt
hat, winter-weight black suit, black shirt, black police shoes. No
gloves? He took off the hat and wiped the sweatband and his
face. He excavated sweat inside the collar with a handkerchief
that had been folded and padded more than once looking for a
dry corner. He wiped the top of his head. He had fine small features and amused eyes. He was I thought quite old but I really
couldn't tell as he had no hair to give me a clue. In retrospect,
he was probably a well-worn sixty.

"How would you like a Coke?" I offered. I kept a few things
with my lunch in a refrigerator in the stockroom. "I never saw
anybody who needed it more."

"Oh thank you very much." His voice was breathy and barely
audible. His head stuck out of his collar like a head at a carnival
to throw a ball at. He screwed up his face to a smile, pure, sweet
and guileless. "Could I have a glass of cold water? That would be
fine."

"You're welcome to a Coke."

"Thank you very much. A glass of cold water would be fine."

15   I asked him to sit down while I filled his order and he was
glad to be off his feet. He disposed of the water with evident
pleasure, saving an inch for later.

"I'm Eleanor MacAlly. It's my store. What can I do for you?"

He had an envelope of credentials and offered each in turn
as he spoke: a worn business card with his photograph and the
imprint of The Lord's Will Church, the last card, shown for
identification only and put back in the envelope; a letter that
had been folded many times, the creases split; a small spiral

notebook in which names had been penciled by a patient, unskilled hand.

"I am Reverend Hesterson of The Lord's Will Church—"

"Which is where?"

20   It broke the trend of his presentation. He regrouped. "We are in Wuster. I move to Hyannis in the summer to do the Lord's work. I came to see if you would help us keep our children in the camp. We bring boys from the city to the outdoors. They so appreciate it. We have many friends who help us with contributions. The folks are good to us. Do you know Mr. Seymour Larrick?" He didn't seem to have enough breath to say all that, but by replenishing as he went along he managed.

Mr. Larrick's torn letter testified that Reverend Zeal Hesterson was well known to the writer and that he did many good works. Mr. Larrick's letter was from five years before. His address was Providence. My impulse was to go into that. I decided not to pry.

Hesterson opened his lined, worn notebook toward me. On each line was a name and an amount. The amounts were mostly one or two dollars. There were fives, very few tens, and a saintly twenty-five. I recognized only a few names. Lou Potch, the oil dealer, president of the Merchant's Association, was down for two dollars. Beth Hannon, who had the Killarney shop, was down for five. I wanted to weep for the artlessness of a solicitation that allowed me to be heroic for five dollars. He took a receipt pad from his pocket and acknowledged my contribution.

"The children will bless you," he assured me.

I said I wished it could be more but this was a new business. He said the Lord would bless me. I said I could use the help.

25   Hesterson passed from my mind until the following August, on a rainy day. The store was flooded with customers. I had my head down at the counter writing a sale and glimpsed him standing quietly aside, under the overhanging black hat. To seal in the steam, a black military raincoat—much oversize—sagged from his shoulders to his knuckles and on toward his ankles. I didn't know how long he had been there. He had done nothing to catch my attention. I motioned him toward the office and got to him as soon as there was a break. The few seconds I could give him

were enough to tell him where to get a glass of water and do anything else he had to do after walking around all day. I raised him to seven dollars.

He came in every year. He showed me pictures of his boys—four of them bunched on a porch swing, another several with their arms around each other buddy-style. One year a woman—also in black from head to toe with the credentials in a big black patent handbag—introduced herself as Sister Marie. Reverend Hesterson wasn't feeling too good and she was doing his rounds. I sent him my best wishes and the ten that had by then become my amount. He survived his indisposition and was back on the beat the next year.

"I'm going to give you fifteen dollars," I said. "Put it in the book for ten. I don't want to stick my head up."

"That is so fine of you. The Lord will bless you."

"You took care of that already."

30   At a dinner meeting of the Merchants somebody said we ought to do something about all these solicitations. We should have a common front. Of course nobody knew what to do, it was just self-expression. I spoke up. "Whatever you do, don't do anything to hurt my friend the Reverend Zeal Hesterson. He does great work. I recommended him to you all."

Not many merchants knew what reverend I was talking about until I identified him as the little black preacher. Then everybody knew him. They traded information around the room. He had been coming ten years—no, it was more like twelve. He wasn't in Hyannis, he was in Centerville. On a pond in Marstons Mills. He wasn't local. We were South Westham merchants, we had enough to do taking care of our own. Well, people could do what they wanted. We passed a motion for the secretary to send a letter to the manager of the mall calling on him to urge all his merchants to support local activities. "Mark on the envelope 'Throw Directly in Waste Basket,'" mumbled Grove Lanpheer.

"They can do what they want with it," the secretary said. "It will make a story in the papers that we asked for support for local activities."

After the meeting, the question occurred to me for the first time: what are the logistics of Hesterson's fund-raising? Why is he all the way down here in South Westham? How does he decide who gets the privilege of a solicitation?

I STOPPED IN TO HAVE THE MOTEL'S CONTINENTAL BREAKFAST with friends staying at Ship Wright's where Center Street comes into town off Route 6. The morning sun hadn't yet come up to speed. We sat on the porch settling world affairs and watching the amazing amount of traffic coming into town that early, a stream of vacationers setting shopping and laundry out of the way so they could go to the beach, a lot of vans and pickups with local workmen headed for jobs; and the Reverend Zeal Hesterson and Sister Marie, parking in the small empty lot next to that important-looking electrical setup; generators or dynamos—a rig of the electric company. Nobody thinks to park there, but it doesn't say No Parking and there is shade all day long.

35   Sister Marie went into the foreign-car agency on the corner. Hesterson crossed the street and went into the bank. I was still telling my friends about Hesterson, when he came out and went into the oculist's shop next door. In a minute or two Sister Marie finished at the car agency and went next-door to Anthony's Letter Shop. I didn't see them when I drove through town to my store. When I came back to the center for lunch I saw him going into the toy store.

He got to me at the usual time, mid-afternoon. We talked about the logistics. He and Sister Marie began on the main street at one end of every town on Cape Cod from Falmouth to Provincetown and went on to the end of the day. Then they walked back and got their car. In some towns like ours they did more than one street, some towns took two or three days, some like Truro they could do in a morning. All summer, rain or shine, door to door, wearing their credentials of respectability.

"That's some schedule," I said.

"The Lord has in mind to ask no more than we can give."

"It doesn't allow you much time for the boys, does it?"

40   "I have good helpers."

I gave him twenty-five. "Show me on the list for ten, same as before."

He thanked me and got up to leave. I noticed that the tops of his shoes were wrinkled and slits showed between the uppers and the soles when he walked. He didn't walk easily. He walked as if he didn't want to roll over on his toes. He walked as if his feet hurt. "Get yourself a pair of shoes sometimes." I went to the register again. "This isn't for the camp. This is for shoes."

He gave me his beatific smile. I said. "Remember, that's for you, nobody else. I want to see you in real shoes the next time."

I didn't exact a promise. The next year he showed me that he had new shoes. *Different* shoes, I would have said. They had a European look, narrowing to an acute point after the breadth at the ball. They had no toe cap or pattern. I could see his toes flex under the soft uppers. He probably picked them up at the Goodwill or a Thrift Shop. I bit my tongue and didn't say anything.

45   IN ADDITION TO HESTERSON, two or three other deserving mendicants were on my summer list. The Cookie Lady came in with packages of marvelous cookies, sugared molasses, oatmeal, fruit hermits. No matter how busy we were I stopped the store and made an announcement. "Friends, this lady sells the most delicious homemade cookies. The proceeds are for a good cause, the Mabel Delcourter House for unfortunate young women in Boston. I recommend her to you."

I broke open a package for customers to sample and the Cookie Lady went around the store selling out of a big wicker basket. The cookies were as good as I said, although on the expensive side. I always took a half dozen packages and doled them out to myself from the freezer, even when I was on a diet. My salespeople took one or two packages, and a few customers always tried them. A leaflet in each package explained that the Mabel Delcourter House gave unfortunate young women a good Christian outlook. It seems to be a characteristic of sacrificial people to print everything in light blue ink. The one card Hesterson showed and put back in the envelope was in light blue ink too.

Another on my list was a guitar player who put on an entertainment in our parking lot every year right after the Fourth of

July for (his blue card said) Something Wildlife. The guitar player and the Cookie Lady and the Reverend Zeal Hesterson were my regulars for a few dollars. If I was going to be out of the store around the time they were expected I left word they were to be taken care of the same as if I were there. They had enough walking around to do without coming back if they missed me.

I don't want to give the impression that I feel superior to two-dollar and no-dollar people. People look at things their own way, and somebody I don't see on a list may be taking care of two grandmothers. I do like a good cookie, and I was brought up to be uncomfortable if I don't tithe. Real tithing is before tax. I'm not as good as the way I was brought up, I'm an after-tax person. At rock bottom I'm a no-tax person. I paid Hesterson and the others out of the cash register and charged it to shortage on the day's tally. I don't think that's the way the Internal Revenue Service likes transactions like that handled, but it was easier for me and works out the same for the government, and I didn't want to set up any of my beneficiaries for an IRS letter by showing their names in my expense ledger.

I see that some billion-dollar companies do everything the IRS way and don't pay any taxes at all. They tithe to tax lawyers. The IRS is comfortable with that. You can make up your own mind which cases are the most deserving.

2

FOR ONLY THE SECOND TIME I CAN REMEMBER, Sister Marie came in at the usual time three or four years ago and said the reverend was peaked. When he felt better he might make a special trip to see come of his good friends, maybe in September. I sent my best wishes and a contribution.

Within a few days, a minor crisis came up and I had to be in Hyannis, a horrendous fate in the summer. We had an artist there who painted scenes on tiles and I needed to see with my own eyes how she was doing on a big order we had for a kitchen wall. I arranged to meet her early to beat the traffic and be back in the shop by ten. You can never quite beat the traffic in summer because there are more people beating the traffic than there is traffic. My session with the tile-painter ran long, and before I was ready to drive back to South Westham it was already late morning.

I thought, while I'm here why not drop in on Hesterson? We had been friends for years and I had never visited the camp. The way things were going I would never visit it, as summer was when I had no time to spare and didn't get on the highway unless I had to, and after Labor Day the camp was gone. I phoned the store to be sure the morning flurry of customers was tapering off and told them I would be back later in the afternoon when everybody was coming off the beach. I had a free day.

The phone book didn't have his name. I hadn't expected it to. I looked up The Church of the Lord's Will under all possible variants and didn't find it. I didn't see anything in the Camps listing. Around the corner at the Chamber of Commerce Hesterson was known but no more than as somebody who had been seen and about whom merchants had made inquiries. I began to feel a challenge.

I asked several merchants who had been established for a long time on Main Street and would have been solicited. They all knew the little black preacher with the collar or Sister Marie but didn't know where they lived or where the camp was. Had I tried the post office?

55   The post office keeps information close to its vest because you may be a bill collector, but if you ask for something reasonable like the location of a store you get an obliging answer. I asked for the camp. The clerk didn't know but he threw the question in the air, "Wilbur! The old black reverend who has a box? You know? The one who wears the collar? You know anything about a camp he has? Where it is?"

He heard an answer I didn't and passed it to me. "We don't know about the camp. You can find him on Rascher's Lane. Take 28 west. Watch for Lester Street about a half mile after the rotary. Take a right. Go in to the second left. It's dirt. That's Rascher's. It's only a block or two long and dead ends. He's in there."

My station wagon was in the lot behind the row of stores across the street. I stood between parked cars waiting for a break in three lanes of traffic to coincide, but when it occurred I didn't dart through in the entrepreneurial way that my son warned me would one day put me in the hospital. A feeling that I had left something undone held me back. Was it that—instead of being a pleasant surprise to Hesterson—I might be intruding? Ought I to have let him know with more than "I'll drop in on you some-day" said the year before last?

Standing in indecision I realized that I had neglected an obvious source of information. Who would have a better line on a children's camp than the Board of Health? The rule is "When in doubt delay," and a delay to seek knowledge is espe-cially praiseworthy. Town offices were in the adjoining building.

Bureaucrats may take long coffee breaks, they may disappear early Friday afternoon, they may be set in concrete; but the blessed thing about them is that they know. If you want to know something don't ask the president of the United States or a selectman, ask whoever has been in that department since Day One. The firmly made woman doubtless had. She nodded before I told her all I already knew.

"We hear about that camp. Wherever it is isn't in this county. I know it isn't in my town. I got curious and asked the towns around. It isn't in any town from Harwich to Falmouth."

"The Reverend Mr. Hesterson is on Rascher's Lane, that's right, isn't it?"

"He's there with his sister. He rents a four-room house on a quarter-acre. It abuts watershed land. There's no camp in there."

Others might have begun to smell fraud sooner, but they had not had Zeal Hesterson's lovely smile laid on them, or known that, rain or shine, he walked the length of August days in black sweat-sodden clothes, in shoes with open seams, and preferred a glass of cold water. What crime would such a man commit? Did he keep a chorus girl? Did he bet on horses? I sat in my car deciding whether to go the ten minutes to Rascher's Lane or mind my own business and get back to my shop. I decided I did not wish to pry.

Still, there is something in us that wants it known that we have not been hoodwinked.

3

65   A REAL-ESTATE MAN CAME IN with an offer for the lot that adjoins the store. I called Mahlon Weber to try it out on him. Mahlon was in his eighties. I always thought of him as a man whose mind would slow down but would retain essential clarity, the way we envision age for sound people.

We had not been together for more than a few words for nearly a year, since he and his wife had gone to Florida for their six-months-and-a-day tax year and returned to the Cape. The interval was long enough to isolate a subtle change. He sat erectly as if slightly distrusting the security of the chair. His hand wavered with the cup. I hadn't noticed that before. His responses required more than the expected amount of time to compose and were delivered with a slight rush as if they had been held phrase-by-phrase in a computer's buffer. He didn't encourage me to sell Cape Cod property before I had to, and then"—not at any price that doesn't net you after tax—the fair-market value of the property—before tax. Somebody will be smart enough—to want it that much." The advice couldn't have been better; it was what I thought.

He observed that I studied his lips, waiting for the phrases to fall.

"I'm getting a little rocky. I have a touch of Alzheimer's, Eleanor. I've known it for two years."

"If you do have it, it's the barest trace. You're going to make it all right, Mahlon."

70   "If I die soon enough. How many years do I have on you? I'm eighty-four."

"Twenty-two. I'm getting there. You're in good shape."

"Save your money, Eleanor. Old age can be expensive. I'm going to pay my own way—all the way—no matter what."

"You did it right."

"I'm lucky. I had an education. I could borrow money to go into business. People came to Cape Cod. For houses. For stores."

75   "Some people have the same luck and don't use it."

"True, Eleanor. True. You and I used our luck. Most people have no luck to use."

I told him about the Reverend Zeal Hesterson. I told him I had sat in the parking lot, making up my mind what do; and then driving to Rascher's Lane, which surprised Mahlon as much as it had me after I had, I thought, decided to leave it alone.

"Did you want to have it out with him?"

"I don't know what I wanted. I wanted at least to see what there was to see with my own eyes. I wanted to know. I seem to have been born wanting to know."

80   I described the neglected street of two short blocks with minimal frame houses on either side and a woods at the end.

"I went to the end of the first block and stopped. There wasn't a soul around. I asked myself what I was doing there. What satisfaction would I have from walking in on him and saying. 'Aha!'? I didn't know if he had ever noticed the station wagon in my lot with the store's card taped to the window. He might be sitting on his porch. I was afraid he might see me. I turned around in a hurry and got out of there."

"Forget it. You did the right thing. People who have no luck—have to be excused some things."

When Mahlon got up to leave, he tested his balance before his first step. He then went on as confidently as a man twenty years younger whose luck might last a few more years.

THE FOLLOWING AUGUST, in the expected week, Zeal Hesterson appeared, wiping the leather of his hat, on an oppressive overcast day a merchant is entitled to after a week of nothing but damn sunshine. Our customers appreciate a day off from the beach too. They like a day in the shops—especially mine—before they go home to Worcester, Syracuse, Cleveland, Des Moines. Where else are they going to find Vicki of Pazcuaro's embroidered Mexican robes and Andersen's Danish pewter and Rose Fox's antique jewelry from New York? The other shops have Cape Cod gifte shoppe stuffe.

85   The Reverend Hesterson found me in what was building up to be the busiest day of the year. Fortunately we were staffed for it, and I wasn't tied down writing sales. My eye was available for

customers who needed a word of information. I greeted customers who were pleased to be recognized after having been in only once before, two years ago. That's the kind of store I have.

I gave Hesterson the keys to the city. After refreshing himself he came to stand beside me in the pottery room, out of the way of the heaviest traffic. I asked him what kind of year it was for the camp.

"It is always a good summer for the boys. It is so different from the city. Is your business successful this year? You have so many customers."

"About as expected. How many boys do you get?"

He ran the numbers in his head. "By the end, more than sixty-five been there. A lot of cars in your parking lot."

I felt welling up a compulsion to go to the edge, to let him suspect that I knew his secret—or might soon come to know it—was capable of knowing it if I chose. "That means that for each one- or two-week period you get—how many boys? Eight or ten?"

"It depends. Some stay longer, some not as long."

"Eight or ten at a time?"

"Something like that. Yes, sometimes twelve."

"I'm coming to visit one of these years if you don't mind."

"I would be happy. One day I saw a station wagon like yours near my house. I thought, our friend Mrs. McAlly is coming to visit us. I was disappointed. Next time."

His face wore its usual innocence, but knowing what I thought I knew, I saw in it the capability of guile. Of course. How could he have survived without guile?

"Someday," I said, and no more. I did not know which of us knew more than the other, more than either of us wanted to know. I didn't want to encourage myself to go further.

He took out the same old notebook—or one worn exactly like it. Pages had lost their grip on the wire binding. He licked two leathery fingers and raised the page with my name and amount penciled in the round childish hand. "You have been good to us. Folks see your name. They give us something because they know you."

All right, then—maybe the camp wasn't in Hyannis. Maybe it wasn't in the county. Maybe it was in the Berkshires or in Maine. Maybe he raised money this way and sent them a check.

100   What difference did it make if it wasn't anywhere?

If the Lord didn't think Hesterson should have the money He shouldn't have sent him in to see me on a day like that in the suit, the hard collar, the hat, the shoes anybody else would have thrown away. The Lord should have had him mail me a brochure printed in blue ink, so I could give it thought and exercise judgment. If I thought he had something good going I would put him on my list to get a check. There would be a paper trail, the IRS would be happy.

I took two twenties and a ten out of the register and wrote a memo on the tally *$50 Hesterson* to remind myself that the shortage was not accountable to one of the summer girls. "I'm relying on you to do good work. You can show in the book that I gave fifty. Maybe somebody else will be inspired."

He laid his benedictory smile on me. "The Lord will bless you."

I thought perhaps not. The Lord knew what fifty dollars amounted to from somebody born lucky. "If He pleases," I said. "Take care of yourself."

105   Under the leather his toes flexed, trying to help his hand write my name and $50. He folded the ledger and returned it to his breast pocket. "The Lord takes care. He puts us in the way of peril to show He is the one who snatches us back to a safe place."

I thought it roundabout, not the way I would choose; a show-off tithe He would not especially appreciate if I did it. I said I would try to stop by when the boys were there, but it was not easy to get away from the store in the summer.

Edna O'Brien

Edna O'Brien is the author of six books of
stories: *The Love Object, A Scandalous Woman, Mrs.
Reinhardt, Returning, A Fanatic Heart,* and *Lantern
Slides.* Among her eight novels are *The Country
Girls, The Lonely Girl, Girls in Their Married Bliss,* and
I Hardly Knew You.

Brother

BAD CESS TO HIM. Thinks I don't know, that
I didn't smell a rat. All them bachelors swaggering in here; calling him out to the haggart in case I twigged. "Tutsy this and Tutsy
that." A few readies in it for them; along with drives and big
feeds. They went the first Sunday to reconnoiter, walk the land
and so forth. The second Sunday they went in for refreshments.
Three married sisters, all gawks. If they're not hitched up by now
there must be something wrong; harelip or a limp or fits. He's
no oil painting, of course. Me doing everything for him; making his porridge and emptying his worshipful Po, for God knows
how many years. Not to mention his lumbago, and the liniment
I rubbed in.

"I'll be good to you, Maisie," he says. Good! A bag of toffees
on a holy day. Takes me for granted. All them fly-boys at thresh-
ing time trying to ogle me up into the loft for a fumble. Puckauns.

I'd take a pitchfork to any one of them; so would he if he knew. I scratched his back many's the night and rubbed the liniment on it. Terrible aul smell. Eucalyptus.

"Lower . . . lower," he'd say, "down there." Down to the puddingy bits, the lupins. All to get to my Mary. He had a Mass said in the house after. Said he saw his mother, our mother; something on her mind. I had to have grapefruit for the Priest's breakfast, had to depip it. These Priests are real gluttons. He ate in the breakfast room and kept admiring things in the cabinet, the china bell and the bog-oak cabin and so forth. Thought I'd part with them. I was running in and out with hot tea, hot water, hot scones; he ate enough for three. Then the big handshake; Matt giving him a tenner. I never had that amount in my whole life. Ten bob on Fridays to get provisions, including sausages for his breakfast. Woeful the way he never consulted me. He began to get hoity-toity, took off that awful trousers with the greasy backside from all the sweating and lathering on horseback, trac- tor and bike; threw it in the fire cavalier-like. Had me airing a suit for three days. I had it on a clotheshorse turning it round every quarter of an hour, for fear of it scorching.

Then the three bachelors come into the yard again, blabbing about buying silage off him. They had silage to burn. It stinks the countryside. He put on his cap and went out to talk to them. They all leant on the gate, cogitating. I knew 'twas fishy but it never dawned on me it could be a wife. I'd had gone out and sent them packing. Talking low they were and at the end they all shook hands. At the supper he said he was going to Galway Sunday.

5   "What's in Galway?" I said.

"A greyhound," he said.

First mention of a greyhound since our little Daisy died. The pride and joy of the Parish she was. Some scoundrels poi- soned her. I found her in a fit outside in the shed, yelps coming out of her, and foam. It nearly killed him. He had a rope that he was ruminating with, for months. Now this bombshell. Galway.

"I'll come with you, I need a sea breeze," I said.

"It's all male, it's stag," he said, and grinned.

10   I might have guessed. Why were they egging him on, I'll never know except 'twas to spite me. Some of them have it in for

me; I drove bullocks of theirs off our land, I don't give them any haults on bonfire night. He went up to the room then and wouldn't budge. I left a slice of griddle bread with golden syrup on it outside the door. He didn't touch it. At dawn I was raking the ashes and he called me, real softsoapy, "Is that you, Maisie, is that you?" Who in blazes' name did he think it was—Bridget, or Mary of the Gods! "Come in for a minute," he said. "There's a flea or some goddamn thing itching me, maybe it's a tick, maybe they've nested." I strip the covers and in thou'll candle-light he's like one of those Saints that they boil, thin and raky. Up to then I only ventured in the dark, on windy nights when he'd say he heard a ghost, and I had to go to him. I reconnoiter his white body while he's muttering on about the itch, said, "Soldiers in the tropics minded itch more than combat." He read that in an almanac.

"Maisie," he says in a watery voice, and puts his hand on mine and steers me to his shorthorn. Pulled the stays off of me. Thinking I don't know what he was after. All pie. Raving about me being the best sister in the wide world and "I'd give my last shilling" and so forth. Talked about his young days when he hunted with a ferret. Babble, babble. His limbs were like jelly and then the grunts and him burying himself under the red flannel eiderdown, saying God would strike us.

The next Sunday he was off again. Not a word to me since the tick mutiny, except to order me to drive cattle or harness the horse. Got a new pullover, a most unfortunate color, like pic-calilli. He didn't get home that Sunday until all hours. I heard the car door banging. He boiled himself milk, because the saucepan was on the range with the skin on it. I went up to the village to get meal for the hens and everyone was gassing about it. My brother had got engaged for the second time in two weeks. First it was a Dymphna and now it was a Tilly. It seemed he was in their parlor—pictures of cows and millstreams on the wall— sitting next to his intended, eating cold ox-tongue and beetroot when he leans across the table, points to Tilly and says, "I think I'd sooner her."

Uproar. They all dropped utensils and gaped at him, think-ing it a joke. He sticks to his guns, so much so that her father and the bachelors drag him out into the garden for a heart-to-heart. Garden. It seems it's only high grass and an obelisk that wobbles. They said, "What the Christ, Matt?" He said, "I prefer Tilly, she's plumper." Tilly was called out and the two of them were told to walk down to the gate and back, to see what they had in common.

In a short time they return and announce that they understand one another and wish to be engaged. Gink. She doesn't know the catastrophe she's in for. She doesn't know about me and my status here. Dymphna had a fit, shouted, threw bits of beetroot and gizzard all about and said, "My sister is a witch." Had to be carried out and put in a box room, where she shrieked and banged with a set of fire irons that were stored there. Parents didn't care, at least they were getting one cissy off their hands. Father breeds French herds, useless at it. A name like Charlemagne. The bachelors said Matt was a brave man, drink was mooted. All the arrangements that had been settled on Dymphna were now transferred to Tilly. My brother drank port wine and got maudlin. Hence the staggers in the yard when he got home and the loud octavians. Never said a word at the breakfast. I had to hear it in the village. She has mousey hair and one of her eyes squints but instead of calling it a squint the family call it a "lazy eye." It is to be a quiet wedding. He hasn't asked me, he won't. Thinks I'm too much of a gawk with my gap teeth, and that I'd pass remarks and say, "I've eaten to my satisfaction and if I ate any more I'll go flippety-floppety," a thing he makes me say here to give him a rise in the wet evenings.

15   All he says is, "There'll be changes, Maisie, and it's for the best." Had the cheek to ask me to make an eiderdown for the bed, rose-colored satin. I'll probably do it, but it will only be a blind. He thinks I'm a softie. I'll be all pie to her at first, bringing her the tea in bed and asking her if she'd like her hair done with the curling tongs. We'll pick elder flowers to make jelly. She'll be in a shroud before the year is out. To think that she's all purty now, like a little peacock, preening herself. She won't even have the last rites. I've seen a photo of her. She sent it to him for under his pillow. I'll take a knife to her, or a hatchet. I've been in Our Lady's once before, it isn't that bad. Big teas on

Sundays, and fags. I'll be out in a couple of years. He'll be so morose from being all alone, he'll welcome me back, with open arms. It's human nature. It stands to reason. The things I did for him, going to him in the dark, rubbing in that aul liniment, washing out at the rain barrel together, mother-naked, my bosoms slapping against him, often saw the stars fading and me bursting my sides with the things he said—"Dotey." Dotey no less. I might do for her out of doors.

Lure her to the waterfall to look for eggs. There're swans up there and geese. He loves the big geese eggs. I'll get behind her when we're on that promontory and give her a shove. It's very slippy from the moss. I can just picture her going down, being swept away like a newspaper or an empty canister, yelling, then not yelling. I'll call the alarm. I'll shout for him. If they do smell a rat and tackle me I'll tell them that I could feel beads of moisture on my brother's poll without even touching it, I was that close to him. There's no other woman could say that, not her, not any woman. I'm all he has, I'm all he'll ever have. Roll on, nuptials. Daughter of death is she.

Richard Ford

Richard Ford, a Pulitzer Prize winner, is the author of *A Piece of My Heart, The Sportswriter, The Ultimate Good Luck, Rock Spring,* and *Wildlife.* He wrote the introduction for *The Best American Short Stories, 1990.*

Electric City

IN THE FALL OF 1960, WHEN I WAS SIXTEEN and my father was for a time not working, my mother met a man named Warren Miller and fell in love with him. This was in Great Falls, Montana, at the time of the Gypsy Basin oil boom, and my father had brought us there in the spring of that year up from Lewiston, Idaho, in the belief that people—small people like him—were making money in Montana or soon would be, and he wanted a piece of that good luck before all of it collapsed and was gone in the wind.

My father was a golfer. A teaching pro. He had been to college though not to the war. And since 1944, the year when I was born and two years after he married my mother, he had worked at that—at golf—at the small country clubs and public courses in the towns near where he'd grown up, around Colfax and the Palouse Hills of eastern Washington State. And during that time, the years when I was growing up, we had lived in Coeur d'Alene and McCall, Idaho, and in Endicott and Pasco and Walla Walla, where both he and my mother had gone to college and where they had met and gotten married.

My father was a natural athlete. His own father had owned a clothing store in Colfax and made a good living, and he had learned to play golf on the kinds of courses he had taught on. He could play every sport—basketball and ice hockey and throw horseshoes, and he had played baseball in college. But he loved the game of golf because it was a game other people found difficult and that was easy for him. He was a smiling, handsome man with dark hair—not tall but with delicate hands and a short fluid swing that was wonderful to see but never strong enough to move him into the higher competition of the game. He was good at teaching people to play golf though. He knew how to discuss the game patiently, in ways to make you think you had talent for it, and people liked being around him. Sometimes he and my mother would play together and I would go along with them and pull their cart, and I knew he knew how they looked—good-looking, young, happy. My father was soft-spoken and good-natured and optimistic—not slick in the way someone might think. And though it is not a usual life to be a golfer, to make your living at it the way anyone does who is a salesman or a doctor, my father was in a sense not a usual kind of man: he was innocent and he was honest, and it is possible he was suited perfectly for the life he had made.

In Great Falls my father took a job two days a week at the air base, at the course there, and worked the rest of the time at the club for-members-only, across the river. The Wheatland Club that was called. He worked extra because, he said, in good times people wanted to learn a game like golf, and good times rarely lasted long enough. He was thirty-nine then, and I think he hoped he'd meet someone there, someone who'd give him a tip, or let him in on a good deal in the oil boom, or offer him a better job, a chance that would lead him and my mother and me to something better.

5   We rented a house on Eighth Street North in an older neighborhood of single-story, brick-and-frame houses. Ours

was yellow and had a low, paled fence across the front of it and a weeping birch tree in the side yard. Those streets are not far from the train tracks and are across the river from the refinery where a bright flame burned at all hours from the stack above the metal tank buildings. I could hear the shift whistles blow in the morning when I woke up, and late at night the loud whooshing of machinery processing crude oil from the wildcat fields north of us.

My mother did not have a job in Great Falls. She had worked as a bookkeeper for a dairy concern in Lewiston, and in the other towns where we had lived she had been a substitute teacher in math and science—subjects she enjoyed. She was a pretty, small woman who had a good sense for a joke and who could make you laugh. She was two years younger than my father, had met him in college in 1941 and liked him, and simply left with him when he'd taken a job in Spokane. I do not know what she thought my father's reasons were for leaving his job in Lewiston and coming to Great Falls. Maybe she noticed something about him—that it was an odd time in his life when his future had begun to seem different to him, as if he couldn't rely on it just to take care of itself as it had up until then. Or maybe there were other reasons, and because she loved him she went along with him. But I do not think she ever wanted to come to Montana. She liked eastern Washington, liked the better weather there, where she had been a girl. She thought it would be too cold and lonely in Great Falls, and people would not be easy to meet. Yet she must've believed at the time that this was a normal life she was living, moving, and working when she could, having a husband and a son, and that it was fine.

THE SUMMER OF THAT YEAR was a time of forest fires. Great Falls is where the plains begin, but south and west and east of there are mountains. You could see mountains on clear days from the streets of town—sixty miles away the high eastern front of the Rocky Mountains themselves, blue and clear-cut, running to Canada. In early July, fires started in the timber canyons beyond Augusta and Choteau, towns that were insignificant to me but that were endangered. Fires began by mysterious causes. They burned on and on through July and August and into September when it was thought that an early fall would bring rains and possibly snow, though that is not what happened.

Spring had been a dry season and lasted dry into summer. I was a city boy and knew nothing about crops of timber, but we all heard that farmers believed dryness forecasted dryness, and read in the paper that standing timber was drier than wood put in a kiln, and that if farmers were smart they would cut their wheat early to save losses. Even the Missouri River dropped to a low stage, and fish died, and dry mud flats opened between the banks and the slow stream, and no one boated there.

My father taught golf every day to groups of airmen and their girlfriends, and at the Wheatland Club he played four-somes with ranchers and oilmen and bankers and their wives, whose games he was paid to improve upon and tried to. In the evenings through that summer he would sit at the kitchen table after work, listening to a ball game from the East and drinking a beer, and read the paper while my mother fixed dinner and I did school work in the livingroom. He would talk about people at the club. 'They're all good enough fellows,' he said to my mother. 'We won't get rich working for rich men, but we might get lucky hanging around them.' He laughed about that. He liked Great Falls. He thought it was wide open and undiscovered, and no one had time to hold you back, and that it was a good time to live there. I don't know what his ideas for himself were then, but he was a man, more than most, who liked to be happy. And it must've seemed as though, just for that time, he had finally come to his right place.

10   By the first of August the timber fires to the west of us had not been put out, and a haze was in the air so that you could sometimes not see the mountains or where the land met the sky. It was a haze you wouldn't detect if you were inside of it, only if you were on a mountain or in an airplane and could see Great Falls from above. At night I stood at the window and looked west up the valley of the Sun River toward the mountains that were blazing, I could believe that I saw flames and hills on fire and men moving, though I couldn't see that, could only see a

brightening, wide and red and deep above the darkness between the fire and all of us. At night I would wake up and taste smoke and smell it. Twice I even dreamed our house had caught fire, a spark travelling miles on a wind and catching in our roof, consuming everything. Though I knew even in this dream that the world would spin on and we would survive, and the fire did not matter so much. I did not understand, of course, what it meant not to survive.

Such a fire could not help changing things, and there was a feeling in Great Falls, some attitude in general, that was like discouragement. There were stories in the paper, wild stories. Indians were said to have set fires to get the jobs putting them out. A man was seen driving a loggers road throwing flaming sticks out his truck window. Poachers were to blame. A peak far back in the Marshall Mountains was said to have been struck by lightning a hundred times in an hour. My father heard on the golf-course that criminals were fighting the fire, murderers and rapists from Deer Lodge, men who'd volunteered but then slipped away and back to civilized life.

No one, I think, thought Great Falls would burn. Too many miles separated us from the fire, too many other towns would have to go first—too much bad luck falling one way. But people wet the roofs of their houses, and planes took off every day carrying men to jump into the flames. West of us smoke rose like thunderheads, as if the fire itself could make rain. And as the wind stiffened in the afternoon, we all knew that the fire had jumped a trench line or rushed forward or exploded into some untouched place, and that we were all affected, even if we never saw flames or felt the heat.

I was then beginning the eleventh grade in Great Falls High School and was trying to play football, a game I did not like and wasn't good at, and tried to play only because my father thought I could make friends by playing. There were days, though, that we sat out football practice because the doctor said smoke would scar our lungs and we wouldn't feel it. I would go on those days and meet my father at the Wheatland Club—the base course having closed because of the fire danger—and hit practice balls with him late in the day. My father began to work fewer days as the summer went on, and was home more. People did not come to the club because of the smoke and the dryness. He taught fewer lessons, saw fewer of the members he had met and made friends with the spring before. He worked more in the pro-shop, sold golf equipment and clothes and magazines, rented carts, spent more time collecting balls along the edge of the river by the willows where the driving range ended.

On an afternoon in late September, two weeks after I had started school and the fires in the mountains west of us seemed to be lasting forever, I walked with my father out on the driving range with wire baskets. One man was hitting balls off the practice tee far back and to the left of us. I could hear the thwock of the club and a hiss as the balls arched out into the twilight, hit and bounced toward us. At home, the night before, he and my mother had talked about the election that was coming. They were Democrats. Both their families had been. But my father said on that night that he was considering the Republicans now. Nixon, he said, was a good lawyer. He was not a personable man, but he would stand up to the labor unions.

My mother laughed at him and put her hands over her eyes as if she didn't want to see him. "Oh, not you, too, Jerry," she said. "Are you becoming a right-to-work advocate?" She was joking. I don't think she cared who he voted for, and they did not talk about politics. We were in the kitchen and food was already set out on the table.

"Things feel like they've gone too far in one direction," my father said. He put his hands on either side of his plate. I heard him breathe. He still had on his golf clothes, green pants and a yellow nylon shirt with a red club emblem on it. There had been a railroad strike during that summer but he had not talked about unions, and I didn't think it had affected us.

My mother was standing and drying her hands at the sink. "You're a working man, I'm not," she said. "I'll just remind you of that, though."

"I wish we had a Roosevelt to vote for," my father said. "He had a feel for the country."

"That was just a different time then," my mother said, and sat down across the metal table from him. She was wearing a blue and white checked dress and an apron. "Everyone was afraid then, including us. Everything's better now. You forget that."

20 "I haven't forgotten anything," my father said. "But I'm interested in thinking about the future now."

"Well," she said. She smiled at him. "That's good. I'm glad to hear that. I'm sure Joe's glad of it, too." And then we ate dinner.

The next afternoon, though, at the end of the driving range by the willows and the river, my father was in a different mood. He had not given a lesson that week, but wasn't tense and didn't seem mad at anything. He was smoking a cigarette, something he didn't ordinarily do.

"It's a shame not to work in warm weather," he said, and smiled. He took one of the golf balls out of his basket, drew back and threw it through the willow branches toward the river where it hit down in the mud without a sound. "How's your football going?" he asked me. "Are you going to be the next Bob Waterfield?"

"No," I said. "I don't think so."

25 "I won't be the next Walter Hagen, either," he said. He liked Walter Hagen. He had a picture of him wearing a broad-brimmed hat and a heavy overcoat, laughing at the camera as he teed off some place where there was snow on the ground. My father kept that picture inside the closet door in his and my mother's bedroom.

He stood and watched the lone golfer who was driving balls out on to the fairway. We could see him silhouetted. "There's a man who hits the ball nicely," he said, watching the man take his club back smoothly, then sweep through his swing. "He doesn't take chances. Get the ball in the middle of the fairway, then take the margin of error. Let the other guy foul up. That's what Walter Hagen did. The game came naturally to him."

"Isn't it the same with you?" I asked, because that's what my mother had said, that my father had never needed to practice.

"Yes it is," my father said, smoking. "I thought it was easy. There's probably something wrong with that."

"I don't like football," I said.

30 My father glanced at me and then stared at the west where the fire was darkening the sun, turning it purple. "I liked it," he said

in a dreamy way. "When I had the ball and ran up the field and dodged people, I liked that."

"I don't dodge enough," I said. I wanted to tell this to him because I wanted him to tell me to quit football and do something else. I liked golf and would've been happy to play it.

"I wasn't going to not play golf, though," he said, "even though I'm probably not cagey enough for it." He was not listening to me, now, though I didn't hold it against him.

Far away at the practice tee I heard a thwock as the lone man drove a ball up into the evening air. There was a silence as my father and I waited for the ball to hit and bounce. But the ball actually hit my father, hit him on the shoulder above the bottom of his sleeve—not hard or even hard enough to cause pain.

My father said, "Well. For Christ's sake. Look at that." He looked down at the ball beside him on the ground, then rubbed his arm. We could see the man who'd hit the ball walking back toward the clubhouse, his driver swinging beside him like a walking cane. He had no idea where the balls were falling. He hadn't dreamed he'd hit my father.

35 My father stood and watched the man disappear into the long white clubhouse building. He stood for a while as if he was listening and could hear something I couldn't hear—laughing, possibly, or music from far away. He had always been a happy man, and I think he may simply have been waiting for something to make him feel that way again.

"If you don't like football,"—and he suddenly looked at me as if he'd forgotten I was there—"then just forget about it. Take up the javelin throw instead. There's a feeling of achievement in that. I did it once."

"All right," I said. And I thought about the javelin throw—about how much a javelin would weigh and what it was made of and how hard it would be to throw the right way.

My father was staring toward where the sky was beautiful and dark and full of colors. "It's on fire out there, isn't it? I can smell it."

"I can too," I said, watching.

40 "You have a clear mind, Joe." He looked at me. "Nothing bad will happen to you."

"I hope not," I said.

"That's good," he said, "I hope so, too." And we went on then picking up golf balls and walking back toward the clubhouse.

WHEN WE HAD WALKED BACK TO THE PRO-SHOP, lights were on inside, and through the glass windows I could see a man sitting alone in a folding chair, smoking a cigar. He had on a business suit, though he had the jacket over his arm and was wearing brown and white golf shoes.

When my father and I stepped inside carrying our baskets of range balls, the man stood up. I could smell the cigar and the clean smell of new golf equipment.

"Hello there, Jerry," the man said, and smiled and stuck out his hand to my father. "How'd my form look to you out there?"

"I didn't realize that was you," my father said, and smiled. He shook the man's hand. "You have a blueprint swing. You can brag about that."

"I spray 'em around a bit," the man said, and put his cigar in his mouth.

"That's everybody's misery," my father said, and brought me to his side. "This is my son, Joe, Clarence. This is Clarence Snow, Joe. He's the president of this club. He's the best golfer out here." I shook hands with Clarence Snow, who was in his fifties and had long fingers, bony and strong, like my father's. He did not shake my hand very hard.

"Did you leave any balls out there, Jerry?" Clarence Snow said, running his hand back through his thin, dark hair and casting a look at the dark course.

"Quite a few," my father said. "We lost our light."

"Do you play this game, too, son?" Clarence Snow smiled at me.

"He's good," my father said before I could answer anything. He sat down on the other folding chair that had his street shoes under it, and began unlacing his white golf shoes. My father was wearing yellow socks that showed his pale, hairless ankles, and he was staring at Clarence Snow while he loosened his laces.

"I need to have a talk with you, Jerry," Clarence Snow said. He glanced at me and sniffed his nose.

"That's fine," my father said. "Can it wait til' tomorrow?"

55   "No it can't," Clarence Snow said. "Would you come up to the office?"

"I certainly will," my father said. He had his golf shoes off and he raised one foot and rubbed it, then squeezed his toes down. "The tools of ignorance," he said, and smiled at me.

"This won't take much time," Clarence Snow said. Then he walked out the front door, leaving my father and me alone in the lighted shop.

My father sat back in his folding chair, stretched his legs in front of him, and wiggled his toes in his yellow socks. "He'll fire me," he said. "That's what this'll be."

"Why do you think that?" I said. And it shocked me.

60   "You don't know about these things, son," my father said. "I've been fired before. These things have a feel to them."

"Why would he do that?" I said.

"Maybe he thinks I fucked his wife," my father said. I hadn't heard him say that kind of thing before, and it shocked me, too. He was staring out the window into the dark. "Of course, I don't know if he has a wife." My father began putting on his street shoes, which were black loafers, shiny and new and thick-soled. "Maybe I won some money from one of his friends. He doesn't have to have a reason." He slid the white shoes under the chair and stood up. "Wait in here," he said. And I knew he was mad, but did not want me to know he was. He liked to make you believe everything was fine and for everybody to be happy if they could be. "Is that OK?" he said.

"It's OK," I said.

"Think about some pretty girls while I'm gone," he said, and smiled at me.

65   Then he walked, almost strolling, out of the little pro-shop and up toward the clubhouse, leaving me by myself with the racks of silver golf clubs and new leather bags and shoes and boxes of balls—all the other tools of my father's trade, still and silent around me like treasures.

WHEN MY FATHER CAME BACK IN TWENTY MINUTES he was walking faster than when he'd left. He had a piece of yellow paper stuck up in his shirt pocket, and his face looked tight. I was sitting on the chair Clarence Snow had sat on. My father picked up his white shoes off the green carpet, put them under his arm, then walked to the cash register and began taking money out of the trays.

"We should go," he said in a soft voice. He was putting money in his pants pocket.

"Did he fire you?" I asked.

"Yes he did." He stood still for a moment behind the open cash register as if the words sounded strange to him or had other meanings. He looked like a boy my own age doing something he shouldn't be doing and trying to do it casually. Though I thought maybe Clarence Snow had told him to clean out the cash register before he left and all that money was his to keep. "Too much of a good living, I guess," he said. Then he said, "Look around here, Joe. See if you see anything you want." He looked around at the clubs and the leather golf bags and shoes, the sweaters and clothes in glass cases. All things that cost a lot of money, things my father liked. "Just take it," he said. "It's yours."

70   "I don't want anything," I said.

My father looked at me from behind the cash register. "You don't want anything? All this expensive stuff?"

"No," I said.

"You've got good character, that's your problem. Not that it's much of a problem." He closed the cash register drawer. "Bad luck's got a sour taste, doesn't it?"

"Yes sir," I said.

75   "Do you want to know what he said to me?" My father leaned on the glass countertop with his palms down. He smiled at me, as if he thought it was funny.

"What?" I said.

"He said he didn't require an answer from me, but he thought I was stealing things. Some yokel lost a wallet out on the course, and they couldn't figure anybody else who could do it. So I was elected." He shook his head. "I'm not a stealer. Do you know it? That's not me."

"I know it," I said. And I didn't think he was. I thought I was more likely to be a stealer than he was, and I wasn't one either.

"I was too well liked out here, that's my problem," he said. "If you help people they don't like you for it. They're like Mormons."

80   "I guess so," I said.

"When you get older," my father said. And then he seemed to stop what he was about to say. "If you want to know the truth don't listen to what people tell you," was all he said.

He walked around the cash register, holding his white shoes, his pants pockets full of money. "Let's go now," he said. He turned off the light when he got to the door, held it open for me, and we walked out into the warm summer night.

WHEN WE'D DRIVEN BACK ACROSS THE RIVER into Great Falls and up Central, my father stopped at the grocery a block from our house, went in and bought a can of beer and came back and sat in the car seat with the door open. It had become cooler with the sun gone and felt like a fall night, although it was dry and the sky was light blue and full of stars. I could smell beer on my father's breath and knew he was thinking about the conversation he would have with my mother when we got home, and what that would be like.

"Do you know what happens," he said, "when the very thing you wanted least to happen happens to you?" We were sitting in the glow of the little grocery store. Traffic was moving behind us along Central Avenue, people going home from work, people with things they liked to do on their minds, things they looked forward to.

85   "No," I said. I was thinking about throwing the javelin at that moment, a high arching throw into clear air, coming down like an arrow, and of my father throwing it when he was my age.

"Nothing at all does," he said, and he was quiet for several seconds. He raised his knees and held his beer can with both hands. "We should probably go on a crime spree. Rob this store or something. Bring everything down on top of us."

"I don't want to do that," I said.

"I'm probably a fool," my father said, and shook his beer can until the beer fizzed softly inside. "It's just hard to see my opportunities right this minute." He didn't say anything else for a while. "Do you love your dad?" he said in a normal voice, after some time had passed.

"Yes," I said.

90   "Do you think I'll take good care of you?"

"Yes," I said. "I think so."

"I will," he said.

My father shut the car door and sat a moment looking out the windshield at the grocery, where people were inside moving back and forth behind the plate-glass windows. "Choices don't always feel exactly like choices," he said. He started the car then, and he put his hand on my hand just like you would on a girl's. "Don't be worried about things," he said. "I feel calm now."

"I'm not worried," I said. And I wasn't, because I thought things would be fine. And even though I was wrong, it is still not so bad a way to set your mind toward the unknown just when you are coming into the face of it.

95   AFTER THAT NIGHT IN EARLY SEPTEMBER things began to move more quickly in our life and to change. Our life at home changed. The life my mother and father lived changed. The world, for as little as I'd thought about it or planned on it, changed. When you are sixteen you do not know what your parents know, or much of what they understand and less of what's in their hearts. This can save you from becoming an adult too early, save your life from becoming only theirs lived over again— which is a loss. But to shield yourself—as I didn't do—seems to be an even greater error, since what's lost is the truth of your parents' life and what you should think about it, and beyond that, how you should estimate the world you are about to live in.

On the night my father came home from losing his job at the Wheatland Club, he told my mother about it straight out and they both acted as if it was a kind of joke. My mother did not get mad or seem upset or ask him why he had gotten fired. They both laughed about it. When we ate supper my mother sat at the table and seemed to be thinking. She said she could not get a job substituting until the term ended, but she would go to the school board and put her name in. She said other people would come to my father for work when it was known he was free, and that this was an opportunity in disguise—the reason we had come here—and that Montanans did not know gold when they saw it. She smiled at him when she said that. She said I could get a job, and I said I would. She said maybe she should become a banker, though she would need to finish college for that. And she laughed. Finally she said. "You can do other things, Jerry. Maybe you've played enough golf for this lifetime."

After dinner, my father went into the living-room and listened to the news from a station we could get from Salt Lake after dark and went to sleep on the couch still wearing his golf clothes. Late in the night they went into their room and closed the door. I heard their voices, talking. I heard my mother laugh again. And then my father laughed and said, loudly, still laughing. "Don't threaten me. I can't be threatened." And later on my mother said. "You've just had your feelings hurt, Jerry, is all." After a while I heard the bathtub running with water, and I knew my father was sitting in the bathroom talking to my mother while she took her bath, which was a thing he liked doing. And later I heard the door close and their light click off and the house become locked in silence.

AND THEN FOR A TIME AFTER THAT my father did not seem to take an interest in working. In a few days the Wheatland Club called—a man who was not Clarence Snow said someone had made a mistake. I talked to the man, who gave me the message to give to my father, but my father did not call back. The air base called him, but again he did not accept. I know he did not sleep well. I could hear doors close at night and glasses tapping together. Some mornings I would look out my bedroom window, and he would be in the backyard in the chill air practicing with a driver, hitting a plastic ball from one property line to the next, walking in his long easy gait as if nothing was bothering him. Other days he would take me on long drives after school, to Highwood and to Belt and Geraldine, which are the towns east of Great Falls, and let me drive the car on the wheat prairie roads where I could be no danger to anyone. And once we drove across the river to Fort Benton and sat in the car and watched golfers playing on the tiny course there above the town.

Eventually, my father began to leave the house in the morning like a man going to a job. And although we did not know where he went, my mother said she thought he went downtown, and that he had left jobs before and that it was always scary for a while, but that finally he would stand up to things and go back and be happy. My father began to wear different kinds of clothes, khaki pants and flannel shirts, regular clothes I saw people wearing, and he did not talk about golf anymore. He talked some about the fires, which still burned late in September in the canyons above Allen Creek and Castle Reef—names I knew about from the *Tribune*. He talked in a more clipped way then. He told me the smoke from such fires went around the world in five days and that the amount of timber lost there would've built 50,000 homes the size of ours. One Friday he and I went to the boxing matches at the City Auditorium and watched boys from Havre fight boys from Glasgow, and afterward in the street outside we could each see the night glow of the fires, pale in the clouds just as it had been in the summer. And my father said, "It could rain up in the canyons now, but the fire wouldn't go out. It would smoulder then start again." He blinked as the boxing crowd shoved around us. "But here we are" he said, and smiled, "safe in Great Falls."

100   It was during this time that my mother began to look for a job. She left an application at the school board. She worked two days at a dress shop, then quit. "I'm lacking in powerful and influential friends," she said to me as if it was a joke. Though it was true that we did not know anyone in Great Falls. My mother knew the people at the grocery store and the druggist's, and my father had known people at the Wheatland Club. But none of them ever came to our house. I think we might've gone someplace new earlier in their life, just picked up and moved away. But no one mentioned that. There was a sense that we were all waiting for something. Out of doors, the trees were through with turning yellow and leaves were dropping onto the cars parked at the curb. It was my first autumn in Montana, and it seemed to me that in our neighborhood the trees looked like an eastern state would and not at all the way I'd thought Montana would be. No trees is what I'd expected, only open prairie, the land and sky joining almost out of sight.

"I COULD GET A JOB TEACHING SWIMMING," my mother said to me on a morning when my father left early and I was looking through the house for my school books. She was standing drinking coffee, looking out the front window, dressed in her yellow bathrobe. "A lady at the Red Cross said I could teach privately if I'd teach a class, too." She smiled at me and crossed her arms. "I'm still a life-saver."

"That sounds good," I said.

"I could teach your dad the backstroke again," she said. My mother had taught me to swim, and she was good at that. She had tried to teach my father the backstroke when we lived in Lewiston, but he had tried and failed at it, and she had made a joke about it afterwards. "The lady said people want to swim in Montana. Why do you think that is? These things always signify a meaning."

"What does it mean?" I said, holding my school books.

She hugged her arms and turned herself a little back and forth as she stood in the window frame watching out. "Oh, that we're all going to be washed away in a big flood. Though I don't believe that. So. Some of us will not be washed away and will float to the top. That's better, isn't it?" She took a drink of coffee.

"It should have a happy ending for the right people," I said.

"That's easy," she said. "Everyone doesn't do it that way, though." She turned and walked away back into the kitchen then to start my breakfast before school.

IN THE DAYS AFTER THAT, my mother went to work at the YWCA in Great Falls, at the brick building that is gone now on Second Street North, near the courthouse. She walked to work from our house and carried her swimming-suit in a vanity case, with a lunch to eat and some makeup articles for when she came home in the afternoon. My father said he was glad if she wanted to work there, and that I should find a job, too, which I had not done. But he didn't mention himself working or how he was spending his days or what he thought about our future or any plans he had made for things. He seemed out of reach to me, as if he had discovered a secret he didn't want to tell. Once, when I walked home from football practice, I saw him inside the

Jack 'n' Jill cafe, sitting at the counter drinking coffee and eating a piece of pie. He was wearing a red plaid shirt and a knitted
cap, and he hadn't shaved. A man I didn't know was sitting on a
stool beside him, reading the *Tribune*. They seemed to be
together. Another time, on a day when the wind was blowing
hard, I saw him walking away from the court-house wearing a
woollen jacket and carrying a book. He turned the corner at the
library and disappeared, and I did not follow him. And one
other time I saw him go into a bar called the Pheasant Lounge
where I thought Great Falls city policemen went. This was at
noon, and I was on my lunch hour and couldn't stay to see more.

When I told my mother that I had seen him these times she
said, "He just hasn't had a chance to get established, yet. This
will be all right finally. There's no lack in him."

110   But I did not think things were all right. I don't believe my
mother knew more than I did then. She was simply surprised,
and she trusted him and thought she could wait longer. But I
wondered if my parents had had troubles that I didn't know
about, or if they had always had their heads turned slightly away
from each other and I hadn't noticed. I know that when they
shut the door to their bedroom at night and I was in my bed
waiting for sleep, listening to the wind come up, I would heard
their door open and close quietly, and my mother come out and
make a bed for herself on the couch in the living-room. Once I
heard my father say, as she was leaving, "You've changed your thinking now, haven't you, Jean?" And my mother say "No." But then
the door closed and she did not say anything else. I do not think
I was supposed to know about this, and I don't know what they
could've said to each other or done during that time. There was
never yelling or arguing involved in it. They simply did not stay
together at night, although during the day when I was present
and life needed to go on normally there was nothing to notice
between them. Coming and going was all. Nothing to make you
think there was trouble or misunderstanding. I simply know
there was, and that my mother for her own reason began to move
away from my father then.

After a time I quit playing football. I wanted to find a job,
though I thought that when spring came, if we were still in Great

Falls, I would try to throw the javelin as my father had said. I had taken the book, *Track and Field for Young Champions,* out of the library and had found the equipment cage in the school basement and inspected the two wooden javelins there, where they were stored against the concrete wall in the shadows. They were slick and polished and thicker than I thought they'd be. Though when I picked one up, it was light and seemed to me perfect for the use it had. And I thought that I would be able to throw it and that it might be a skill—even if it was a peculiar one—that I might some-day excel at in a way my father would like.

I had not made friends in Great Falls. The boys on the foot-ball team lived farther downtown and across the river in Black Eagle. I had had friends in Lewiston, in particular a girlfriend named Iris, who went to the Catholic school and who I had exchanged letters with for several weeks when we had come to Great Falls in the spring. But she had gone to Seattle for the summer and had not written to me. Her father was an Army officer, and it could be her family had moved. I had not thought about her in a while, did not care about her really. It should've been a time when I cared about more things—a new girlfriend or books—or when I had an idea of some kind. But I only cared about my mother and my father then, and in the time since then I have realized that we were not a family who ever cared about much more than that.

THE JOB I FOUND was in the photographer's studio on Third Avenue. It was the place that took airmen's photographs, and engagement and class pictures, and what I did was clean up when school was over, replace bulbs in the photographer's lamps, and rearrange the posing furniture for the next day.

I finished work by five o'clock, and sometimes I would walk home past the YWCA and slip through the back door and down into the long tiled pool room where my mother taught her classes of adults until five, and from five to six was free to teach privately and be paid for it. I would stand at the far end behind the tiers of empty bleachers and watch her, hear her voice, which seemed happy and lively, encouraging and giving instruction. She would stand on the side in her black bathing suit, her skin pale, and make swimming motions with her arms for the students standing in the shallow water. Mostly they were old women, and old men with speckled bald heads. From time to time they ducked their faces into the water and made the swimming motions my mother made—slow, jerky grasps—without really swimming or ever moving, just staying still, standing and pretending. "It's so easy," I would hear my mother say in her bright voice, her arms working the thick air as she talked. "Don't be afraid of it. It's all fun. Think about all you've missed." She'd smile at them when their faces were up, dripping and blinking, some of them coughing. And she would say, "Watch me now." Then she'd pull down her bathing cap, point her hands over her head to a peak, bend her knees and dive straight in, coasting for a moment, then breaking the surface and swimming with her arms bent and her fingers together, cutting the water in easy reaching motions to the far side and back again. The old people—ranchers, I thought, and the divorced wives of farmers—watched her in envy and silence. And I watched, thinking as I did that someone else who saw my mother, not me or my father, but someone who had never seen her before, would think something different. They would think: "Here is a woman whose life is happy"; or "Here is woman with a nice figure to her credit"; or "Here is a woman I wish I could know better, though I never will." And I thought to myself that my father was not a stupid man, and that love was permanent, even though sometimes it seemed to recede and leave no trace at all.

115   ON THE FIRST TUESDAY IN OCTOBER, the day before the World Series began, my father came back to the house after dark. It was chill and dry outside, and when he came in the back door his eyes were bright and his face was flushed and he seemed as if he had been running.

"Look who's here now," my mother said, though in a nice way. She was cutting tomatoes at the sink board and looked around at him and smiled.

"I've got to pack a bag," my father said. "I won't have dinner here tonight, Jean." He went straight back to their room. I was sitting beside the radio waiting to turn on some baseball news, and I could hear him opening a closet door and shoving coat hangers.

My mother looked at me, then she spoke toward the hallway in a calm voice. "Where are you going, Jerry?" She was holding a paring knife in her hand.

"I'm going to that fire," my father said loudly from the bedroom. He was excited. "I've been waiting for my chance. I just heard thirty minutes ago that there's a place. I know it's unexpected."

120   "Do you know anything about fires?" My mother kept watching the empty doorway as if my father was standing in it. "I know about them," she said. "My father was an estimator. Do you remember that?"

"I had to make some contacts in town," my father said. I knew he was sitting on the bed putting on different shoes. The overhead light was on and his bag was out. "It's not easy to get this job."

"Did you hear me?" my mother said. She had an impatient look on her face. "I said you don't know anything about fires. You'll get burned up." She looked at the back door, which he'd left partway open, but she didn't go to close it.

"I've been reading about fires in the library," my father said. He came down the hall and went into the bathroom where he turned on the light and opened the medicine cabinet. "I think I know enough not to get killed."

"Could you have said something to me about this?" my mother said.

125   I heard the medicine cabinet close and my father stepped into the kitchen doorway. He looked different. He looked like he was sure that he was right.

"I should've done that," he said. "I just didn't." He had his shaving-bag in his hand.

"You're not going out there." My mother looked at my father across the kitchen, across over my head in fact, and seemed to smile. "This is a . . . stupid idea," she said, and shook her head.

"No it's not," my father said.

"It isn't your business," my mother said, and pulled up the front of her blue apron and wiped her hands on it, though I don't think her hands were wet. She was nervous. "You don't have to do this. I'm working now."

130 "I know you are," my father said. He turned and went back into the bedroom. I wanted to move from where I was but I didn't know where a better place was to be, because I wanted to hear what they would say. "We're going to dig firebreaks up there," he said from the bedroom. I heard the locks on his bag snap closed. He appeared again in the doorway, holding a gladstone bag, a bag his father had given him when he had gone away to college. "You're not in any danger," he said.

"I might die while you're gone," my mother said. She sat down at the metal table and stared at him. She was angry. Her mouth looked hardened. "You have a son here," she said.

"This won't be for very long," my father said. "It'll snow pretty soon, and that'll be that." He looked at me. "What do you think, Joe? Is this a bad idea?"

"No," I said. And I said it too fast, without thinking what it meant to my mother.

"You'd do it, wouldn't you?" my father said.

135 "Will you like it if your father gets burned up out there and you never see him again?" my mother said to me. "Then you and I go straight to hell together. How will that be?"

"Don't say that, Jean," my father said. He put his bag on the kitchen table and came and knelt beside my mother and tried to put his arms around her. But she got up from her chair and walked back to where she had been cutting tomatoes and picked up the knife and pointed it at him, where he was still kneeling beside the empty chair.

"I'm a grown woman," she said, and she was very angry now. "Why don't you act like a grown man, Jerry?"

"You can't explain everything," my father said.

"I can explain everything," my mother said. She put the knife down and walked out the kitchen door and into the bedroom, the one she had not been sleeping in with my father, and closed the door behind her.

140   My father looked at me from where he was still beside her chair. "I guess my judgement's no good now," he said. "Is that what you think, Joe?"

"No," I said. "I think it is."

And I thought his judgement was good, and that going to fight the fire was a good idea even though he might go and get killed because he knew nothing about it. But I did not want to say all of that to him because of how it would make him feel.

MY FATHER AND I WALKED FROM HOME in the dark down to the Masonic Temple on Central. A yellow Cascade Country school bus was parked at the corner of Ninth, and men were standing in groups waiting to go. Some of the men were bums. I could tell by their shoes and their coats. Though some were just regular men who were out of work, I thought, from other jobs. Three women who were going waited together under the streetlight. And inside the bus, in the dark, I could see Indians were in some of the seats. I could see their round faces, their slick hair, the tint of light off their eyeglasses in the darkness. No one would get in with them, and some men were drinking. I could smell whiskey in the night air.

My father put his bag on a stack of bags beside the bus, then came and stood next to me. Inside the Masonic Temple—which had high steps up to a glass center door—all the lights were on. Several men inside were looking out. One, who was the man I had seen with my father in the Jack 'n' Jill, held a clipboard and was talking to an Indian man beside him. My father gestured to him.

145   "People categorize other people," my father said. "But you shouldn't do that. They should teach you that in school."

I looked at the men around me. Most of them were not dressed warmly enough and were shifting from foot to foot. They looked like men used to work, though they did not seem glad to be going to fight a fire at night. None of them looked like my father, who seemed eager.

"What will you do out there?" I said.

"Work on a fire line," my father said. "They dig trenches the fire won't cross. I don't know much more, to tell you the truth."

He put his hands in his jacket pockets and blew down into his shirt. "I've got this hum in my head now. I need to do something about it."

"I understand," I said.

150 "Tell your mother I didn't mean to make her mad."

"I will," I said.

"We don't want to wake up in our coffins, though, do we? That'd be a rude surprise." He put a hand on my shoulder and pulled me close to him and squeezed me and laughed an odd little laugh, as if the idea had actually given him a scare. He looked across Central Avenue at the Pheasant Lounge, the place I had seen him go into the week before. On the red neon sign over the door a big cock pheasant was busting up into the night air, its wings stretched into the darkness—escaping. Some men waiting at the Masonic Temple had begun to go across the street into the bar. "I'm only thinking about right this minute now," he said. He squeezed my shoulder again, then put his hands back into his jacket pockets. "Aren't you cold?"

"I'm a little cold," I said.

"Then go back home," he said. "You don't need to watch me get on a bus. It might be a long time. Your mother's probably thinking about you."

155 "All right," I said.

"She doesn't need to get mad at you. She's mad enough at me."

I looked at my father. I tried to see his face in the streetlight. He was smiling and looking at me, and I think he was happy for that moment, happy for me to be with him, happy that he was going to a fire now to risk whatever he cared about risking. It seemed strange to me, though, that he could be a man who played golf for a living and then one day become a man who fought forest fires. But it's what was happening, and I thought I would get used to it.

"Are you too old now to give your old dad a kiss?" my father said. "Men love each other, too. You know that, don't you?"

"Yes," I said. And he took my cheeks in his hands and kissed me on the mouth, and squeezed my face. His breath smelled sweet to me and his face was rough.

160 "Don't let what your parents do disappoint you," he said.

"All right," I said. "I won't." I felt afraid then for some reason, and I thought if I stayed there I would show him that I was,
so I turned around and started back up Central in the dark and
the growing cold. When I got to the corner I turned to wave
good-bye. But my father was not in sight, and I thought that he
had already gotten onto the bus and was waiting in his seat
among the Indians.

Mona Simpson

Mona Simpson has published several novels, including *Anywhere But Here* and *The Lost Father.* Her stories have been included in *The Best American Short Stories, The Pushcart Prize* annual, and *Twenty Under Thirty.*

I Am Here to Tell You It Can Be Done

USED TO BE, I WAS ALWAYS SAYING, *This doesn't count.* I lived my life in secret, like if nobody saw, I didn't really have it. I was barely there. I wouldn't admit to a thing. Now I know that what humans observe and talk about is less than what I do alone, without live eyes on me. I want to tell you, don't believe what you've already heard about me. Believe this here alone. I'll tell you far worse than what they know. You see, I'm famous for the wrong reasons. The money girl. For nerving enough to say I care about other than money while I'm still making money. If you quit earning, they'll let you be as high holy as you want. I'm not famous for baking prayer bread, as if just bread weren't good enough for human gossip.

This doesn't count. I won't say that to you about us here today. This counts. For me this counts.

We don't really need this place, any of it, the nice light, they made the windows high so it waterfalls this time of day, the stone, cool, all these architect-made wonders. The first course I led like this, I ran it from behind the teacher's desk of a fourth grade classroom. All of you would have been sitting in rows in those funny little chairs, the men's knees knocking the bellies of the desk part, everybody's back out of joint. People just naturally folded their hands on those desktops, all ready to be ordered.

But it worked. Lot of people got help. Changed. In my office; I have an office, top of this church, in that square steeple, I always wanted a building with arches like we have here on top with nothing in the cutout part so you can see sky, on my wall, I keep pictures of every class. Some send me letters, you know, where they are, just what they're doing.

5   They send presents sometimes. And I'll tell you one funny thing about this course. You know how you get presents you don't like and your first thought is, what can I do with it, how to get rid of it? Well, every present I've ever opened from somebody who knew me here like this, was right. No other way to say it. Just right. You're all going to know each other that much.

I get to feeling like any old teacher. Cept I'm not old. Twenty-five still. But you age fast in religion. You're the Baby Baba and then you're just one of the cons. If you live. Or else you take the institution way. You teach at Harvard, Columbia or Berkeley, on one of those hills. Everything's hush-hush there. You don't hear many souls. Just buildings. Or the mish path. Learn a language with Berlitz tapes and then take a steamship to save the other people. I think we've got enough trouble right here.

You all came today. Big group. Maybe you saw an ad, the brochure, maybe you heard about it on TV, from somebody you know, but you filled out your form, and got here on time this morning to this church. You paid your good money. Thank you for it. I know I am not cheap.

But I am here to tell you that you made no mistake. I am no fraud.

I am somebody who came back from the other side. And I don't mean from life after death. I mean from the dead in life.

10   My name is Dawn. I took it for myself when I ran away from the minister's family I'd been warded to and came out here to our state. I didn't know then that I'd be making sermons myself. I thought I was just another runaway orphan on a greyhound bus out of hell with my last baloney sandwich from home in a brown bag wrinkled up between my feet.

When I turn thirty, I'm changing my name again, to Star Duke. From morning to evening. I was born in Missouri. Baptized Dorothy Ann Maria Matsky.

We have an order to this class. You're going to live here, in the new dorm, for seven days. We will have Confession, Fasting, Penance, Conversion, Communion, Gospel (mine and a little bit from everywhere), and Prayer.

My church is a school. I always liked school, I felt safe in it. But then, too, the studies always seemed beside the point. The real problems never got whispered while we scribbled away with soft pencils solving abstractions on blue-lined paper, so thick so you could still see the wood in it. Where I lived was a papermill town.

Most of you, going on your shoes and the way your hands fold on your laps, look like working people who saved good money to come here. You can tell a lot from people by their shoes. Shoes and handbags. My two aunts taught me that and they meant for money. Cul-lass, they would say. They meant you can tell who's rich. I say, you can tell who is good, who is false, what lies they tell, what they try, how they manage, from a shoe and how a person wears it. An old worn shoe can be a beautiful thing, like a body that's been made to shape by its soul.

15   Who've we got here today? Lot of women. Always. The women make less money in this world but it's the women who can scrape up the dollars, save, scrimp, it's the women who go to the therapists, it's the women who buy the books, all trying to improve their lot and their lot is usually some man. That's not feminist. That's fact. And a lot of you women probably're down about love. Well, we'll get to that too. All in turn.

And some men, I see. Of color, most of you. You seen some too, I know that.

Never too many white men in my course, but a few of you, I count what, four, five. I commend you. Commend anyone who cuts out of his herd. We had one man, he sent his secretary here. Let me tell you something. You can't get nobody to do your soulwork for you. That's one activity you cannot delegate. I sent her packing right back to her typewriter. She didn't want to go. He'd instructed her to take notes, she said. He wouldn't like it, her coming back early.

WELL, I'LL TELL YOU NOW, you can start thinking about relaxing, because your days of drugs are over. Your days of drink, your days of gambling. I had a lifetime gambler in here and he stopped, like that. Smokers we get all the time. They don't use anything. They just quit. I'll have you done with meat too before you go back out there. You'll crave a nice plate of rice and beans with Tabasco and vinegar.

Lot of programs, lot of therapists, they'll say to you, There are no guarantees. I give guarantees.

20   I know it's not easy to listen to a young preacher. The freckles don't help.

A couple of you probably came here today because of religion. And most of you are here because you know I'm a woman in business. And you want to figure out how to build up what I did. That's all right. Don't have to feel bad about it. I know that's the hook, okay, I use it too. So you don't have to sneak around about what you want.

The first year I was in business, I made one million dollars selling Prayer Bread in shopping malls. Two dollars a loaf. I opened one store and I worked. Then it was two, then ten. I brought my bread hot to that banker who wasn't going to give me a loan. I was waiting outside the door with the bread in a basket when they came with their keys in the morning. I will tell you step by step how I made my first million dollars, which unlike a lot of religious leaders in the state of California, I did not spend on myself. I don't save it either. I spend it. On this.

I don't have no fancy house. Nuh-uh. You can see my home. It's here, down outside, the stone cabin. On this property.

I maintain, I will tell you, exactly twenty-five thousand dollars savings. I drive a new but mid-priced car. American. Ford.

There is something you can get from me, not like money, and it will last.

25 MOST OF WHAT YOU'VE LEARNED ALREADY won't work in this world. Else you wouldn't be here. And most of what they taught you, you didn't even know that they were teaching you that then and you sure as hell didn't know why. They were teaching it because they wanted you to be a certain way. Not for your own good like they told you. That's why we have so many falldowns.

You'll notice these days—especially here in our state, there's help for everybody for their everything.

If you drink, you can go to a meeting with alcoholics, any hour of the day, starting every fifteen minutes to the hour.

And with drugs. Same with gambling, eating, sexual problems.

There's groups and groups and groups. And you can talk and talk and talk about drink and drugs and dependency and whatever.

30 As *if all anybody can ever be is what happened to them.*

You notice a lot of people who went through some of what I went through, you went through, who had the same things happen to them—they take those outside garments and they go and make a career out of it.

Women whose husbands beat them, they go and be counselors to other women being beaten up. The incest people write books about being the incest people. The handicapped spend their lives in jobs trying to prove that being handicapped is no handicap. It all has a sad quality, like trying too hard, because why not just take that as given truth and be something else, like a gardener, or a lawyer. Alcoholics, the same thing, well you all know. The rape girls.

I myself didn't want to be no counselor. I didn't want to write down about what happened to me. I didn't want to be any social worker.

I wanted to be what I would have been otherwise.

35   *I wanted to be what I would of if the bad hadn't happened.*
    I wanted to get back what I was before.
    And I want that same for you.
    I want you to be what you're meant to, from the start.
    Now let me sit down and tell you how the world made my outside. The what happened to me part.

40   First of all, there is no such thing as pure. Ain't nowhere. There is good. And that's about as much as you're gonna grasp in this life.

    There is no such thing as pure. I wasn't even back then—before. Though I started out lucky, grew up back of a store with my mama. My daddy was long gone but what did we care. We had more than enough. You never are hungry living back of a store, and for special memories, we had delicacies come in trucks from far-away cities. Fancy papered jars and cans. In the Midwest in those days we had fancy Chinese oranges packed in syrup.

    And the world was jungle. Everything smelled. The leaves in the morning gave a fresh tart taste so it almost hurt. I learned God way back then and had planted in me my calling. Prettinear every day, I went down to the river where it was all mud with the neighbor boy. I took a big glass jar—this jar was the pride of our kitchen, this one jar, olives had come in it, from Europe—it was so big and shaped and thick good glass but my mama still let me take it down to the river to catch minnows in the muddy shallow.

    We kept going and it was a long warm day on one or the other side of summer and we walked into a baptism by the great Reverend Arthur B. Sands Gray. He is the man that day who dropped the seed in my heart that later grew into my profession. He didn't have to plant much. The hole was already here. He just dropped the word in and flicked some soil over it light, like—with a fingernail.

    It went on a long time, his baptism there, and first the neighbor boy and me lagged back on those muddy banks. I had a sack dress, no underwear, no shoes, nothing, but I was all browned colors same as the water. The neighbor boy had britches cut halfway down his calf and he was pale and got little pink bites all over him. The Reverend had a close group of six or eight but they were decent grownups dressed in clothes that were the colors they started as, they held their little shoes in their hands. He preached to them but more and more he kept glancing up at us kids clinging with our hands and feet to the cottonwoods.

45   *You kids know you're gonna die,* he shouted.

You kids understand you poor?

People gonna tell you wrong things all you life, people gonna try make you believe you wrong and if you let them you're gonna curl up and grow in funny like toes in a bad shoe.

They gonna try and stunt you.

Is no such thing as justice in this here world and they not going to see in you what I see in you through them grey and green eyes today.

50   The neighbor boy squatted down pouring out river water with the guppies bellying desperate down the slow red banks.

Most of you probably don't know rivertime. There are different things you come to feel about religion if you grow up around a river not an ocean. When I first came here and I became Dawn and I was fifteen I got off the bus with my duffle and it was Santa Monica and I walked down to the pier and on the sand and into the water and the water was like nothing I'd ever seen—that color. And it was big and it came leaping at me like dogs and it was clear and it was clean.

I stripped my clothes down to the bottom peel and left my everything including money hidden in a split between the sole of my shoe and went in. I remember those waves coming up around my bare hips all foamy like a shower or a co'cola but blue a color the only thing I'd seen like that before was an eye.

Rivertime is different: water is brown, plainer than you can imagine here. Bushes that grow by the sides, blooming on top, smelling delicate in wind, riverplants stay the same, mile after mile. And a dirty slime gag pulls under like the mineral in shit, the half of vegetable rot. The day goes on longer. You do get time. We went baptized that day and the Reverend told us we would never die now, no matter what they did to us, we could live always, they couldn't take away our eternity. We would get ours after. Somewhere else.

And when he pushed my head down in the water he pressed something sharp and pointy in my hand.

55 *Keep you own self dignity. Mind you soul.*

That was what he said that day when there was time for every-thing. The neighbor boy and I, far down the river in a shade ditch, under dizzy willows, took our clothes off, the one thing we each had and lay with our bodies matching leg by leg, knee fac-ing into knee, chests pressing. We were the same length exactly.

We figured out the beginning of the world ourselves. No one had told us yet. Everything there, the trees gathering and rip-pling above us, the river sound, a spring rise smell and its back-yank under, all was still. But he pushed against me and stopped as if the fabric of my dress held it back, but I had no dress it was skin and then he raised himself up, I swear so he was levitated off the ground balancing on me, like an acrobat in the air held by one baton jabbed on a taut trampoline, and then I broke and he fell down, my hand clutching the thing in my fist, we fell through such hot pain. But then he moved again and the pain tunneled, it was different. My other hand, not the one holding the sharp thing the Reverend gave me, settled on top of his butt, a hard place, light skin over bone, I thought then and do now, the most arrogant place in a man.

Then I convulsed. I didn't know what it was but I didn't know what any of it was, it was us a way we hadn't been before. First my mouth filled with water, then I looked down and the bodies of us were moving I couldn't tell which was me and which was him and then for a moment after it was like fire went out from where we joined and I felt his thighs and my thighs both, my body went ahead far beyond me, ran away, like two dogs along the water and when it came back—it seemed like minutes later— I had light inside.

My fist was still closed over whatever it was the Reverend had put there. On my left side sat the empty glass jar. For a moment when our bodies left and ran away like dogs just running fast and greedy on mud, I'd see the glass go different, all its cells, a crys-tal honeycomb but still clear and the leaf next to it opened thick.

60 But then I was back in gravity. I felt the weight of his leg on mine. And when I turned the jar was still honeycomb but filling with gold yellow, a liquid light and I knew that was the Lord emptying himself into my soul just pouring at the moment we

discovered the stickiness on us. I took some with a finger and tasted. It was like milkweed milk. We ran to the river and went in, just floating there, try-hard messy swimmers the same as always. Those days they never taught kids to swim, you just beat around in the water, praying. I switched the sharp thing to my other hand.

We were at a age when it amazed us what could be made in the world out of free other things. We had made milkweed milk.

When I finally opened my hand that night, I saw it was a pop bottle top, painted on the inside gold, with a little picture of Jesus pressed in. It'd made cuts in my hands and my mama took my palms in her lap and saw the little stars of dried blood and said, Girl you scare me.

I LOST MY RIGHT EYE TO THAT RIVER before I left Missouri. I was flop-legged over an innertube, got caught in rapids and cottonwood branches—thin little pointed ones, red-tipped—scratched my eye out bloody as a raccoon would.

That's why my eyes don't match. When we were in the store picking out, where they have all the parts of the body, I picked violet, I didn't want it green like the left.

Then my mama died—tumors—and that was the end of my good childhood. Twelve-years-old and I had to pick. I had two aunts up in the Twin Cities, live-together spinsters. They would've taken me. But I chose for my profession. The young minister in town had been promoted to a new parish in Iowa and he and his wife and girl took me along. I thought I'd learn.

And I did. Some. Sunday mornings the man made an oracle. It was a white church with a white steeple over miles and miles of combed perfect corn. He set the pews trembling. Full of farmers. I knew what the backstage was like, the sink, with his comb in the cup and Listerine on the ledge, the ironing board, where he kept the Band-Aids. I lived there all of four years. I learned some miracles, small ones. The border between trick and miracle is thin.

He went and drank Saturday nights in his so-called ceramics workshop down the basement. He went, Going to work on the wheel, Mother. He always called his wife mother. She called him father to him and us. I never saw him make very much of clay. Liquor was a bad magic thing in him. He came back late, walked to my room, and opened me up, like fingering through the middle of a flower. His breath poured me in bitter. I felt the inside of me stretch to fit him, organs crowding. I never felt the trembling. I never convulsed. I never confused his with mine. I knew exactly what sticky stuff was him, what was me.

Sunday morning, he'd be waiting bottom of the banister to take us all to church. I don't know if he remembered a thing or not. But he had a perfect daughter. Sarah. She was younger than me but just as tall. She had long blonde hair, grey eyes, everything right. She had one of those heads and bodies like made on a lathe. From every angle, you looked and it was even. We wore the same size dresses, and when the mother bought her new, I got the old.

Pretty soon then I started ministering myself. They billed me, THE PREACHER'S PROTÉGÉ, and at one October corn roast I lectured fifty people about loss and gift, and at the end I took out my eye and showed.

70   After that he and I started fighting and it ended up him hitting bad. He beat me up underneath the kitchen table. That was more alive than his Saturday nights. Our fights flashed with gold and ardor. I hated him for blood. The first night it happened, next morning on my sheet I found a smear of brown. That was from me. I knew. I threw away the pop top from the old Reverend, buried it in the ground under a hickory tree. By then I was twelve and knew about hymen. But I figured I'd lost all that a long time ago.

If I'd known I still had it I might of done more.

That Sunday morning I was in the bathroom before any of them for an hour with soap and that sheet scratching it out of the fabric with my fingernails.

Then I did the worst thing I ever did in my life and I'm going to tell it to you now. Later on today, I want you to start touching for that—the true worst sin you have ever done. Your first assignment for me here is to go to your room tonight and find the worst thing you ever done. You're going to tell them aloud here to each other tomorrow morning. You'll be close to each other forever. Your second assignment's going to be a wish, called What I Never Got in My Life.

You cannot be clean until you show the dirt. It is part of knowing somebody. It is communion, with the Lord and with anybody here.

75   I don't know how far ahead I planned. I know Saturday nights I started wearing an old flannel nightgown and covered my face with white cream thick as Crisco. I kept my hair back in a tight bun, full of pins. I had a kerchief compress over my eyes. I made out that this was all for my night sleep restoration beautification, but I thought at first it'd keep him away from me.

But nothing did.

I kept slapping on the cold cream and tying the kerchief. I started talking to Sarah, about consummation with the angel. I told her I left my window open Saturday nights and God's own angel, maybe God himself came into me, filled me, ravaged me, tickled me with feathers, blew on me, filled me with exquisite blooming light, everywhere under skin.

Go on, she said.

In those days there, you saw traveling holy people. They came through town, sold their relics and left. Autumn and spring, they stayed in our house. These things happened to them all the time. Holy spirits made them get out of bed and kneel on all fours. They groaned while spirits sucked, drinking from their souls and blowing up into them, wind scraping up all their orifices with celestial sand.

80   At night I'd lie on the floor of her room and slowly describe the angel's sweet ministrations.

I could feel her limbs move itchy on the bed in that first shrill of yearning. It took a month or so but finally Sarah told me—she wanted to taste the angel too.

That Saturday night I got her ready. I stripped her and dressed her in my room. I remember it was an October night, blowy, the trees outside black and dry, ticking the walls of the house. Light was far away and deep orange. I put her in my old nightgown that I always wore. I made her hair like mine, bunned and pinned. I put the cream on thick, tied the blindfold. The hardest thing was getting her to take her underwear off. She was one of those girls that put fresh panties on to sleep. I turned her around like for Pin-the-Tail-on-the-Donkey. The day before I'd snuck down to the basement and stole three thimblesfull of whiskey in a waterglass. I wanted her deep asleep.

I stayed awake in her bed, flat up, waiting. It seemed later and later. I worried about moonlight. But there was a scarce October moon and the stars, though sharp, were small. It was black. Late, finally, I heard his footsteps climbing to my door, then the door closed. He was in. I didn't dare go listen. I was scared to leave the bed. It was dark, my door was closed. I thought if he ever caught me he would kill me and he would be right.

Nothing happened for a long time. I went through every-thing, alone, face up in that bed. I couldn't hear a sound. I knew what everyone knows once at the worst when they have done something this bad and cannot stop it anymore.

85   I half expected them to discover each other and both come out and kill me. I half wanted that, but it stayed quiet.

A long time later I heard him walk out and I heard him clear his throat and cough, the same way he did when he left me each week. He went down to the kitchen sink, washed his hands and gulped a glass of water. Sometimes in the morning, we found bits of silver clay in the metal sink. He told us that was porcelain.

I heard him take his shoes off before he went in his own bed-room.

I wanted to rush in and see Sarah, make sure she was alive, I felt like sisters now, I only loved her. But something strapped my limbs down to the bed. I didn't sleep at all that night. Hours later, but still before light, I heard her in the bathroom. Then I got up and listened outside the door and I heard the fingernails scratching on cloth like I had done.

I opened the door. Spikes of light bounced off the tiles. Her face hung flat and older, laundry on a line.

90   That was my father, she said. He used us. There was no blame in it. I guess she still thought I believed he was an angel.

I wondered when she knew. Did she look down and see the same trash biscuit colored skin that had made her, part her? I didn't know. I never had a daddy.

Could he tell you knew?

I saw his ring, she said.

That is it. My worst thing I ever did. Later on, I found something like this in the Bible too. And then for a while I felt better. For a long time I used to feel better about things if it happened in the Bible. Don't laugh. It was written down, other people read it too. I heard since of kinds of people who have sacrificed themselves for years but turned steel and hero to protect a little sister or brother. But not me. I was not that good. I wanted him to spoil his own the way he'd spoiled me.

95   And I got my due. I had a child stuck on the inside blood wall of me, growing, and this was the worst that was done to me. When they found out, they locked me in the upstairs garage room all day, no more school, after five months when I showed. There was no toilet in there. They gave me a blackpainted chipping pail, dent-bottomed, that had been for picking cherries. I number-twoed in that. For number one, I had the glass jar from my home. All those four years I never heard the minister's wife talk about bodies as anything but number one and number two. Shelley, her real name was.

I had a bed in there and a year's worth of Ladies Home Journals, which I read again and again, especially the recipes. The bucket in the corner. Him coming in and out. He was the only one besides his wife with a key. Me climbing the ladder up the web of light.

They took away the baby. It was a boy. They gave him away through something Christian, I don't even know what city, what they said for his name. And then as soon as I could walk again, I left. The day I went to the bus station with my duffle, I passed Sarah outside the high school. She was a bad kid now. She just stood there, her hair darker, with oil on both sides of her nose, her skin not clean anymore, ashes from her cigarette just dropping on the thigh of her jeans.

My first job here was waitress in the Venice New Day Cafe. Old-fashioned original health food. Vegetarian without too many vegetables. A lot of things with sprouts and melted cheese. Lots of peanut butter and heavy, heavy bread. Everything sopped with oil. I joined the church. And a couple there, took me with them to the valley, Sherman Oaks, I could live in their house, go to high school. I was behind but not that much behind. And that's when I met my first love. I knew the day I sat across from him in the McDonald's dallying with my hair. I thought I'd found the Lord again and this time I was gonna marry him.

I worried all that day what he'd think, I had no family, nothing, I wasn't good enough. And then I found out his mama was blind. And I knew. I had him. We both went to school, they had me over to their house, everything. They even got me a tutor so I could learn tennis, so I could be up to him in doubles. I lucked out. I'd found one of the richest boys in Encino.

100   LOVE, IN MY LIFE, WAS NOT MY OWN DOING. There I got help. I needed it. And it came to me, luck, like an angel.

I started out falling that time in high school and went on right through college and after. I fell and fell and fell. And always, it grew, a long painful thing.

I seemed to be a hard one to love. Even now, I am not sure why. I've got some ideas. But it is very difficult, ever, to know yourself the way other people can. You see yourself better and worse. There are some people who just find themselves the center of great many affections, the core of a flower with numberless petals. I studied those girls, not being one of them. The boys too. There were boys like that also. I knew. I was always one of those hundred petals ringing.

They did have some characteristics, I gathered. They kept something for almost everyone, gave a compliment, a gentleness, just a slowing down, a hand someplace. They took time for a lot of different people. They didn't pick one and knock over life in a straight line to that person. No. They weren't like that at all. They were softer meanderers, spread-palmed, seeing just what the world put in their way.

Maybe a long time later I tried to be like that but not at first. Anyway, you can't try so hard to be different with lists and all. Won't work.

105   If I liked a guy enough, I got ashamed. I couldn't hardly look straight at him. Talk, if I did at all, went nasty. That was bad.

And the first one lasted all my twenties. A guy named Ricky S. His house at home literally had a white picket fence with each picket pointed in an upside down V. This is what our dinners consisted of: a protein, a vegetable and a starch. The three different-colored things on a plate that had ridges to separate the compartments. Every time. But he had other women. He always did.

My aunts in the Midwest, never-married women who maintained a hat closet, educated me to believe you could always tell a woman's wealth by her accessories. They sent me gifts so I could up myself a little, look like more than I was. I've always made a point of wearing cowboy boots and sneakers, plain joke belts and leather backpacks.

I never wanted to fool nobody.

I was poor. You grow up poor to the age of fifteen, you always poor.

110   You get so . . . you wanna be.

My name is Hungry. I said that once at a dress-up party when somebody asked who I was. Oh-oh, the person said, and what is your occupation. I said, real loud, I'm a preacher. My date then was Ricky S. and we'd had a fight. Can't you just say you're in school studying theology, he'd been saying. Come on, you weren't exactly poor, your family was in business in Missouri, they did well. If they'd been here, in California, they would have been California-prosperous. It's just a different scale.

He was the last of my spiritual loves that would not work in this world. Marriage is a way different thing.

Parties like that one, I couldn't survive in. When I feel slave I have to get out.

Biology made him love me, finally. It was the teacher. Mr. Glinton, Ricky's original god. But he took a liking for me. I used to go into his office hours and he kept me for as long as I wanted. I sat different ways in my chair. With Ricky, I used to worry what he saw. I'd sit the way I thought made me best. I wanted him on my right side, with my good eye, I didn't want him overemphasized on my calves. But with Mr. Glinton, I just didn't care. He always smiled when he saw a certain new part of me, as if he liked it all, the full and roughnesses.

115   He got me to tell all my stories, my whole life. He knew way more than anybody else did. And then he tinkered, toyed with Ricky's heart. He reached in and adjusted things a way I never could have, but he did easy, without any trouble. He said to him once, You'll be in love with girls like Dawn when you're older, but you can't really understand her now. She's too much for you.

     After that Ricky looked at me twice always, the second time to check, a little scared.

     I wanted to be one of those people who gets what they want easily without asking

     I wasn't one.

     That was a mistake to want. Mr. Glinton helped me with more than just Ricky S. He made me understand, when you fall in love with somebody, it isn't them. You fall in love with world. That's why I wasn't attracting and people like Ricky were. They grew up in that house with that family and protein and vegetable and starch and everything. I was just on my own. I started to look at the other people around campus and see, yup, she's got world, he has it, he's carrying it. Ricky S. had world orbiting around him. Mr. Glinton had world. So even my own love wasn't pure. I stopped believing in the possibility of perfection on the earth. And that was the first moment I began to learn how to live. Everyone here is beloved, yes, but only so much. Mr. Glinton tried to show me step by step how to add my own world around me.

120   The thing was, I had time.

THAT IS ALL OLD.

     I am here to tell you that it can be done. I changed. What you see here now . . . is new.

     You over there?

     You know a lady who acts everyday like a man left her yesterday and she was shattered like a clay pot in pieces on the floor? And then you find out it was twenty years ago? That was me.

125   And you, you know somebody who's got these big ideas but just don't have the confidence to see it all through. Don't ever finish any one thing? That was me.

I'm gonna write down four words: WOULDA COULDA SHOULDA and SORTA. Words we are going to learn to erase out of us. You're going to be DOING every day by the time I'm done with you.

I'm not much interested in punishment. I've done too much wrong myself.

I want all this out here in our group. Everything you did bad. You will be close forever to this group.

See, I am here for my son. I hope my child will walk into one of these courses someday. He does not need to know who I am to him. He does not need to recognize me. I just want him to recognize God. And that's what I can do for you. I can touch you to God. Make that introduction.

130   My born name was Dorothy Matsky. I have already built ninety-two shelters in this state. I have furnished three schools with libraries and my congregation numbers three thousand, not counting TV. And there'll be more.

Nobody is doing what I am doing.

I'm weird. I'm weird for my age and for here, for California, and now I'm weird for my profession.

At the bottom of each of you, there is a picture of you failing. And I want to tell you something. That is one beautiful picture. Yours over there, yours may be a laugh rising up from a back porch with your old gramma, a laugh about how you were gonna make it someday far anyway, even though you didn't get those queenly things you thought of, jewels and all, when you were a little girl. For you there, it might be lying down in some field with the weeds higher than your face with your lost dumb brother, just slowing your time down to him, like a clock running out of winding.

You have a choice. And tearing that picture in half, letting that paper flow and frill in the water, I guarantee that will be the hardest choice you will ever make in your life. Whether to live in this life or the next. To be the one or the many.

135   God is not a social worker. He is too big for that. Too diffuse. How do you know he is alive at all? You will know. You can always tell if you pay attention.

Okay. Now. That's all right, let her leave, that's fine. One's not bad.

Some never understand: Bread is religion. That's what all the journalists miss. If you just make money, they leave you alone. If you want to give it away, you better be pure perfect. I mean do you see them going after Mrs. Fields? No, cookies they get. But bread is too mystical.

Now, I've got one more confession to you all. I might have lured you here with some kind of trick. I know, a lot of you are here, thinking now, well what's she gonna do for us? How's she gonna change me?

And I'll tell you how. It might not be the way you want. It's not the straight way, it's not the short way.

140   You are probably thinking, she got from A to B, from poor nothing country girl to millionaire, you're probably thinking, well I can bake too. But I am not going to teach you how to get to B.

B is nowhere. B is another A. There are more and more des- tinations beyond it and the ambitious heart is always hungry.

I want you to forget B and meet God.

I will help you arrange the meeting.

All you need to live this life, is food and light.

145   I cannot give you the light because I do not own it. I could not even give you B if I wanted to, I have B because I do not need B, I do not want B, B is beside the point. It is only safe to be famous if you'd rather not be. The best way to be rich is to be rich not for long.

I can help you with food. Starting today, we will fast and after three days, we will break bread together on our knees, I can give you food and I can help you empty yourself for the Lord, sweep the room that holds the chair of your soul.

The Lord does not want your money. He wants yourself. Your whole love. It is like jumping off a cliff and falling in love with a person.

I CAN TELL YOU HOW I FOUND GOD. I didn't. He found me. I did nothing. Twice I was ready to die. The first time was underneath the minister's kitchen table. He'd beat me blind again, I guess you'd call it unconscious. And I felt that tinny tin-kling of noise above as the world began again, the minister's wife's shoes shuffled the ground, a tin frypan hit the stovetop and I closed my eyes and felt, ENOUGH. I did not want to live. To rise up again from under that cover of bruised blackness, each time from unconscious, I had to work and I didn't want to work anymore. One spark of my calling, my vocation—this, stuck in me, like a safety-pin in skin reminding. But I decided no. Let somebody else do it. I was not going to be what I been before. I had not been given enough in the world to get by. Let some-body else do it. That spark snagged but it was one of point of light. The other won. In everything, there exists in small meas-ure, its exact opposite.

I closed my eyes and decided to let myself die. I just lay there and the sounds around the kitchen grew faint, they were still there, I heard people walk around the table, a drawer opened, but they were very faint, like noise from a volume turned down TV, the sounds of another world.

150   BUT I DID NOT DIE.

He saved me.

Each of you will meet him in a different way. You over there, you will meet him timidly. You will have a shy meeting, just like you might meet somebody important in your life, still even though it's quiet and private you know all the time that it mat-ters, the silence doesn't make it matter any less. You will cry, I can tell you will cry. You will tremble and shout, you'll be a reg-ular circus. I don't know how I can tell. For you it will be sex, yes it will. For you, sir, I believe it will be a small thing. But no less treasured, no less profound. Like a jewel kept in a velvet box.

For those of you who came for other aims, you may consider yourself tricked. But let me tell you why I didn't clear this car-lier. I consider everyone alive on this earth, somewhere on the road to salvation.

No thief wants to be himself stolen from.

155   No liar wants to be lied to.

A jeerer's worst fear is you laughing at him.

No molester, no taker, wants his own home ravaged.

No rich man wants to be poor.

No woman who has servants wants herself to be servant.

160 And what is profit but theft?

No matter how bad you think you are, you're no worse than anybody else. Everybody has murdered some part of another person. Everybody who owns two of shoes instead of one has, in some measure, stolen.

See this jar. My jar. This is a jar full of hundred dollar bills all together the amount you paid to come here today. I'm going to set it right here and if anyone wants to leave you are welcome to come take your money and go on.

No one?

Really?

165 Don't worry about offending. I'm beyond offense. Used to it.

The second time I wanted to die was just ordinary time, nothing really wrong. You see faith is slippery. And I have that in me, that is my charm for success in shopping malls, the locket I carry on me is a relic of that feeling—that, let somebody else do it, I don't care, I am ready to go.

Every thing contains a small measure, its opposite.

ABIDING is a beautiful word.

DON'T TAKE THINGS AGAINST YOUR INTEREST as absolute true. Every law, every document, even our Bible needs revision. The Old Testament will have God taking revenge on the children of children of families. I will not accept that.

170 I never thought I was so great. But He did.

Today is only our first day. Confession. Tomorrow we'll fast, Wednesday do penance, Thursday is conversion, Friday communion and gospel and Saturday, prayer. So these are the days of our week here.

You've heard my confession.

Now I want to learn yours. Think about it a minute. Now that you know, see if you still want to open yourself and try and believe in somebody like me.

Lee K. Abbott

Lee K. Abbott is the author of *The Heart Never Fits Its Wanting, Love Is the Crooked Thing,* and *Dreams of Distant Lives.*

Freedom, A Theory of

THE STORY MY FATHER TOLD—before he abandoned my mother and me, before he reappeared years and years later to beat the stuffings out of me—concerned his sister Shirley who, at seven years old in 1927, burst out of the ladies' room on the third level of the old steamship *Seeandbee,* a five-hundred-foot, all-steel sidewheeler from the Cleveland & Buffalo Transit Company, went through the railing ("Stumbled," my father insisted), and pitched overboard.

"Presumed drowned," he always said. "Body never recovered. Four days of dragging, searching."

I began hearing this story, I am told, only months after my birth in 1947; truth to say, there was not a time before he walked out on us—drove, actually—in September of 1956 when I can't remember hearing it, or some detail, week in, week out. I heard about the condition of Lake Erie ("Few waves, excellent visibility, water temperature moderate"); what celebrities were on

board (Johnny Risko, the heavyweight who'd fought Gene
Tunney, and his manager, Dapper Danny Dunn); the men with
whom his own father, the Judge, was that night playing poker in
one starboard parlour (Shondor Birns, a gangster from the
Ten-Eleven Club; WJAY personality Red Manning; musician
Pee Wee Jackson from the Smiling Dog Saloon; and W. Burr
Gongwer, eventually Cuyahoga County's Democratic party
boss). I heard what band was playing (Shaw Sissle from the
Trianon Ballroom); what was eaten by those gentlemen (the deli
trays, Schimdt's beer, several bottles of bootleg Canadian
whiskey); and what, other than *va-va-va-voom,* could be said
about certain hootchie-kootchie sorts.

"The details," my father used to remark. "I just can't get
over the details. Stupid, huh?"

5   I wondered, a kid decades removed from the event itself,
what all this had to do with me; for there were thousands of
times, hearing him tramp up the stairs in our house in Shaker
Heights to wish me sweet dreams, when I knew, and dreaded,
that he was bringing me something new, or newly discovered,
about Shirley. Her favorite ice cream (toffee vanilla). How
expertly she tap-danced. That her middle name was Nemea—
which is a valley in ancient Argolis. More than once, buried
under the covers, I curled myself up to look like sleep and said,
"My name is Carter Hopkins Garner. I like blue. I like Y.A.
Tittle. God is great. Five times six is thirty."

He was obsessed, yes, though haunted is, I think, a better
word. You could see him—at the dinner table, say, standing to
carve a roast, bone-handled knife clutched, his vest unbut-
toned—open his mouth, perhaps to make an observation about
the gravy boat or the flatware, then pause, eyes narrowing, his
head suddenly tilted, as though he'd heard, faint but clear, her
voice, any of the help-words she might have hollered in panic
in the water. Or, bent over a putt at the Canterbury Golf Club,
me to one side holding his bag, he'd suddenly pull himself
upright, thrust a hand out to hush the rest of his foursome, and
empty his face of everything except a single horrible thought—
the way he looked, in fact, the day he drove past me in his Dodge,

mechanically waving bye-bye to me, to my mother, to autumn itself; to a world that had, one cloudless night in the 20s, wobbled out of its precious and perfect groove.

I NEVER REALLY TOOK NOTE OF MY FATHER as a creature independent of his Shirley stories until, the afternoon he left us, I walked home from Geoffrey "Jeep" Freeman's house, where I had been playing, and found my mother, composed as a movie star, reclining on the divan in the sun room, radio playing, smoking a Viceroy cigarette as though, any minute now, a brass band, its oomm-pah-pah deafening enough to be impressive in New York City, might march through our front door to whisk her away.

"What is it you'd like for dinner, Carter?" She was looking yonder, beyond the flagstone patio, to the oaks that are the rough for the eighth fairway at the Shaker Country Club. "Marie has ribeye, I believe. That would be lovely, wouldn't it?"

I could hear Marie, our cook, in the kitchen, pans banging.

10   "Could I," I wondered, "have cereal?"

She looked at me then, straight on, the way my wife Alison looks at me when what she has to say must be absorbed one significant syllable at a time.

"He's not coming back, you know."

I was nine years old, wearing a Santone Manner surcoat, my hands out of my pockets as I'd been taught, and I believed that mother—a Smith College graduate, a woman who'd met Consuelo Roosevelt and could tell you what to do with bagworms—never looked more beautiful than she did the moment I said, too grown up for the hour, "I know."

"He isn't a bad man, Carter. Not bad at all." I understood that too, and said so. "If you're thinking," she said, "that I know where he's going, then you're mistaken."

15   "Yes," I said, very much not wanting ever to be mistaken.

"Nor does Marie," she said. "Or Mr. Abel."

I thought of Abel, our gardener, and how fussy he could be about dirt I was not welcome to dig in.

"Is this a tragedy, Mother?"

She took her time then, a wonderful amount of time as big and sun-filled as the room itself, and came round to my question in at least seven or eight visible ways, her chin going up and sideways, a gold earring dangling, her eyes blinking as if I'd asked how far Neptune was from this very spot.

20 "It's a setback, darling. A serious inconvenience."

That was how we talked in that household: *inculcate, deliberate, insouciant*—a high-falutin language to describe the few we were and what we did.

"We shan't speak of this again, Carter."

She wanted agreement and I gave it to her, ignoring the rattle in me.

"The Judge will look after us."

25 I said "Yes, ma'am," a phrase I wasn't absolutely connected to, and thought to leave—to go where, I had no idea—when she stood, as though a bell had clanged, and gave a sigh so theatrical it could have come from Deborah Kerr in *Tea and Sympathy*, one movie in Metrocolor we'd seen. "Give us a kiss, Mister."

Cheek to cheek we stood, her bent and me on tip-toes, me thinking about the Judge and his moustaches and his wall-wiggling way of going "ha-ha-ha," before I realized she had more to say and would not let me go until she said it.

"Don't hate him, Carter. Promise?"

She smelled like lilacs and cigarettes and gin.

"I won't, Mother."

30 She squeezed me a little and I was no longer a boy talking like a grown-up or able to know much more than my name and street address.

"The Garner family does not hate," she said. "Ever."

She was wrong about that as she was wrong about Elvis Presley ("Whoever heard of a song about, gracious, a hound dog?") and Bishop Fulton Sheen ("To me he looks like a rodent"); as she would, before her brain cracked, be wrong about Fidel Castro and what to do with *Lady Chatterly's Lover*. In fact, I began to hate my father—feel for him all the contrary and cowardly thoughts the word suggests—less than a week later when I found myself in his second floor study.

"What is all this?" I said.

I had been standing behind his desk, observing his clutter, one-hundred-percent fascinated by a book, *Decedents' Estates & Trusts* (The Foundation Press), and watching phrases like *inter vivos* and *per curiam* rise up from his well-scribbled yellow tablet. He had been struggling with a case that required him to know "Nontestamentary Acts" and "Death Without Issue," as well as what had been decided in Root v. Arnold and Spencer v. Childs, and now, wherever he was—in Outer Mongolia, in Timbuktu—he was no longer an attorney for Andrew Squire or obliged to speak about "Rules Restricting Creation of Remainders to Heirs."

35   I touched nothing. Not his files on the floor like oversize playing cards. Not his Crosley TV. Not his Julius La Rosa and Perez Prado records on the desk chair. "Breathe," I told myself, and did, taking in a room that smelled like Vitalis Hair Tonic and the Old Forester he liked.

"Father," I said, a word it was possible to utter without heart or anything else essential.

Across the room in his closet hung his three-button, center-vent Hart Shaffner & Marx suitcoats, his Dobbs hat, his ties from the Haband Tie Company of Paterson, New Jersey. "Details," I may have said. "I can't get over the details." He wore shoes from the Massagic Company and Kara-Lon sweaters and used Scuff-Kote shoe polish from Esquire. As still as a sentinel, I studied his room, saw a hair on his blotter, observed that he'd made a note—in handwriting as formal and forward as the way he sat in a chair—about a Montclair hardtop coupe in persimmon and classic white.

He was not here and yet I could sense him, imagine him completely from the *x* and *y* and *z* he'd left behind. Two incidents came to mind. In one, a year earlier, he was standing deep in the back yard, by the arbor, with Abel. There had been a discussion about weeds—or compost, or pruning—and so, me at Father's side, under our umbrella while Abel stood an arm's length away, water streaming off his hat, my father cleared his throat. A question had occurred to him, something vital, and, still staring at the squishy ground, he said, "Abel, do you believe in life after death?"

Abel's head turned slowly, as if on a screw. In his eyes were amazement and wariness, one then the other.

40 "I believe in just rewards," he said. "I don't have a clear picture of heaven."

My father, still concentrating on the earth, nodded, and I remember watching Abel swallow—he had an enormous Adam's apple—scratch lazily at his ear, and turn his head so that they, not exactly shoulder to shoulder, were again focusing on whatever problem they'd discovered at their feet.

"From now on, Abel," my father said, "call me Willy."

I was hearing something, I thought, something new and special, and I watched Abel, whose surname was a Polish jawbreaker with too many *c*'s and *y*'s, hear it too.

"Good, Mister Willy," Abel said. "Heaven, Mister Willy."

45 "Everybody calls me William. Or Bill. But I like Willy. It implies—what?—brio maybe."

The second incident that occurred to me the day that I began to hate my father also involved Abel: we were playing checkers in the dining room, my father and I, and Abel came in, hat literally in hand, to complain about the climbing roses behind the garage.

"Mister Willy," he began, "no good. No good for nothing, those roses."

My father jumped several of my checkers, said "King me," and then flung himself into a paragraph six or seven minutes long, about "use" and "meaning" and "authenticity," using the sort of sentences I remembered from summer camp—dense and flopped back on themselves, singsongy and always barbed at the end. He began slowly, fingers stabbing the air, until, just before he ran down and the light came back to Abel's eyes, my father was yattering headlong, not out of control but excited, as if the only sense worth having was sense you discovered by going loopy and inside out and topsy-turvy.

"I am talking about reconciling desire to responsibility," he concluded.

50 Abel agreed, quietly.

"I am talking about urges which we have, and their denial. Say this with me, Abel. Say—"

It took Abel another twenty minutes to get out of that room, words like "evidentiary" and "testator" zooming at him, and me, like wasps. I remembered this, I say, that afternoon I stood in his office, my mother having told me not to hate him, and I swear I didn't until I recalled that, speaking of "mettle" and "modesty" and "rage," my father had plucked from his jacket pocket his Ace comb and, still hollering about time and what can be lost or won by it, had begun, fussily and furiously, combing his hair.

"Freedom," he had shouted that afternoon. "A Theory of."

Days had passed, days and days and days: He had driven away, Mother had spoken to me, I had come to his study, and suddenly, as able to do this as I was to give my height or the color of my own hair, I went out his door (which is now my own and behind which I figure out who's owed what), shut it carefully, and said, "I do hate you."

55 JEEP FREEMAN, MY BEST FRIEND, noticed my father first. Jeep, who now knows what high and low there is to brag about in real estate plus the fortune you can make from it, had just caught the football I'd thrown, made a wiggle-waggle on the model of Alan "The Horse" Ameche of the Baltimore Colts, squeaked when I tackled him, and thumped backwards with the words, "Isn't that your father?"

Down the way, past several yards of what *greensward* was probably invented to describe, my father was painstakingly backing out his Dodge, his every movement, like burlesque, an exaggeration of what gets taught in Driver's Education: adjusting the mirrors, rear and side; scooting his seat back; locking his door; engaging this, releasing that; hands at ten and two, as erect behind the wheel as Higbee's store window mannequin.

"Where's he going?" Jeep wondered.

We were standing, nine year olds with grass stains on our knees and little to be entertained by, and for the life of me—a cliché I use deliberately, with respect for the sentiment it originally expressed—I couldn't figure out what my father was doing at home. It was three-thirty, and he was supposed to be downtown, at Ninth and Superior Avenues, his a life—like my own now—of putting wealth into words, of puzzling out how to pass on the lowboy and the pewter and the mutual funds to Cousin Mable, to a dog named Fifi, to the Wicked Witch of the West.

"You want something to drink?" Jeep asked. "I'm thirsty."

60   I had taken two giant steps toward the street my father was in the middle of, and it is more true than less that Jeep Freeman, thirsty best friend, had disappeared from me; he would only reappear after my father was well up the road when I could snatch my football away and say for him, schoolmate and buddy, to mind his own damn business and to leave me alone and to go wherever it was fat boys like him went when they weren't being pests or know-it-all busybodies.

I was watching my father and his car rolling toward me—odd to say—a piece at a time: hubcap, grill, hood ornament, windshield, headlamp, Dobbs hat, hand, eyes, door handle, light and shadow and silence the size of winter. As distant from myself as I sometimes get when I drink too much, I approached the curb. There was a crack to stand on, a leaf. There was a spot near the street, I knew, for me to occupy, an X on the earth I can still see from my study window.

"One-Mississippi," I mumbled, aiming to count high as need be, until I would be yammering numbers it takes several breaths to complete. I had put the trees out of mind. And the grass and the clouds, the big houses there and there and there. And then my father, sitting high as a pasha, pulled abreast, head turned a fraction my way, his hand ticking back and forth like a metronome.

Goodbye, that gesture was saying. *Good luck.*

I was full of question marks—*huhs* and *whats* and *whys.*

65   To and fro went his hand, manicured and long-fingered, more suited for piano-playing than pencil-pushing: *So long, kiddo.*

Yes, I thought. *No.*

He was thinking of Shirley, I guessed. Of deck rails to slip over, of edges to tumble from, of corners to step around, and of darkness, like death, to vanish into.

"Wait," I said, my first words aloud.

But he was already past me, indifferent as stone, attending to what lay in front of him and away, and I had only me to wonder

about and one thousand thoughts to fumble through before I
could face Jeep Freeman and say where he could go with his
Erector Set and Lincoln Logs and likewise cheap view of life.

II

70   Correct: I became as obsessed with my father and his disap-
pearance as he had been with his sister and hers; and over the
years I told that story as often as he'd told his. The next fall, in
Mrs. Sweeney's fourth grade class at Hawken, the prep school
which raised me up and made me a spelling champ, I made it the
subject of an essay. "Where My Father Went," an essay surely as
which-away and inside out as this story but filled with lingo like
"scoundrel" and "blackguard" and "scalawag," words as mean as
I could make them. Later, at the Upper Campus, I afflicted him
with scabies and lesions, likened him to a viper, made him a
drunk or bully who'd cheat at bridge. I cast him (yes: *cast,* whose
proper use you can look up in John Milton) as far from me and
my mother and our house as I could, given how little I knew of
the big world: in Narbada, among thieves and cutthroats; in
Nara, among yellow barbarians; in the Lesser Sunda Islands,
among lepers and animals happy only in the dark and the wet.

Still, there was a part of me—is there a bone for this idea, or
a tissue?—that thought he might return, and so, on important
occasions (graduation, my birthday, Christmas), I kept expecting him—still slender, I thought, still as smooth as a Beau
Brummell—to step again into my life. The Fourth of July after
my sophomore year at Yale, for example, I felt sure he was close—
on the next block, maybe, on Public Square downtown, on
Fairmount Boulevard. I couldn't sit, nor go a step without turning. I picked at my fingers, read the paper haphazardly, brushed
my teeth again and again. In the back yard my mother, wearing
a straw hat the size of a parasol, sat in a chaise reading, next to
her a highball (that's what she called it). It was afternoon, bright
as a postcard; the radio was saying what was up with Muhammed
Ali and what folks my own age were doing in Haight-Ashbury;
Jeep Freeman, still my best friend, was waiting for me to pick
him up so we could go to the stadium to see the Indians play the
Tigers; and I, watchful and nervous and stupid, was standing on

my front porch, listening to the neighborhood go about its holiday. "Okay," I told myself. "Okay." Up the street, far enough away to be possible, a car had turned my direction. It was a Dodge. A Ford. A Cadillac. "Yes," I said. "Of course." I managed a step toward the sidewalk, now miles and miles away. That car was green. It was red. It was persimmon and classic white. And I was moving, the heart of me going *click-click-click*. It wasn't Father, in fact, but the part of me that hated him didn't know that. A thought came—having to do, I believe, with fear. And another—this as black-minded as any from a storybook villain. "Yes," I said, this with hiss enough to be meaningful. "Come on," I said. I had my fists up—not for the last time, it would turn out—and was jumpy the way the frightened are. And then the car swerved into a drive a few up from my own. Out climbed a woman and three children, in swimsuits and towels, noise reaching me that was neither important nor dire; and immediately I was grateful no one was nearby to see me, trembling, rig myself together one ragged piece at a time.

I last expected him in 1974, the year of the oil embargo, the year Hank Aaron clobbered the home run that gave him one more than Babe Ruth. I was a lawyer by then ("Say attorney," my mother always insisted, "Lawyers are what crooks have") for Jones Day, a firm too big to do anything but make money. The occasion was the death of Judge Garner, my grandfather, my father's father, who is buried in Lakeview Cemetery with President Garfield and three or four stingy Rockefellers. It wasn't a wake we were having at our house as much as it was, well, a cocktail party, entertainment provided by old Freddie Webster from Val's in the Alley, a nightclub the Judge was a cut-up at, and GAR disc jockey Harry Pildner, who had eyebrows bushy enough for Congress. Everybody was there—old-timers mostly, from the *Buckeye Press* and the defunct *Cleveland World,* papers the Judge had written for when he was known as Mad Manny Garner, when he played the tenor sax and was secretary for the American Federation of Musicians, Local No. 4.

"Isn't it marvelous?" Mother kept saying, cornering me every hour or so to read a telegram from this muckety-muck or that, urging me to introduce myself to Mrs. Dorothea Beal of

Gates Mills or to D. P. Sells, Jr., of Medusa Cement. "The Judge would have loved this," she said. "Hoopla, you know. He dearly loved hurly-burly."

Yes, the Judge would have loved the celebration. There were women with heavy perfume and men in green suits, not to mention ruder sorts who called me "Bub" and laughed with their mouths full; there was high-stakes chitchat, more than one fist-fight in the garden, an awning that collapsed, a redhead named Reva Something-or-other who showed us her garter belt and sang in French, a Victor Borge look-alike who tried to sell me a Vermont Christmas tree farm, three tubs of crushed ice—and it was no work at all to imagine the Judge in the dining room, surprisingly nimble for the roly-poly he was, doing the Cleveland Chicken, a dance with too much elbow and knee for the unpracticed, his head shiny as a light bulb. And then somewhere in here—after the street lights flickered on but before Meech Sims toppled into the liver pâté—the air went funny and cold.

75   "What's wrong, Carter?" It was Alison, my girlfriend then, my wife now. She was wearing a hat my mother had pressed on her, a cockeyed contraption with feathers of which, so the joke went, there were only a dozen of in Ohio.

"He's here," I said.

She was seeing what I was, I think: Elmer Smits telling an Apache story, Libby Wellington tugging at her girdle, Otis P. Miller doing an imitation of the Bishop of Pittsburgh in an inner tube.

"He's not here, Carter. He's not anywhere."

I was trying to move, telling my legs to move, intending to go room by room by room.

80   "Stop it," Alison said, gripping me at the biceps. "You'll embarrass your mother."

I yanked myself free. My mother was in the library. My mother was with her lady friends—Alice Tipton, Dottie and Marion Levisay, Margaret Harding's snooty sister. She was laughing. She was guzzling vodka. She was singing a verse from "The Courtship of Yongy-Bonghy-Bo," stuck on the verse where "the early pumpkins blow." She needn't know what I was doing. She needn't

"Wait here," I told Alison.

I was a fool, she said. An ignoramus.

I believe I put my finger to my lips, scrunched my face up tight—evil à la Vincent Price or other matinee ghoul.

85 "Shhhhh," I whispered. "Don't move."

In the pantry I found Shelby Humes, a cousin by marriage, a sissy I meant to shove sidelong with a shoulder. "Pardonnez-moi," he said, wiping his Manhattan off his shirtfront, "aren't we a rough customer." My father was here, I was convinced. He was in the sun room with the Lewellyn twins, or in the kitchen peering into the refrigerator. In the back yard by the peonies, or in the front leaning like a *boulevardier* against the willow. He stood in the light. In the shadows. By the foyer. Next to the parson's bench in the center hall. He was on the tree lawn, perfecting his wedge shot; in the garage, banging on a steam pipe.

"Are you satisfied?" Alison asked when I passed her a second time. She looked collapsed, thoroughly defeated by my craziness. With an ache I wondered how it was that she, a blonde *cum laude* economics major who could cuss you out in German and hit a volleyball as fiercely as any Olympian, had found herself with me.

"Please," I said, not certain what to be asking for. "Just give me a minute here, okay?"

Again I was gone, racing up the stairs, heading for the study—once his, now mine.

90 At the door, I tucked my shirt in, smoothed my hair. I had carted all his stuff—his papers, his handsome clothes and pricey toilet articles—to the basement years before, after I'd moved home; and so I wondered, light-headed and antsy, what he could be looking at in there. I had clutter, yes, mounds of it. I was not as persnickety as he. So what could he make of my books, the trash I got lost in, like *I, the Jury,* or of my brilliant college papers, on that shrieking yakety-yak by Faulkner, say, or what drippy insight Wordsworth had about tintinnabulation. I imagined my father, suspicious as a cop, studying the ticky-tacky on my walls: a picture from a catalogue of a trout that would, if you snapped your fingers at its mouth, wag its tail; a business card from the Medical Mission Sisters of Our Lady of the Highway;

the complete lyrics to "Louie, Louie," supposedly the dirtiest song in America.

"Father," I said.

I was not going in. There was no reason to. Instead, I was taking in the character of my hall, the gloomy it was, the shabby. Down a few doors, past my own room, was my mother's, the bedroom—now that Mother is in a nursing home—that Alison and I share. The floor near me was stained, white spots like bleach on the hardwood; the carpet runner, once festive-seeming, its print intricate and tidy as long-lost needlework, seemed threadbare and dusty. The wallpaper had peeled in spots above the wainscotting, itself scratched, its walnut-panel inlays wobbly and cracked in places. Plaster was loose, you could see that, and three bulbs were out in the chandelier at the far end, and instantly, to the hand of me that let go of the doorknob and to the legs of me that backed up unsteadily, as if the whole place were rocking wildly in a storm, it made more sense to be somewhere, anywhere else—downstairs, for instance, by the living room fireplace, hearing Baron Henley tell us for the zillionth time how a gentleman shines his shoes.

"You're right," I said to Alison much later. I was drunk then, all of real life draining with a gurgle into a hole between my feet.

"I know," she said, patting my head.

95   I was a boy again—ill-behaved, ashamed, very sleepy. I had an idea, once as important as money or love or death.

"Alison." Her name came out with too many syllables and not enough breath to be beautiful. "You will marry me, won't you?"

There were two of her, then three, each blurry at the edge, wobbling round and round like cars in a Ferris wheel.

"We'll see, Carter," they were saying to the left and right of me. "We shall see."

THESE ARE THE FACTS as I learned them from my father the afternoon, only a few years ago, he reappeared to beat me up: In Calumet City, Illinois, he led a labor strike at the Globe Iron Works; he gave a lecture at the Harvard Club in Newburgh

Heights; he worked for the Pfaff Company in Los Angeles, for
the El Dorado Golf Club in Arkansas, the Surf Club of Miami.
He'd met the Chicago *Tribune* cartoonist John T. McCutcheon
and, at the Porcupine Club, the novelist J. P. Marquand. He'd
danced the cha-cha-cha with Clare Booth Luce, toasted the
Broadway opening of *Repent in Haste.* He'd toured the carrier
Tarawa at Norfolk, taught one semester at the Windsor School,
had his appendix removed at the Anna Jacques Hospital in
Newburyport, gave orders for a month to the staff of *Cosmo-*
politan, rode in a golfmobile manufactured by the Ford Motor
Company. He had dreams of going to Bangkok, to Cairo, of visiting Pandit Nehru, of staying at the Savoy in London. He'd
been drunk with men named Cabot and Denny, women named
Adelaide and Pearl. He'd fixed a typewriter, blown a bugle, ped-
dled kitchen cutlery. He'd sailed a yacht named *Stormie Seas,*
saddled a quarter horse named Thomas Harrow, lassoed an
ostrich.

100   "I have cavorted and raised Cain and mingled like a savage,"
he announced that afternoon. "What in hell, boy, have you
done?"

We saw him at Eaton Road where it crosses the Shaker
Country Club golf course between the eleventh green and the
twelfth tee, a figure as out of place in 1980 as Popeye the Sailor.

"Who's that?" Jeep Freeman asked, the two of us men of
leisure and would-be robber barons.

"Don't know," I said. "Don't care."

I was in my element here, I say. I was married, the father of
twin girls, thrifty enough to vacation three times a year, knowledgeable about wraparound bonds and what gets reported in
Gourmet magazine, able to tell Mozart from Mahler, and slick
enough to get in and out of every soirée in the United States.
Plus, that day I was blasting the ball like Jack Nicklaus.

105   "It's your honor," Jeep said, sour-mouthed as it is possible
to look when you have lipped out a thirty-dollar, three-foot
gimme.

I was happy—pleased with the bees, the birds, the clouds
tumbling my way from the west.

"Life is easy," I said. "Watch this."

Here it was that I noticed the man—not my father yet—
standing to one side of us, his a suit you might find on a
Hollywood has-been. Wide lapels, cut too full through the chest,
necktie like a dinner napkin.

"Pardon me," he said, addressing Jeep Freeman. "Would
you excuse us for a second?"

110   Jeep looked confused, perplexed, his face doing all the
things I like it for—opening, closing, wrinkling, grinning. Then
he shrugged, said, "Sure, what the hell." He'd just go in the
woods there, he said. Take a leak. Maybe pray a little. Maybe
shoot himself.

"Thank you," the man said, and for a minute we watched
Jeep haul himself over a hill, his a green and yellow ensemble
you could see flickering now and then through the trees. "Fine
young man, that Jeep Freeman."

Something hardened in me, my loose insides settling with a
clatter in the flat, hard bottom of me. I was cold, I believe, the
winds from a million directions, the world part water, part
whoosh. I had recognized him.

"You," I said.

He winked, still a sly man. "Me."

115   I would like to report that something dramatic happened
immediately, a set-to as slapdash and colorful and heedless as
that in prime time, but except for a truck honking and dog barking, there was nothing to concentrate on but the production,
fussy as any biddy you might know, William H. Garner, Esq.,
made of stripping himself to his shirtsleeves.

"Do you know boxing?" he asked.

Instantly, I became a youngster answering a grown-up: "Yes, sir."

He had folded his jacket over a bench, pulled out a tiny
notebook.

"I understand you've had ugly things to say about me," he
said, flipping pages. He'd kept track, he said. Of all I'd said—the
ugly things, the cruel, the unwarranted. I didn't know, he said.
I hadn't the vaguest idea. I was as unthinking as a stump. He had
contacts, associates, companions with wonderful memories.

120   "How'd you find me?" I wanted a cigarette, business to do
with my hands and mouth. "I mean, how'd you know I'd be here?"

He'd called my secretary. He'd called Alison, claimed to be a client. He'd even talked to Beth Ann, Jeep's wife.

"Nice woman," he said, "if a bit bubbly for my taste. Tedious, you know. Too much gosh and golly."

In the trees, Jeep was singing, a yodel-like enterprise with too much nose, being the clown he's famous at parties for, and half of me—that part now tired and slack-kneed—wanted to be in there with him messing up lines from the Rolling Stones.

"What I propose is this," my father began. "A punch-up, a settling of old scores."

125   Was he thinking of Shirley again? Or of what, stupidly, she and her death stood for? I didn't know. I just remembered the times he'd come to my room or besieged me in the backyard— not with discoveries, I think now, but with illustrations of how tenuous it was, our life. How we are knocked together and tipped headlong by luck, good and bad. How, mostly, it is chaos we learn from. How broken-off and hit-or-miss life is. How cramped and split we are inside.

"I go first?" I said.

"Then I go," he said. "Let's try to do this with honor, Carter, shall we?" Something was being settled here, decided as are wars and games.

"We don't have to do this," I said.

"Oh, but we do."

130   I could say I took an inventory of myself at this point—the in and out I am, the up and down—but I did not. Instead I was looking at my hands, pleased at how soft they were. I was not a fighter. I was not violent. I was not angry. These are the things, I contend, that I was not.

"I don't hate you anymore," I said.

"Of course you don't," he said.

He had his legs flexed, as white-haired as Santa Claus but too skinny to sock in the jaw.

"We'll have a drink afterwards," he said. "Some civilized palaver."

135   That was a good idea, I thought, and said so, strangely proud of myself.

"You'll be going away again?" I asked, relieved to hear him say, yes, alas, he had engagements, appointments, faraway places to be.

"Any time you're ready," he declared.

I put down my golf club, oddly aware of how expensive it was. The sky was like poster paint, primary and impossible. I could hear a bird and traffic, not sure what to make of either. Yes, I thought. Yes. I hung on to myself, the rips and ruins and jags I was. And then, at the moment Jeep Freeman stumbled out of the woods whistling, I flew forward with a fist.

Richard Bausch

Richard Bausch's *"The Man Who Knew Belle Starr"* is in his first collection, *Spirits and Other Stories,* and was featured in *Ellery Queen Magazine* as a "distinguished reprint." *The Fireman's Wife and Other Stories* is his second collection. He has published several novels including, *Real Presence, Hello To the Cannibals, The Last Good Time,* and *Mr. Field's Daughter.*

The Man Who Knew Belle Starr

MCRAE PICKED UP A HITCHER ON HIS WAY WEST. It was a young woman, carrying a paper bag and a leather purse, wearing jeans and a shawl—which she didn't take off, though it was more than ninety degrees out and Mcrae had no air conditioning. He was driving an old Dodge Charger with a bad exhaust system and one long crack in the wraparound windshield. He pulled over for her and she got right in, set the leather purse on the seat between them, and settled herself with the paper bag on her lap between her hands. He had just crossed into Texas.

"Where you headed?" he said.

She said, "What about you?"

"Nevada, maybe."

5   "Why maybe?"

And that fast he was answering *her* questions. "I just got out of the Air Force," he told her, though this wasn't exactly true. The Air Force had put him out with a dishonorable discharge after three years at Leavenworth for beating up a staff sergeant. He was a bad character. He had a bad temper that had got him into a load of trouble already and he just wanted to get out West, out to the wide-open spaces. It was just to see it, really. He had the feeling people didn't require as much from a person way out where there was that kind of room. He didn't have any family now. He had five thousand dollars from his father's insurance policy and he was going to make the money last him a while. He said, "I'm sort of undecided about a lot of things."

"Not me," she said.

"You figured out where you were going," he said.

"You could say that."

10   "So where might that be?"

She made a fist and then extended her thumb and turned it over.

"Under," she said; "down."

"Excuse me?"

"Does the radio work?" she asked, reaching for it.

15   "It's on the blink," he said.

She turned the knob anyway, then sat back and folded her arms over the paper bag.

He took a glance at her. She was skinny and long-necked, and her hair was the color of water in a metal pail. She looked just old enough for high school.

"What's in the bag?" he said.

She sat up a little. "Nothing. Another blouse."

20   "Well, so what did you mean back there?"

"Back where?"

"Look," he said, "we don't have to do any talking if you don't want to."

"Then what will we do?"

"Anything you want," he said.

25   "What if I just want to sit here and let you drive me all the
way to Nevada?" "That's fine," he said.
      "That's just fine."
      "Well, I won't do that. We can talk."
      "Are *you* going to Nevada?" he asked.
      She gave a little shrug of her shoulders. "Why not?"
30   "All right," he said, and for some reason he offered her his
hand. She looked at it, and then smiled at him, and he put his
hand back on the wheel.

IT GOT A LITTLE AWKWARD almost right away. The heat was
awful, and she sat there sweating, not saying much. He never
thought he was very smooth or anything, and he had been in
prison: it had been a long time since he had found himself in
the company of a woman. Finally she fell asleep, and for a few
miles he could look at her without worrying about anything but
staying on the road. He decided she was kind of good-looking
around the eyes and mouth. If she ever filled out, she might be
something. He caught himself wondering what might happen,
thinking of sex. A girl who traveled alone like this was probably
pretty loose. Without quite realizing it, he began to daydream
about her, and when he got aroused by the daydream he tried to
concentrate on figuring his chances, playing his cards right, not
messing up any opportunities—but being gentlemanly, too. He
was not the sort of person who forced himself on young women.
She slept very quietly, not breathing loudly or sighing or moving
much; and then she simply sat up and folded her arms over the
bag again and stared out at the road.
      "God," she said, "I went out."
      "You hungry?" he asked.
      "No."
35   "What's your name?" he said. "I never got your name."
      "Belle Starr," she said, and, winking at him, she made a
clicking sound out of the side of her mouth.
      "Belle Starr," he said.
      "Don't you know who Belle Starr was?"

All he knew was that it was a familiar-sounding name. "Belle Starr."

40 She put her index finger to the side of his head and said, "Bang."

"Belle Starr," he said.

"Come on," she said. "Annie Oakley. Wild Bill Hickok."

"Oh," Mcrae said. "Okay."

"That's me," she said, sliding down in the seat. "Belle Starr."

45 "That's not your real name."

"It's the only one I go by these days."

They rode on in silence for a time. "What's *your* name?" she said.

He told her.

"Irish?"

50 "I never thought about it."

"Where you from, Mcrae?"

"Washington, D.C."

"Long way from home."

"I haven't been there in years."

55 "Where *have* you been?"

"Prison," he said. He hadn't known he would say it, and now that he had, he kept his eyes on the road. He might as well have been posing for her; he had an image of himself as he must look from the side, and he shifted his weight a little, sucked in his belly. When he stole a glance at her he saw that she was simply gazing out at the Panhandle, one hand up like a visor to shade her eyes.

"What about you?" he said, and felt like somebody in a movie—two people with a past come together on the open road. He wondered how he could get the talk around to the subject of love.

"What *about* me?"

"Where're you from?"

60 "I don't want to bore you with all the facts," she said.

"I don't mind," Mcrae said. "I got nothing else to do."

"I'm from way up North."

"Okay," he said, "you want me to guess?"

"Maine," she said. "Land of Moose and Lobster."

65   He said, "Maine. Well, now."

"See? The facts are just a lot of things that don't change."

"Unless you change them," Mcrae said.

She reached down and, with elaborate care, as if it were fragile, put the paper bag on the floor. Then she leaned back and put
her feet up on the dash. She was wearing low-cut tennis shoes.

"You going to sleep?" he asked.

70   "Just relaxing," she said.

But a moment later, when he asked if she wanted to stop and
eat, she didn't answer, and he looked over to see that she was
sound asleep.

HIS FATHER HAD DIED while he was at Leavenworth. The last
time Mcrae saw him, he was lying on a gurney in one of the bays
of D.C. General's emergency ward, a plastic tube in his mouth,
an IV set into an ugly yellow–blue bruise on his wrist. Mcrae had
come home on his first leave from the Air Force—which he had
joined at the order of a juvenile judge—to find his father on the
floor in the living room, in a pile of old newspapers and bottles,
wearing his good suit, with no socks or shoes and no shirt. It
looked as if he were dead. But the ambulance drivers found a
pulse and rushed him off to the hospital. Mcrae cleaned the
house up a little and then followed in the Charger. The old man
had been steadily going downhill from the time Mcrae was a boy
and so this latest trouble wasn't new.

In the hospital, they got the tube into his mouth and hooked
him to the IV, and then left him there on the gurney. Mcrae
stood at his side, still in uniform, and when the old man opened
his eyes and looked at him it was clear that he didn't know who it
was. The old man blinked, stared, and then sat up, took the tube
out of his mouth, and spat something terrible-looking into a
small metal dish which was suspended from the complicated
apparatus of the room and made a continual water-dropping
sound like a leaking sink. He looked at Mcrae again, and then he
looked at the tube. "Jesus Christ," he said.

"Hey," Mcrae said.

75   "What?"

"It's me."

The old man put the tube back into his mouth and looked away.

"Pops," Mcrae said. He didn't feel anything.

The tube came out. "Don't look at me, boy. You got your-self into it. Getting into trouble, stealing and running around. You got yourself into it."

80   "I don't mind it, Pops. It's three meals and a place to sleep."

"Yeah," the old man said, and then seemed to gargle some-thing. He spit into the little metal dish again.

"I got thirty days of leave, Pops."

"Eh?"

"I don't have to go back for a month."

85   "Where are you going?"

"Around," Mcrae said.

The truth was that he hated the Air Force, and he was think-ing of taking the Charger and driving to Canada or someplace like that and hiding out the rest of his life—the Air Force felt like punishment, it *was* punishment, and he had already been in trouble for his quick temper and his attitude.

That afternoon, he'd left his father to whatever would hap-pen, got into the Charger, and started North. But he hadn't made it. He'd lost heart a few miles south of New York City, and he turned around and came back. The old man had been moved to a room in the alcoholic ward, but Mcrae didn't go to see him. He stayed in the house, watching television and drinking beer, and when old high-school buddies came by he went around with them a little. Mostly he stayed home, though, and at the end of his leave he locked the place and drove back to Chanute, in Illinois where he was stationed. He wasn't there two months before the staff sergeant caught him drinking beer in the day-room of one of the training barracks and asked for his name. Mcrae walked over to him, said, "My name is trouble," and at the word *trouble,* struck the other man in the face. He'd had a lot of beer, and he had been sitting there in the dark, drinking the last of it, going over everything in his mind, and the staff sergeant, a baby-faced man with a spare tire of flesh around his waist and an attitude about the stripes on his sleeves, had just walked into it. Mcrae didn't even know him. Yet he stood over him where he had fallen, and then he found himself kicking him. It took two other men to get him off the poor man, who wound up in the hospital with a broken jaw (the first punch had done it), a few cracked ribs, and multiple lacerations and bruises.

The court-martial was swift. The sentence was three years at hard labor, along with the dishonorable discharge. He'd had less than a month to go on the sentence when he got the news about his father. He felt no surprise, nor, really, any grief; yet there was a little thrill of something like fear. He was in his cell, and for an instant some part of him actually wanted to remain there, inside walls, where things were certain and there weren't any decisions to make. A week later, he learned of the money from the insurance, which would have been more than the five thousand except that his father had been a few months behind on the rent, and on other payments. Mcrae settled what he had to of those things and kept the rest. He had started to feel like a happy man, out of Leavenworth and the Air Force, and now he was on his way to Nevada or someplace like that—and he had picked up a girl.

90   HE DROVE ON UNTIL DUSK, stopping only for gas, and the girl slept right through. Just past the line into New Mexico, he pulled off the interstate and went north for a mile or so, looking for someplace other than a chain restaurant to eat. She sat up straight, pushed the hair back away from her face. "Where are we?"

"New Mexico," he said. "I'm looking for a place to eat."

"I'm not hungry."

"Well," he said, "*you* might be able to go all day without anything to eat, but I got a three-meal-a-day habit to support."

She brought the paper bag up from the floor and held it in her lap.

95   "You got food in there?" he asked.

"No."

"You're very pretty—childlike, sort of—when you sleep."

"I didn't snore?"

"You were quiet as a mouse."

100   "And you think I'm pretty?"

"I guess you know a thing like that. I hope I didn't offend you."

"I don't like dirty remarks," she said. "But I don't guess you meant to be dirty."

"Dirty."

"Sometimes people can say a thing like that and mean it very dirty, but I could tell you didn't."

105 He pulled in at a roadside diner and turned off the ignition. "Well?" he said.

She sat there with the bag on her lap. "I don't think I'll go in with you."

"You can have a cold drink or something." he said.

"You go in. I'll wait out here."

"Come on in there with me and have a cold drink," Mcrae said. "I'll buy it for you. I'll buy you dinner if you want."

110 "I don't want to," she said.

He got out and started for the entrance, and before he reached it he heard her door open and close, and turned to watch her come toward him, thin and waiflike in the shawl, which hid her arms and hands.

The diner was empty. There was a long low bar, with soda fountains on the other side of it, and glass cases in which pies and cakes were set; and there were booths along one wall. Everything seemed in order, except that no one was around. Mcrae and the girl stood in the doorway for a moment and waited, and finally she stepped in and took a seat in the first booth. "I guess we're supposed to seat ourselves," she said.

"This is weird," said Mcrae.

"Hey," she said, rising, "there's a jukebox." She strode over to it and leaned on it, crossing one leg behind the other at the ankle, her hair falling down to hide her face.

115 "Hello?" Mcrae said. "Anybody here?"

"Got any change?" asked the girl.

He gave her a quarter and then sat at the bar. The door at the far end swung in and a big red-faced man entered, wearing a white cook's apron over a sweat-stained baby-blue shirt whose sleeves he had rolled up past the meaty curve of his elbows. "Yeah?" he said.

"You open?" Mcrae asked.

"That jukebox don't work, honey," the man said.

120   "You open?" Mcrae said as the girl came and sat down beside him.

    "Sure, why not?"

    "Place is kind of empty."

    "What do you want to eat?"

    "You got a menu?"

125   "You want a menu?"

    "Sure," Mcrae said, "why not?"

    "Truth is," the big man said, "I'm selling this place. I don't have menus any more. I make hamburgers and breakfast stuff. Some french fries and cold drinks. A hot dog maybe. I'm not keeping track."

    "Let's go somewhere else," the girl said.

    "Yeah," said the big man, "why don't you do that?"

130   "Look," said Mcrae, "what's the story here?"

    The other man shrugged. "You came in at the end of the run, you know what I mean? I'm going out of business. Sit down and I'll make you a hamburger on the house."

    Mcrae looked at the girl.

    "Okay," she said, in a tone which made it clear that she would've been happier to leave.

    The big man put his hands on the bar and leaned toward her. "Miss, if I were you I wouldn't look a gift horse in the mouth."

135   "I don't like hamburger," she said.

    "You want a hot dog?" the man said. "I got a hot dog for you. Guaranteed to please."

    "I'll have some french fries," she said.

    The big man turned to the grill and opened the metal drawer under it. He was very wide at the hips and his legs were like trunks. "I get out of the Army after twenty years," he said, "and I got a little money put aside. The wife and I decide we want to get into the restaurant business. The government's going to be paying me a nice pension and we got the savings, so we sink it all in this goddamn diner. Six and a half miles from the interstate. You get the picture? The guy's selling us this diner at a great price, you know? A terrific price. For a song, I'm in the restaurant business. The wife will cook the food and I'll wait tables, you know, until we start to make a little extra, and then we'll hire somebody—a high-school kid or somebody like that. We might even open another restaurant if the going gets good enough. But, of course, this is New Mexico. This is six and a half miles from the interstate. There's nothing here any more because there's nothing up the road. You know what's up the road? Nothing."

He had put the hamburger on, and a basket of frozen french fries.

140   "Now the wife decides she's had enough of life on the border, and off she goes to Seattle to sit in the rain with her mother and here I am trying to sell a place nobody else is dumb enough to buy. You know what I mean?"

"That's rough," Mcrae said.

"You're the second customer I've had all *week*, bub."

The girl said, "I guess that cash register's empty then, huh?"

"It ain't full, honey."

145   She got up and wandered across the room. For a while she stood gazing out the windows over the booths, her hands invisible under the woolen shawl. When she came back to sit next to Mcrae again, the hamburger and french fries were ready.

"On the house," the big man said.

And the girl brought a gun out of the shawl—a pistol that looked like a toy. "Suppose you open up that register, Mr. Poormouth," she said.

The big man looked at her, then at Mcrae, who had taken a large bite of his hamburger and had it bulging in his cheeks.

"This thing is loaded and I'll use it."

150   "Well, for Christ's sake," the big man said.

Mcrae started to get off the stool. "Hold on a minute," he said to them both, his words garbled by the mouthful of food, and then everything started happening all at once. The girl aimed the pistol, there was a popping sound—a single, small pop, not much louder than the sound of a cap gun—and the big man took a step back against the counter, into the dishes and pans there. He stared at the girl, wide-eyed, for what seemed a long time, then went down, pulling dishes with him in a tremendous shattering.

"Jesus Christ!" Mcrae said, swallowing, standing back from her, raising his hands.

She put the pistol back in her jeans under the shawl and then went around the counter and opened the cash register.

"Damn," she said.

155   Mcrae said, low, "Jesus Christ."

And now she looked at him—it was as if she had forgotten he was there. "What're you standing there with your hands up like that?"

"God," he said. "Oh, God."

"Stop it," she said. "Put your hands down."

He did so.

160   "Cash register's empty." She sat down on one of the stools and gazed over at the body of the man where it had fallen. "Damn."

"Look," Mcrae said, "take my car. You—you can have my car."

She seemed puzzled. "I don't want your car. What do I want your car for?"

"You—" he said. He couldn't talk, couldn't focus clearly, or think. He looked at the man, who lay very still, and then he began to cry.

"Will you stop it?" she said, coming off the stool, reaching under the shawl and bringing out the pistol again.

165   "Jesus," he said. "Good Jesus."

She pointed the pistol at his forehead. "Bang," she said. "What's my name?"

"Your name?"

"My name."

"Belle—" he managed.

170   "Come on," she said. "The whole thing—you remember."

"Belle—Belle Starr."

"Right." She let the gun hand drop to her side, into one of the folds of the shawl. "I like that so much better than Annie Oakley."

"Please," Mcrae said.

She took a few steps away from him and then whirled and aimed the gun. "I think we better get out of here, what do you think?"

175   "Take the car," he said, almost with exasperation. It frightened him to hear it in his own voice.

     "I can't drive," she said simply. "Never learned."

     "Jesus," he said. It went out of him like a sigh.

     "God," she said, gesturing with the pistol for him to move
to the door, "it's hard to believe you were ever in *prison*."

     THE ROAD WENT ON INTO THE DARK, beyond the fan of
the headlights. He lost track of miles, road signs, other traffic,
time. Trucks came by and surprised him, and other cars seemed
to materialize as they started the lane change that would bring
them over in front of him. He watched their taillights grow small
in the distance, and all the while the girl sat watching him, her
hands somewhere under the shawl. For a long time there was just
the sound of the rushing night air at the windows, and then she
moved a little, shifted her weight, bringing one leg up on the seat.

180   "What were you in prison for, anyway?"

     Her voice startled him, and for a moment he couldn't think
to answer.

     "Come on," she said, "I'm getting bored with all this quiet.
What were you in prison for?"

     "I—beat up a guy."

     "That's all?"

185   "Yes, that's all." He couldn't keep the irritation out of his voice.

     "Tell me about it."

     "It was just—I just beat up a guy. It wasn't anything."

     "I didn't shoot that man for money, you know."

     Mcrae said nothing.

190   "I shot him because he made a nasty remark to me about the
hot dogs."

     "I didn't hear any nasty remark."

     "He shouldn't have said it or else he'd still be alive."

     Mcrae held tight to the wheel.

     "Don't you wish it was the Wild West?" she said.

195   "Wild West," he said, "yeah." He could barely speak for the
dryness in his mouth and the deep ache of his own breathing.

     "You know," she said, "I'm not really from Maine."

He nodded.

"I'm from Florida."

"Florida," he managed.

200 "Yes. Only I don't have a Southern accent, so people think I'm not from there. Do you hear any trace of a Southern accent at all when I talk?"

"No," he said.

"Now you—you've got an accent. A definite Southern accent."

He was silent.

"Talk to me," she said.

205 "What do you want me to say?" he said. "Jesus."

"You could ask me things."

"Ask you things—"

"Ask me what my name is."

Without hesitating, Mcrae said, "What's your name?"

210 "You know."

"No, really," he said, trying to play along.

"It's Belle Starr."

"Belle Starr," he said.

"Nobody *but,*" she said.

215 "Good," he said.

"And I don't care about money, either," she said. "That's not what I'm after."

"No," Mcrae said.

"What I'm after is adventure."

"Right," said Mcrae.

220 "Fast living."

"Fast living, right."

"A good time."

"Good," he said.

"I'm going to live a ton before I die."

225 "A ton, yes."

"What about you?" she said.

"Yes," he said, "me, too."

"Want to join up with me?"

"Join up," he said. "Right." He was watching the road.

230 She leaned toward him a little. "Do you think I'm lying about my name?"

"No."

"Good," she said.

He had begun to feel as though he might start throwing up what he'd had of the hamburger. His stomach was cramping on him and he was dizzy. He might even be having a heart attack.

"Your eyes are as big as saucers," she said.

235   He tried to narrow them a little. His whole body was shaking now.

"You know how old I am, Mcrae? I'm nineteen."

He nodded, glanced at her and then at the road again.

"How old are you?"

"Twenty-three."

240   "Do you believe people go to heaven when they die?"

"Oh, God," he said.

"Look, I'm not going to shoot you while you're driving the car. We'd crash if I did that."

"Oh," he said. "Oh, Jesus, please—look, I never saw anybody shot before—"

"Will you *stop it?*"

245   He put one hand to his mouth. He was soaked. He felt the sweat on his upper lip and then he felt the dampness all through his clothes.

She said, "I don't kill everybody I meet, you know."

"No," he said. "Of course not." The absurdity of this exchange almost brought a laugh up out of him. It was astonishing that such a thing as a laugh could be anywhere in him at such a time, but here it was, rising up in his throat like some loosened part of his anatomy. He held on with his whole mind, and it was a moment before he realized that *she* was laughing.

"Actually," she said, "I haven't killed all that many people."

"How—" he began. Then he had to stop to breathe. "How many?"

250   "Take a guess."

"I don't have any idea," he said.

"Well," she said, "you'll just have to guess. And you'll notice that I haven't spent any time in prison."

He was quiet.

"*Guess*," she said.

255   Mcrae said, "Ten?"

"No."

He waited.

"Come on, keep guessing."

"More than ten?"

260   "Well, all right. Less than ten."

"Less than ten," he said.

"Guess," she said.

"Nine."

"No."

265   "Eight."

"No, not eight."

"Six?"

"Not six."

"Five?"

270   "Five and a half people," she said. "You almost hit it right on the button."

"Five and a half people," said Mcrae.

"Right. A kid who was hitchhiking, like me. A guy at a gas station. A dog that must've got lost—I count him as the half. Another guy at a gas station. A guy that took me to a motel and made an obscene gesture to me. And the guy at the diner. That makes five and a half."

"Five and a half," Mcrae said.

"You keep repeating everything I say. I wish you'd quit that."

275   He wiped his hand across his mouth and then feigned a cough to keep from having to speak.

"Five and a half people," she said, turning a little in the seat, putting her knees up on the dash. "Have you ever met anybody like me? Tell the truth."

"No," Mcrae said, "nobody."

"Just think about it, Mcrae. You can say you rode with Belle Starr. You can tell your grandchildren."

He was afraid to say anything to this, for fear of changing the delicate balance of the thought. Yet he knew the worst mistake would be to say nothing at all. He was beginning to feel something of the cunning that he would need to survive, even as he knew the slightest miscalculation would mean the end of him. He said, with fake wonder, "I knew Belle Starr."

280 She said, "Think of it."

"Something," he said.

And she sat farther down in the seat. "Amazing."

HE KEPT TO FIFTY-FIVE MILES AN HOUR. Everyone else was speeding. The girl sat straight up now, nearly facing him on the seat. For long periods she had been quiet, simply watching him drive, and soon they were going to need gas. There was now less than half a tank.

"Look at these people speeding," she said. "We're the only ones obeying the speed limit. Look at them."

285 "Do you want me to speed up?" he asked.

"I think they ought to get tickets for speeding, that's what I think. Sometimes I wish I was a policeman."

"Look," Mcrae said, "we're going to need gas pretty soon."

"No, let's just run it until it quits. We can always hitch a ride with somebody."

"This car's got a great engine," Mcrae said. "We might have to outrun the police and I wouldn't want to do that in any other car."

290 "This old thing? It's got a crack in the windshield. The radio doesn't work."

"Right. But it's a fast car. It'll outrun a police car."

She put one arm over the back seat and looked out the rear window. "You really think the police are chasing us?"

"They might be," he said.

She stared at him a moment. "No. There's no reason. Nobody saw us."

295 "But if somebody did—this car, I mean, it'll go like *crazy.*"

"I'm afraid of speeding, though," she said. "Besides, you know what I found out? If you run slow enough the cops go right past you. Right on past you looking for somebody who's in a hurry. No, I think it's best if we just let it run until it quits and then get out and hitch."

Mcrae thought he knew what might happen when the gas ran out. She'd make him push the car to the side of the road, and then she'd walk him back into the cactus and brush there, and when they were far enough from the road she'd shoot him. He knew this as if she'd spelled it all out, and he began again to try for the cunning he would need. "Belle," he said, "why don't we lay low for a few days in Albuquerque?"

"Is that an obscene gesture?" she said.

"No!" he said, almost shouted. "No! That's—it's outlaw talk. You know. Hide out from the cops—lay low. It's—it's prison talk."

300 "Well, I've never been in prison."

"That's all I meant."

"You want to hide out?"

"Right," he said.

"You and me?"

305 "You—you asked if I wanted to join up with you."

"Did I?" She seemed puzzled by this.

"Yes," he said, feeling himself press it a little. "Don't you remember?"

"I guess I do."

"You did," he said.

310 "I don't know."

"Belle Starr had a gang," he said.

"She did."

"I could be the first member of your gang."

She sat there thinking this over. Mcrae's blood moved at the thought that she was deciding whether or not he would live. "Well," she said, "maybe."

315 "You've got to have a gang, Belle."

"We'll see," she said.

A moment later, she said, "How much money do you have?"

"I have enough to start a gang."

"It takes money to start a gang?"

320 "Well—" He was at a loss.

"How much do you have?"

He said, "A few hundred."

"Really?" she said. "That much?"

"Just enough to—just enough to get to Nevada."

325 "Can I have it?"

He said, "Sure." He was holding the wheel and looking out into the night.

"And we'll be a gang?"

"Right," he said.

"I like the idea. Belle Starr and her gang."

330   Mcrae started talking about what the gang could do, making it up as he went along, trying to sound like all the gangster movies he'd seen. He heard himself talking about things like robbery and getaway and staying out of prison, and then, as she sat there staring at him, he started talking about being at Leavenworth, what it was like.

He went on about it, the hours of forced work, and the time alone—the harsh day-to-day routines, the bad food. Before he was through, feeling the necessity of deepening her sense of him as her new accomplice—and feeling strangely as though in some way he had indeed become exactly that—he was telling her every-thing, all the bad times he'd had, his father's alcoholism, and growing up wanting to hit something for the anger that was in him, the years of getting into trouble, the fighting and the kick-ing and what it had got him. He embellished it all, made it sound worse than it really was because she seemed to be going for it, and because, telling it to her, he felt oddly sorry for himself—a version of this story of pain and neglect and lonely rage was true. He had been through a lot. And as he finished, describing for her the scene at the hospital the last time he saw his father, he was almost certain that he had struck a cord in her. He thought he saw it in the rapt expression on her face.

"Anyway," he said, and smiled at her.

"Mcrae?" she said.

"Yeah?"

335   "Can you pull over?"

"Well," he said, his voice shaking, "why don't we wait until it runs out of gas?"

She was silent.

"We'll be that much farther down the road," he said.

"I don't really want a gang," she said. "I don't like dealing with other people that much. I mean, I don't think I'm a leader."

340   "Oh, yes," Mcrae said. "No—you're a leader. You're defi-nitely a leader. I was in the Air Force and I know leaders, and you are definitely what I'd call a leader."

"Really?"

"Absolutely. You are leadership material all the way."

"I wouldn't have thought so."

"Definitely," he said. "Definitely a leader."

345 "But I don't really like people around, you know."

"That's a leadership quality. Not wanting people around. It is definitely a leadership quality."

"Boy," she said, "the things you learn."

He waited. If he could only think himself through to the way out. If he could get her to trust him, get the car stopped—be there when she turned her back.

"You want to be in my gang, huh?"

350 "I sure do," he said.

"Well, I guess I'll have to think about it."

"I'm surprised nobody's mentioned it to you before."

"You're just saying that."

"No, really."

355 "Were you ever married?" she asked.

"Married?" he said, and then stammered over the answer. "Ah—uh, no."

"You ever been in a gang before?"

"A couple of times, but—but they never had good leadership."

"You're giving me a line, huh?"

360 "No," he said, "it's true. No good leadership. It was always a problem."

"I'm tired," she said, shifting toward him a little. "I'm tired of talking."

The steering wheel was hurting the insides of his hands. He held tight, looking at the coming-on of the white stripes in the road. There were no other cars now, and not a glimmer of light anywhere beyond the headlights.

"Don't you ever get tired of talking sometimes?"

"I never was much of a talker," he said.

365 "I guess I don't mind talking as much as I mind listening," she said.

He made a sound in his throat that he hoped she took for agreement.

"That's just when I'm tired, though."

"Why don't you take a nap?" he said.

She leaned back against the door and regarded him. "There's plenty of time for that later."

370   "SO," HE WANTED TO SAY, "you're not going to kill me— we're a gang?"

They had gone for a long time without speaking, a nerve-wrecking hour of minutes during which the gas gauge had sunk to just above empty—and finally she had begun talking about herself, mostly in the third person. It was hard to make sense of most of it, yet he listened as if to instructions concerning how to extricate himself. She talked about growing up in Florida, in the country, and owning a horse. She remembered when she was taught to swim by somebody she called Bill, as if Mcrae would know who that was, and then she told him how when her father ran away with her mother's sister her mother started having men friends over all the time. "There was a lot of obscene goings-on," she said, and her voice tightened a little.

"Some people don't care what happens to their kids," said Mcrae.

"Isn't it the truth?" she said. Then she took the pistol out of the shawl. "Take this exit."

He pulled onto the ramp and up an incline to a two-lane road that went off through the desert, toward a glow that burned on the horizon. For perhaps five miles the road was straight as a plumb line and then it curved into long, low undulations of sand and mesquite and cactus.

375   "My mother's men friends used to do whatever they wanted to me," she said. "It went on all the time. All sorts of obscene goings-on."

Mcrae said, "I'm sorry that happened to you, Belle." And for an instant he was surprised by the sincerity of his feeling—it was as if he couldn't feel sorry enough. Yet it was genuine: it all had to do with his own unhappy story. The whole world seemed very, very sad to him. "I'm really very sorry," he said.

She was quiet a moment, as if thinking about this. Then she said, "Let's pull over now. I'm tired of riding."

"It's almost out of gas," he said.

"I know, but pull it over anyway."

380 "You sure you want to do that?"

"See?" she said. "That's what I mean. I wouldn't like being told what I should do all the time, or asked if I was sure of what I wanted or not."

He pulled the car over and slowed to a stop. "You're right," he said. "See? Leadership. I'm just not used to somebody with leadership qualities."

She took the gun out and held it a little toward him. He was looking at the perfect dark little circle of the end of the barrel. "I guess we should get out, huh?" she said.

"I guess so," he said. He hadn't even heard himself.

385 "Do you have any relatives left anywhere?" she said.

"No."

"Your folks are both dead?"

"Right, yes."

"Which one died first?"

390 "I told you," he said, "didn't I? My mother—my mother died first."

"Do you feel like an orphan?"

He sighed. "Sometimes." The whole thing was slipping away from him.

"I guess I do, too." She reached back and opened her door. "Let's get out now." And when he opened his door she aimed the gun at his head. "Get out slow."

"Aw, Jesus," he said, "look, you're not going to do this, are you? I mean I thought we were friends and all."

395 "Just get out real slow, like I said to."

"Okay," he said, "I'm getting out." He opened his door, and the ceiling light surprised and frightened him. Some wordless part of himself understood that this was it, and all his talk had come to nothing. All the questions she had asked him and everything he had told her—it was all completely useless. This was going to happen to him, and it wouldn't mean anything. It would just be what happened.

"Real slow," she said. "Come on."

"Why are you doing this?" he said. "You've got to tell me that before you do it."

"Will you please get out of the car now?"

400 He just stared at her.

"All right, I'll shoot you where you sit."

"Okay," he said, "don't shoot."

She said, in an irritable voice, as though she were talking to a recalcitrant child, "You're just putting it off."

He was backing himself out, keeping his eyes on the little barrel of the gun, and he could hear something coming, seemed to notice it in the same instant that she said, "Wait." He stood half in and half out of the car, doing as she said, and a truck came over the hill ahead of them, a tractor trailer, all white light and roaring.

405 "Stay still," she said, crouching, aiming the gun at him.

The truck came fast, was only fifty yards away, and without having to decide about it, without even knowing that he would do it, Mcrae bolted into the road.

He was running—there was the exhausted sound of his own breath, the truck horn blaring, coming on louder, the thing bearing down on him, something buzzing past his head. Time slowed. His legs faltered under him, were heavy, all the nerves gone out of them. In the light of the oncoming truck, he saw his own white hands outstretched as if to grasp something in the air before him, and then the truck was past him, the blast of air from it propelling him over the side of the road and down an embankment in high, dry grass, which pricked his skin and crackled like hay.

HE WAS ALIVE. He lay very still. Above him was the long shape of the road, curving off in the distance, the light of the truck going on. The noise faded and was nothing. A little wind stirred. He heard the car door close. Carefully, he got to all fours and crawled a few yards away from where he had fallen. He couldn't be sure of which direction—he only knew he couldn't stay where he was. Then he heard what he thought were her footsteps in the road and he froze. He lay on his side, facing the embankment. When she appeared there, he almost cried out.

"Mcrae?" she said. "Did I get you?" Her eyes went over where he was, and he stopped breathing. "Mcrae?"

410   He watched her move along the edge of the embankment.

"Mcrae?" She put one hand over her eyes and stared at a place a few feet from him, then she turned and went back out of sight. He heard the car door again, and again he began to crawl farther away. The ground was cold and rough and there was a lot of sand.

He heard her put the key in the trunk, and he stood up, began to run, he was getting away, but something went wrong in his leg, something sent him sprawling, and a sound came out of him that seemed to echo, to stay on the air, as if to call her to him. He tried to be perfectly still, tried not to breathe, hearing now the small pop of the gun. He counted the reports—one, two, three. She was just standing there at the edge of the road, firing into the dark toward where she must have thought she heard the sound. Then she was rattling the paper bag, reloading. He could hear the click of the gun. He tried to get up and couldn't. He had sprained his ankle, had done something very bad to it. Now he was crawling wildly, blindly, through the tall grass, hearing again the small report of the pistol. At last he rolled into a shallow gully and lay there with his face down, breathing the dust, his own voice leaving him in a whimpering animal-like sound that he couldn't stop, even as he held both shaking hands over his mouth.

"Mcrae?" She sounded so close. "Hey," she said. "Mcrae?"

He didn't move. He lay there perfectly still, trying to stop himself from crying. He was sorry for everything he had ever done. He didn't care about the money, or the car or going out West or anything. When he lifted his head to peer over the lip of the gully, and saw that she had started down the embankment with his flashlight, he lost his sense of himself as Mcrae: he was just something crippled and breathing in the dark, lying flat in a little winding gully of weeds and sand. Mcrae was gone, was someone far, far away, from ages ago—a man fresh out of prison, with the whole country to wander in, and insurance money in his pocket, who had headed West with the idea that maybe his luck, at long last, had changed.

Lynna Williams

Lynna Williams is an emerging writer who had two stories in *The Atlantic* in 1990.

Personal Testimony

THE LAST NIGHT OF CHURCH CAMP, 1963, and I am sitting in the front row of the Junior Mixed-Voice Choir looking out on the crowd in the big sanctuary tent. The tent glows, green and white and unexpected, in the Oklahoma night; our choir director, Dr. Bledsoe, has schooled us in the sudden crescendos needed to compete with the sounds cars make when their drivers cut the corner after a night at the bars on Highway 10 and see the tent rising out of the plain for the first time. The tent is new to Faith Camp this year, a gift to God and the Southern Baptist Convention from the owner of a small circus who repented, and then retired, in nearby Oklahoma City. It is widely rumored among the campers that Mr. Talliferro came to Jesus late in life, after having what my mother would call Life Experiences. Now he walks through camp with the unfailing good humor of a man who, after years of begging hardscrabble farmers to forsake their fields for an afternoon of elephants and acrobats, has finally found a real draw: His weekly talks to the senior boys on "Sin and the Circus" incorporate a standing room only question-and-answer period, and no one ever leaves early.

Although I know I will never be allowed in the tent to hear one of Mr. Talliferro's talks—I will not be 12 forever, but I will always be a girl—I am encouraged by his late arrival into our Fellowship of Believers. I will take my time, too, I think: First, I will go to high school, to college, to bed with a boy, to New York. (I think of the last two items as one since, as little as I know about sex, I do know it is not something I will ever be able to do if my mother is in the same time zone.) Then when I'm 52 or so and have had, like Mr. Talliferro, sufficient Life Experiences, I'll move back to West Texas and Repent.

Normally thoughts of that touching—and distant—scene of repentance are how I entertain myself during evening worship service. But tonight I am unable to work up any enthusiasm for the vision of myself sweeping into my hometown to Be Forgiven. For once my thoughts are entirely on the worship service ahead.

My place in the choir is in the middle of six other girls from my father's church in Fort Worth; we are dressed alike in white, lace-trimmed wash-and-wear blouses from J.C. Penney and modest navy pedal pushers that stop exactly three inches from our white socks and tennis shoes. We are also alike in having mothers who regard travel irons as an essential accessory to Christian Young Womanhood; our matching outfits are neatly ironed.

5   At least their outfits are. I have been coming to this camp in the southwestern equivalent of the Sahara desert for six years now, and I know that when it is 100 degrees at sunset, cotton wilts. When I used my iron I did the front of my blouse and pants, so I wouldn't stand out, and trusted anyone standing behind me would think I was wrinkled from the heat.

Last summer, or the summer before, when I was still riding the line that separates good girls from bad, the small deception would have bothered me. This year I am 12 and a criminal. Moral niceties are lost on me. I am singing "Just as I Am" with the choir and I have $300 in my white Bible, folded and taped over John 3:16.

Since camp started three weeks ago I have operated a business in the arts and crafts cabin in the break between afternoon Bible study and segregated (boys only/girls only) swimming. The senior boys, the same ones who are learning critical new information from

Mr. Talliferro every week, are paying me to write the personal testimonies we are all expected to give at evening worship service.

WE DO NOT DWELL ON PERSONAL MOTIVATION in my
family. When my brother David and I sin it is the deed my parents talk about, not mitigating circumstances, and the deed they
punish. This careful emphasis on what we do, never on why we
do it, has affected David and me differently. He is a good boy,
endlessly kind and cheerful and responsible, but his heroes are
not the men my father followed into the ministry. David gives
God and our father every outward sign of respect, but he wor-
ships Clarence Darrow and the law. At 15 he has been my defense
lawyer for years.

While David wants to defend the world, I am only interested
in defending myself. I know exactly why I have started the testimony business. I am doing it to get back at my father. I am doing
it because I am adopted.

10   Even though I assure my customers with every sale that we will
not get caught, I never write a testimony without imagining public
exposure of my wrongdoing. The scene is so familiar to me I do
not have to close my eyes to see it: The summons to the camp
director's office and the door closing behind me; the shocked faces
of other campers when the news leaks out; the Baptist Academy
girls who comb their hair and go in pairs, bravely, to offer my
brother comfort; the automatic rotation of my name to the top of
everyone's prayer list. I spend hours imagining the smallest details
of my shame, leading always to the moment when my father, called
from Fort Worth to take me home, arrives at camp.

That will be my moment. I have done something so terrible
even my father will not be able to keep it a secret. I am doing this
because of my father's secrets.

WE HAD ONLY BEEN HOME FROM CHURCH A FEW
MINUTES; it was my ninth birthday and when my father called
me to come downstairs to his study, I was still wearing the dress

my mother had made for the occasion, pink dotted swiss with a white satin sash. David came out of his room to ask me what I had done this time—he liked to be prepared for court—but I told him not to worry, that I was wholly innocent of any crime in the period just before my birthday. At the bottom of the stairs I saw my mother walk out of the study and I knew I was right not to be concerned: In matters of discipline my mother and father never worked alone. At the door it came to me: My father was going to tell me I was old enough to go with him now and then to churches in other cities. David had been to Atlanta and New Orleans and a dozen little Texas towns; my turn had finally come.

My father was standing by the window. At the sound my patent leather shoes made sliding across the hardwood floor, he turned and motioned for me to sit on the sofa. He cleared his throat; it was a sermon noise I had heard hundreds of times, and I knew that he had prepared whatever he was going to say.

All thoughts of ordering room service hamburgers in an Atlanta hotel left me—prepared remarks meant we were dealing with life or death or salvation—and I wished for my mother and David. My father said, "This is hard for your mother; she wanted to be here but it upsets her so, we thought I should talk to you alone." We had left any territory I knew, and I sat up straight to listen as though I were still in church.

15   My father, still talking, took my hands in his; after a moment I recognized the weight of his Baylor ring against my skin as something from my old life, the one in which I woke up that morning a nine-year-old, dressed for church in my birthday dress, and came home.

My father talked and talked and talked; I stopped listening. I had grown up singing about the power of blood. I required no lengthy explanation of what it meant to be adopted. It meant I was not my father's child. It meant I was a secret, even from myself.

IN THE THREE YEARS SINCE THAT DAY IN MY FATHER'S STUDY, I have realized, of course, that I am not my mother's child either. But I have never believed the lie about my birth is her responsibility. It is my father I blame. I am not allowed to talk about my adoption outside my family ("It would only hurt your mother," my father says. "Do you want to hurt your mother?"). Although I am universally regarded by the women of the church as a Child Who Wouldn't Know a Rule if One Reached Up and Bit Her in the Face, I do keep this one. My stomach hurts when I even think about telling anyone, but it hurts, too, when I think about having another mother and father somewhere. When the pain is enough to make me cry, I try to talk to my parents about it, but my mother's face changes even before I get the first question out and my father follows her out of the room. "You're our child," he says when he returns. "We love you, and you're ours." I let him hug me, but I am thinking that I have never heard my father tell a lie before. I am not his child. Not in the way David is, not in the way I believed I was. Later I remember that lie and decide that all the secrecy is for my father's benefit, that he is ashamed to tell the world I am not his child because he is ashamed of me. I think about the Ford my father bought in Dallas three years ago; it has never run right but he will not take it back. I think about that when I am sitting in my bunk with a flashlight, writing testimonies to the power of God's love.

MY FATHER IS ONE REASON I AM HANDCRAFTING Christian testimonies when my bunkmates are making place mats from Popsicle sticks. There is one other reason: I'm good at it.

Nothing else has changed. I remain Left Fielder for Life in the daily softball games. The sincerity of my belief in Jesus is perennially suspect among the most pious, the popular, campers. And I am still the only girl who, in six years of regular attendance, has failed to advance even one step in Girls' Auxiliary. (Other, younger, girls have made it all the way to Queen Regent with Sceptre while I remain a perpetual Lady-in-Waiting.) Until this year, only the strength of my family connections has kept me from sinking as low in the camp hierarchy as Cassie Mosely, who lisps and wears colorful native costumes her missionary parents send from Africa.

20   I arrived at camp as I did every year, resigned and braced to endure but buoyed by a fantasy life I believe is unrivaled among

12-year-old Baptist girls. But on our second night here, the promise of fish sticks and carrot salad hanging in the air, Bobby Dunn came and stood behind me in the cafeteria line.

Bobby Dunn, blond, ambitious, and in love with Jesus, is Faith Camp's standard for male perfection. He is David's friend, but he has spoken to me only once, on the baseball field last year, when he suggested that my unhealthy fear of the ball was really a failure to trust God's plan for my life. Since that day I have taken some comfort in noticing that Bobby Dunn follows the Scripture reading by moving his finger along the text.

Feeling him next to me, I take a breath, wondering if Bobby, like other campers, other years, has decided to attempt to bring me to a better understanding of what it means to serve Jesus. But he is already talking, congratulating me on my testimony at evening worship service the night before. (I speak publicly at camp twice every summer, the exact number required by some mysterious formula that allows me to be left alone the rest of the time.)

"You put it just right," he says. "Now me, I know what I want to say but it comes out all wrong. I've prayed about it, and it seems to me God wants me to do better."

He looks at me hard, and I realize it is my turn to say something. Nothing comes to me, though, since I agree with him completely. He does suffer from what my saintly brother, after one particularly gruesome revival meeting, took to calling "Jesus Jaw," a malady that makes it impossible for the devoted to say what they mean and sit down. Finally I say what my mother says to the ladies seeking comfort in the Dorcas Bible class: "Can I help?" Before I can take it back, Bobby Dunn has me by the hand, pulling me across the cafeteria to a table in the far corner.

25   The idea that I will write testimonies for other campers—a sort of ghostwriting service for Jesus, as Bobby Dunn sees it—is Bobby's, but before we get up from the table I have refined it and made it mine. The next afternoon in the arts and crafts cabin I make my first sale: $5 for a two-minute testimony detailing how God has given Michael Bush the strength to stop swearing. Bobby is shocked when money changes hands—I can see him thinking, "Temple. Moneylenders. Jee-sus!"—but Michael Bush

is the son of an Austin car dealer, and he quotes his earthly father's Scripture: "You get what you pay for."

Michael, who has made me a professional writer with money earned from polishing used station wagons, is a sweet, slow-talking athlete from Bishop Military School. He's been dateless for months and is convinced it is because the Baptist Academy girls have heard that he has a tendency to take the Lord's name in vain on difficult fourth downs. After his testimony that night Michael leaves the tent with Patsy Lewis, but he waves good night to me.

For an underground business I have as much word-of-mouth trade from the senior boys as I can handle. I estimate my volume is second only to the snack stand that sells snow cones. Like the snow cone stand, I have high prices and limited hours of operation. I arrive at the arts and crafts cabin every day at 2:00 P.M., carrying half-finished pot holders from the day before, and senior boys drift in and out for the next 20 minutes. I talk to each customer, take notes, and deliver the finished product by 5:00 P.M. the next night. My prices start at $5 for words only, and go up to $20 for words *and* concept.

Bobby Dunn has appointed himself my sales force; he recruits customers he thinks need my services and gives each one a talk about the need for secrecy. Bobby will not accept money from me as payment—he reminds me hourly he is doing this for Jesus—but he is glad to be thanked in testimonies.

By the beginning of the second week of camp, our director, Reverend Stewart, and the camp counselors are openly rejoicing about the power of the Spirit, as reflected in the moving personal testimonies being given night after night. Bobby Dunn testifies every other night and smiles at me at breakfast every morning. Patsy Lewis teaches me how to set my hair on big rollers, and I let it dry while I sit up at night writing testimonies. I have a perfect pageboy, a white Bible bulging with $5 bills, and I am popular. There are times when I forget my father.

30   ON THIS LAST NIGHT OF CAMP I AM STILL AT LARGE. But, although I have not been caught, I have decided I am not cut out to be a small business. There is the question of good help,

for one thing. Bobby Dunn is no good for detail work—clearly
the less he knows about how my mind works, the better—and so
I have turned to Angela Tucker. Angela loves Jesus and her father
and disapproves of everything about me. She has been my best
friend since first grade. I love her because she truly believes I can
be saved and, until that happens, she is willing to get into almost
any trouble I can think of, provided I do not try to stop her quoting the appropriate Scripture. She has resisted being drawn into
the testimony business for more than a week, though, giving in
only after I sink low enough to introduce her to Bobby Dunn and
point out she will be able to apply her cut to the high cost of braces.

The truth is the business needs Angela. I am no better a dis-
ciple of the Palmer handwriting method than I am of Christ
and my mother's standards of behavior. No one can read my writing. Angela has won the penmanship medal at E. M. Morrow
Elementary School so many years there is talk it will be retired
when we go off to junior high in the fall. When she's done writing,
my testimonies look like poems.

The value of Angela's superior cursive writing, however, is
offset by the ways in which she manifests herself as a true
believer. I can tolerate the Scripture quoting, but her fears are
something else. I am afraid of snakes and not being asked to
pledge my mother's sorority at Baylor, both standard fears in
Cabin A. Angela is terrified of Eastern religions.

Her father, a religion professor at a small Baptist college,
has two passions: world religions and big game hunting. In our
neighborhood, where not rotating the tires on the family Ford
on schedule is considered eccentric, Dr. Tucker wears a safari
jacket to class and greets everyone the same way: "Hi, wallaby."
Angela is not allowed to be afraid of the dead animals in her
father's den, but a pronounced sensitivity to Oriental mysticism
is considered acceptable in a young girl.

Unless I watch her, Angela cannot be trusted to resist insert-
ing a paragraph into every testimony in which the speaker thanks
the Lord Jesus for not having allowed him or her to be born a
Buddhist. I tell Angela repeatedly that if every member of the
camp baseball team suddenly begins to compare and contrast
Zen and the tenets of Southern Baptist fundamentalism in their

three-minute testimonies, someone—even in this trusting place—
is going to start to wonder.

35   She says she sees my point but keeps arguing for more "spiritual" content in the testimonies, a position in which she is
enthusiastically supported by Bobby Dunn. Angela and Bobby
have fallen in love; Bobby asked her to wear his friendship ring
two nights ago using his own words. What is art to me is faith—
and now love—to Angela, and we are not as close as we were three
weeks ago.

    I am a success, although a lonely one, and there is no one I can
talk to about either my success or my feelings. My brother David,
who normally can be counted on to protect me from myself and
others, has only vague, Christian concern for me these days. He
has fallen in love with Denise Meeker, universally regarded as the
most spiritually developed girl in camp history, and he is talking
about following my father into the ministry. I believe that when
Denise goes home to Corpus Christi, David will remember law
school, but in the meantime he is no comfort to me.

NOW FROM MY PLACE IN THE FRONT ROW of the choir,
I know that I will not have to worry about a going-out-of-busi-
ness sale. What I have secretly wished for all summer is about to
happen. I am going to get caught.

    Ten minutes ago, during Reverend Stewart's introduction of
visitors from the pulpit, I looked out at the crowd in the tent and
saw my father walking down the center aisle. As I watched he
stopped every few rows to shake hands and say hello, as casual and
full of good humor as though this were his church on a Sunday
morning. He is a handsome man, and when he stops at the pew
near the front where David is sitting, I am struck by how much my
father and brother look alike, their dark heads together as they
smile and hug. I think of David as belonging to me, not my father,
but there is an unmistakable sameness in their movements that
catches me by surprise, and my eyes fill with tears. Suddenly David
points toward the choir at me, and my father nods his head and
continues walking toward the front of the tent. I know he has seen
me, and I concentrate on looking straight ahead as he mounts the

stairs to the stage and takes a seat to the left of the altar. Reverend Stewart introduces him as the special guest preacher for our last night of camp, and for an instant I let myself believe that is the only reason he has come. He will preach and we will go home together tomorrow. Everything will be all right.

I hear a choked off sound from my left and know without turning to look that it is Angela about to cry. She has seen my father too, and I touch her hand to remind her no one will believe she was at fault. Because of me, teachers have been patiently writing "easily led" and "cries often" on Angela's report cards for years, and she is still considered a good girl. She won't get braces this year, I think, but she will be all right.

In the next moment two things happen at once. Angela starts to cry, really cry, and my father turns in his seat, looks at me, and then away. It is then I realize Angela has decided, without telling me, that straight teeth are not worth eternal damnation. She and Bobby Dunn have confessed, and my father has been called. Now as he sits with his Bible in his hands and his head bowed, his profile shows none of the cheer of a moment before, and none of the successful Baptist preacher expressions I can identify. He does not look spiritual or joyful or weighed down by the burden of God's expectations. He looks furious.

THERE ARE MORE ANNOUNCEMENTS THAN I EVER REMEMBER on a last night of camp: prayer lists, final volley-ball standings, bus departure times, a Lottie Moon Stewardship Award for Denise Meeker. After each item is read I forget I have no reason to expect Jesus to help me, and I pray for one more; I know that as soon as the last announcement is read, Reverend Stewart will call for a time of personal testimonies before my father's sermon.

Even with my head down I can see Bobby Dunn sinking lower into a center pew and, next to him, Tom Bailey leaning forward, wanting to be first at the microphone. Tom is another of the Bishop School jocks, and he has combed his hair back with Vitalis and put on Sunday clothes. In his left hand he is holding my masterwork reproduced in Angela's handwriting on 3 x 5 cards. He paid me $25 for it—the most I have ever charged—and it is the best piece of my career. The script calls for Tom to talk movingly about meeting God in a car–truck accident near El Paso when he was ten. In a dramatic touch of which I am especially proud, he seems to imply that God was driving the truck.

Tom, I know, is doing this to impress a Baptist Academy girl who has told him she will go to her cotillion alone before she goes with a boy who doesn't know Jesus as his personal Lord and Savior. He is gripping the note cards as though they are Didi Thornton and for the first time in a life full of Bible verses, I see an application to my daily life. I am truly about to reap what I have sown.

THE ANNOUNCEMENTS END, and Reverend Stewart calls for testimonies. As Tom Bailey rises, so does my father. As he straightens up he turns again to look at me and, this time, makes a gesture toward the pulpit. It is a mock gallant motion, the kind I have seen him make to let my mother go first at miniature golf. For an instant that simple reminder that I am not an evil mutant—I have a family that plays miniature golf—makes me think everything will be all right. Then I realize what my father is telling me. Tom Bailey will never get to the pulpit to give my testimony. My father will get there first, telling the worshipers in the packed tent his sorrow and regret over the misdeeds of his little girl. His little girl. He is going to do what I have never imagined in all my fantasies about this moment: He is going to forgive me.

45   Without knowing exactly how it has happened, I am standing up, half running from the choir seats to the pulpit. I get there first, before either my father or Tom, and before Reverend Stewart can even say my name, I give my personal testimony.

I BEGAN BY ADMITTING what I have been doing the past three weeks. I talk about being gripped with hate, unable to appreciate the love of my wonderful parents or Jesus. I talk about making money from other campers who, in their honest desire to honor the Lord, became trapped in my web of wrongdoing.

Bobby Dunn is crying. To his left I can see Mr. Talliferro; something in his face, intent and unsmiling, makes me relax: I am a Draw. Everyone is with me now. I can hear Angela behind me, still sobbing into her hymnal, and to prove I can make it work, I talk about realizing how blessed I am to have been born within easy reach of God's healing love. I could have been born a Buddhist, I say, and the gratifying gasps from the audience make me certain I can say anything I want now.

For a moment I lose control and begin quoting poetry instead of Scripture. There is a shaky moment when all I can remember are bits of "Stopping by Woods on a Snowy Evening," but I manage to tie the verses back to a point about Christian choices. The puzzled looks on some faces give way to shouts of "Amen!" I ask for forgiveness then, theirs and the Lord's, and as I look out at the rows of people in the green and white striped tent, I know I have won. I have done it. I have written the best testimony anyone at camp has ever given.

I feel, rather than see, my father come to stand beside me, but I do not stop. As I have heard him do hundreds of times, I ask the choir to sing an invitational hymn and begin singing with them "Softly and tenderly, Jesus is calling, calling to you and to me. Come home, come home. Ye who are weary, come home." My father never does give a sermon.

While the hymn still is being sung Bobby Dunn moves from his pew to the stage and others follow. They hug me; they say they understand; they say they forgive me. As each one moves on to my father, I can hear him thanking them for their concern and saying yes, he knows they will be praying for the family.

By 10:00 P.M., the last knot of worshipers has left the tent, and my father and I are alone on the stage. He is looking at me without speaking; there is no expression on his face that I have seen before. "Daddy," I surprise myself by saying. Daddy is a baby name I have not used since my ninth birthday. My father raises his left hand and slaps me, hard, on my right cheek. He catches me as I start to fall, and we sit down together on the steps leading from the altar. He uses his handkerchief to clean blood from underneath my eye, where his Baylor ring has opened the skin. As he works the white square cloth carefully around my face, I hear a sound I have never heard before and realize my father is crying. I am crying, too, and the mixture of tears and blood on my face makes it impossible to see him clearly. I reach for him anyway, and am only a little surprised when he is there.

John McCluskey

John McCluskey is the author of several
novels, including *Look What They Done to My Song,
Mr. America's Last Season Blues,* and *The River People.*
He edited *Blacks in History, Vol. II* and *Stories from
Black History.* His stories and poems have been
reprinted in many anthologies.

Lush Life

Dayton, Ohio
Late September, 1955

BEHIND THE DANCE HALL the first of the
car doors were banging shut, motors starting up, and from
somewhere—a backyard, an alley—dogs barked. The band's bus
was parked at one darkened corner of the parking lot. Empty, it
was a mute and hulking barn at this hour. Along its side in
slanted, bold-red letters was painted a sign: Earl Ferguson and
America's Greatest Band.

Suddenly, the back door to the dance hall swung open and
loud laughter rushed out on a thick pillow of cigarette smoke.
Ahead of others, two men in suits—the taller one in plaids and
the other in stripes—walked quickly, talking, smoking. They
stopped at a convertible, a dark-red Buick Dynaflow, dew already
sprouting across its canvas top. Other men, all members of the

band, in twos or threes, would come up, slap each other's backs, share a joke or two, then drift toward the bus. In the light over the back door, moths played.

The shorter man, Billy Cox, took off his glasses, fogged the lens twice, then cleaned them with his polka-dot silk square. He reached a hand toward Tommy, the bassist, approaching.

"I'm gone say see y'all further up the road in Cleveland," Tommy said. "But after a night like tonight, it's gone be one hell of a struggle to tear ourselves from this town. Am I right about that, Billy C.?"

5   Tommy laughed, gold tooth showing, and patted his impeccable "do." More than once it had been said that Tommy sweated ice water. With his face dry, hair in place, tie straightened after three hours of furious work, no one could doubt it now.

Tommy spoke again, this time stern, wide-legged and gesturing grandly. "Just you two don't get high and drive off into some damn ditch." His usual farewell slid toward a cackle. Billy waved him off.

In the Scout Car, as the Dynaflow was called, Billy and Earl Ferguson would drive through the night to the next date. Throughout the night, they would stay at least an hour or so ahead of the bus. They would breakfast and be nearly asleep by the time the bus pulled into the same hotel parking lot, the men emerging, looking stunned from a fitful sleep on a noisy bus.

From a nearby car, a woman's throaty laugh lit up the night. They turned to see Pretty Horace leaning into a car, the passenger's side, smoothing down the back edges of his hair and rolling his rump as he ran his game.

"Man, stop your lying!" came her voice. She, too, was toying with the ends of her hair, dyed bright red and glowing in that light. Her friend from the driver's seat, with nothing better to do perhaps, leaned to hear, to signify, her face round as the moon's.

10   Moving with a pickpocket's stealth and slow grin spreading, Poo moved up to the driver's side of the car and whispered something. The driver jerked back, then gave him her best attention, smiling. One hand to her throat, she moistened her lips, glistened a smile.

In unison, Billy and Earl shook their heads while watching it all. Billy slid one hand down a lapel, pulled a cigarette from the corner of his mouth. "Some of the boys gone make a long night of this one."

Earl nodded. "Some mean mistreaters fixing to hit that bus late and do a whole lot of shucking, man."

Yes, some would dare the bus's deadline by tipping into an after-hours party, by following some smiling woman home. The rules were simple, however: if you missed the bus and could not make practice the next day, you were fined fifty dollars. If you missed the date because you missed the bus or train, you were fired. Daring these, you could seek adventure that broke the monotony of long road trips. You could bring stories that released bubbles of laughter throughout an overheated and smoke-filled bus.

Cars were rolling out of the side parking lot and, passing members of the band, the drivers honked in appreciation. Earl bowed slowly and waved an arm wide and high toward his men, some still walking out of the back door of the dance hall. Then he embraced Billy, mugged, and pointed to Billy's chest as if branding there all the credit for a magnificent night. After all, they had done Basie and Ellington to perfection. Their own original tunes had been wonders to behold. From the very beginning the audience had been with them and danced and danced, heads bobbing and shoulders rocking, cheering every solo. The dancers had fun on the stairstep of every melody; hugging tightly, they did the slow grind to the promise of every ballad. Now they thanked the band again with the toot of their horns, shouts, and the wave of their hands.

15   Within an hour, the bus would start up, all the equipment packed and stored below. Then it would roll slowly out of the parking lot. Some of the men would already be snoring. By the outskirts of town, a car might catch up to it, tires squealing as the car rocked to a stop. One of the men—usually McTee or "Rabbit" Ousley, as myth might have it—would climb out and blow a kiss to some grinning woman behind the wheel and strut onto the bus like some wide-legged conqueror. The doors to the bus would close behind him, sealing his stories from any verification and sealing the band against the long, long night.

But it was the Dynaflow, Earl and Billy inside, pulling away first. They would leave before these tales of triumph, outright lies about quick and furious love in a drafty backroom or tales of a young wife whispering "run! run!" and the scramble for a window after the husband's key slid into the lock downstairs. Yes, before all that, Earl and Billy would pull from the parking lot and start away, slow at first, like they had all the time in the world.

Well before the edge of town, they would have checked for cigarettes, surely, and from some magical place on a side street, a jukebox blaring and the smell of fried chicken meeting them at the door with its judas-hole, they would find their coffee in Mason jars, coffee heavily sugared and creamed, and steaming chicken sandwiches wrapped neatly in waxed paper. Older women, who would do double duty at Sunday church dinners, would smile and wipe their hands on their aprons. And, bless them, these good and prodigal sons with conked hair. Then, moving toward the door, Billy and Earl would be greeted by achingly beautiful women with late-night joy lacing their hoarse voices. Billy and Earl would take turns joking and pulling each other away, then, outside and laughing, climb back into the car for the journey through the night.

For the first few minutes, the lights of Dayton thinning, used car lots and a roller rink as outposts, they were silent before nervous energy swept over them. It was that unsettling bath of exhaustion and exuberance, rising to a tingle at the base of the neck, so familiar at the end of a performance. With Earl at the wheel, they began to harmonize and scat their way through "Take the A Train," "One O'Clock Jump," and their own wonderful collaboration, "October Mellow." In this way they would ride for a while. They would sing in ragged breaths before they gave out in laughter. The radio might go on, and there would be mostly the crackle of static, or, faintly, a late-night gospel concert with harmonies rising and falling, like a prayer song tossed to the wind. Stray cars would rush past in the next lane, headed back toward Dayton. They passed a trailer groaning under its load, one or two squat Fords, then settled back. The night's first chapter was closed behind them with the noise from the motor, with smears of light.

Like a sudden tree in the car's lights, a sign sprouted and announced the city limits of Springfield.

20   Billy started nodding as if answering some ancient question. "Springfield got more fine women than they got in two St. Louises or five New Orleans, I'm here to tell you."

"Wake up, Billy. Find me a place with women finer than they got in St. Louis or New Orleans or Harlem—think I'm gone let Harlem slide?—find me such a place and you got a easy one hundred bill in your hand and I'll be in heaven. I'm talking serious now."

Billy snorted, sitting up straight and shaking his head. "I ain't hardly sleeping. Just remembering it all. See, I ain't been through here since 1952, but I can call some preacher's daughter right now—brown skin and about yeah-tall—yeah, at this very hour. Lord, she would be so fine that you and me both would run up the side of a mountain and holler like a mountain jack."

Then Earl blew a smoke ring and watched its rise; maybe it would halo the rear-view mirror. "Well, okay, I'll take your word for it now, but if we're ever back through here, I definitely want to stop and see if these women are as pretty as you say."

"They pretty, they mamas pretty, they grandmamas pretty. . . ."

25   Earl laughed his high-pitched laugh. "You get crazier every day, Billy Cox." He pushed the accelerator, slamming them deeper into their seats.

Earl leveled off at sixty and for minutes was content to enjoy the regular beat of the wheels hitting the seams across the pavement, pa-poom, pa-poom, pa-poom. It was the next stretch of road, ten miles outside of Springfield, that they truly sensed the flatness of the place. In the darkness there were no distant hills promising contour, variety, or perspective. Fields to the left? Woods to the right? They were silent for a minute or so. Crackling music flared up once again from the radio, then died.

"What do you think of the new boy's work tonight?" Billy asked.

"Who, 'Big City'? Not bad, man. Not bad at all." Earl snapped his fingers. "He's swinging more now. Matter of fact, he's driving the entire trumpet section, Big Joe included. You get the prize on that one, you brought him in. I remember you kept saying he could play the sweetest ballads, could curl up inside something like Strayhorn's 'Daydream' as easy as a cat curl up on a bed."

Billy nodded and looked out the side window. "I knew he had it in him the first time I heard him. His problem was hanging around Kansas City too long with that little jive band and just playing careful music. Sometimes you can't tell what's on the inside—just fast or slow, just hard or soft, just mean or laughing sweet. Can't never tell with some. But I had that feeling, know what I'm saying? Had the feeling that if we cut him loose, let him roam a little taste, that he could be all them combinations, that he could be what a tune needed him to be."

30   Earl tossed a cigarette stub out the window. He remembered the night he had met young Harold. The band was on break, and Harold walked up slowly, head down. The trumpet player had been nervous in his too-tight suit. Earl had later confided to Billy that he looked like he had just come in from plowing a corn field and that if he joined the band he would have to learn how to dress, to coordinate the colors of his ties and suits, shine his shoes. When you joined the Ferguson band, you joined class. Style was more than your sound. It was your walk, the way you sat during the solos by others, the way you met the night. Earl had promptly nicknamed him 'Big City.'

"He said meeting you was like meeting God," Billy had said the next morning over hash browns and lukewarm coffee.

Earl smiled now. He was not God, true. He did know that among bandleaders roaming with their groups across this country, he was one of the best. He knew, too, that soft-spoken Billy Cox, five years younger, was the best composer in the business, period. Together they worked an easy magic. Few could weave sounds the way they could, few could get twelve voices, twelve rambunctious personalities, to shout or moan as one. And with it all was the trademark sound: the perfect blend of brass and reeds. Basie might have a stronger reed section, with the force of a melodic hurricane; Ellington, a brass section with bite and unmatchable brightness. But they had the blend. Within the first few notes you knew that it was Earl Ferguson's band and nobody else's. Now and then players would leave to join other caravans inching across the continent, but the sound, their mix, stayed the same.

The scattered lights of Springfield were far behind them now, merged to a dull electric glow in the rearview mirror. And out from the town there were only occasional lights along State Route 42, one or two on front porches, lights bathing narrow, weathered and wooded fronts, wood swings perfectly still in that time. Tightly-closed shutters, silences inside. Both tried to imagine the front of the houses at noon—children pushing the porch swing? a dog napping in the shade nearby? clothes flapping on a line running from behind the house? Gone suddenly, a blur to pinpoint, then out.

From a pocket Billy had taken out a matchbook. A few chord progressions had been scribbled on the inside cover. Then drawing out a small lined tablet from beneath the seat, he quickly drew a bass staff and started humming.

35   "You got something going?" Earl asked.

"I think, yeah. A little light something, you know, like bright light and springtime and whatnot."

Earl tapped the wheel lightly with the palm of his free hand. "Toss in a small woman's bouncy walk, and I might get excited with you."

"Well, help me then. This time you use the woman—tight yellow skirt, right?—and I'll use the light, the light of mid-May, and when they don't work together, I think we'll both know."

"Solid. What you got so far?"

40   Billy did not answer. He kept a finger to his ear, staring from the matchbook cover to the tablet. Earl let it run. You don't interrupt when the idea is so young.

More often than not, Billy and Earl brought opposites, or, at least, unlikely combinations together. One of the band's more popular numbers, a blues, was the result of Billy's meditations on the richly perfumed arms of a large and fleshy woman, arms tightly holding a man who mistook her short laugh for joy. To this, Earl had brought the memory of a rainy night and a long soft moan carried in the wind, something heard from the end of an alley. They used only the colors and sounds from these images, and only later when the songs were fully arranged did the smell and the touch and the smell of them sweep in. There had been other songs which resolved the contrasts, the differences, between the drone of a distant train and an empty glass of gin, a lipstick print at its rim, fingerprints around it. A baby's whimpering and a man grinning as he counted a night's big take from the poker table, painted bright red fingernails tapping lightly down a lover's arm and the cold of a lonely apartment. How much did the dancing couples, whose whispering and holding close as second skins or those bouncing and whirling tirelessly feel these things, too? Or did they bring something entirely different to the rhythms, something of their own?

Earl and Billy had talked about this many times. They had concluded that it was enough to bring contexts to dreams, to strengthen those who listened and danced. And there were those moments, magical, alive, when the dance hall was torn from the night and whirled, spinning like a top, a half mile from heaven.

Billy started whistling and tapping his thigh. Then he hummed a fragment of a song loudly.

Earl was nodding. "Nice. Already I can hear Slick Harry taking off with Ousley just under him with the alto. In triplets? Let's see, go through it again right quick."

45 Again Billy hummed and Earl brought in high triplets, nervous wings snagged to the thread of the melody, lifting the piece toward brightness. They stopped, and Billy, smiling now, worked quickly, a draftsman on fire, adding another line or two, crossing out, scribbling notes. He would look up to follow the front edges of the car's lights, then away to the darkness and back to the page.

"Listen up." Billy gave the next lines flats predominating, while offering harsh counterpoint to the first two lines and snatching the song away from a tender playfulness for a moment. He scratched his chin and nodded. Pointed to the darkness.

"This is what I got so far." And he sang the line in a strong tenor voice, his melody now seeming to double the notes from the last line, though the rhythm did not vary. It was the kind of thing Art Tatum might do with "Tea for Two" or something equally simple. The song moved swiftly from a lyrical indulgence to a catch-me-if-you-can show of speed.

"Watch it now," Earl said, "or they will figure us for one of those be-boppers." He chuckled. The woman in his mind

walked faster, traffic about her thickened, the streets sent up jar-
ring sounds. Those would be trumpets, probably. Surroundings
leaned in. Trombones and tenor saxophones playing in the lowest octaves announced their possibilities.

Earl offered a line of his own. His woman walked quickly up
the steps of a brownstone. In. Common enough sequence, but
no surprise there. Whatever prompted it, though, was fleeting.
Gone. Then he said. "Okay, forget mine for now. Let's stay with
what you got."

50   Billy shrugged and marked off another staff, then glanced
again to the match cover. He let out a long, low whistle. "Now we
come to the bridge."

"This is when we need a piano, Earl. I bet the closest one to
here is probably some ole beat-up thing in one of these country
churches out here. Or something sitting in the front parlor of
one of these farmer's houses and the farmer's daughter playing
'Jingle Bells' after bringing in the eggs."

Hip and arrogant city was in their laughter, of funky cafes
where fights might break out and beer bottles fly as the piano
man bobbed and weaved, keeping time on scarred pianos that
leaned and offered sticky keys in the lowest and highest octaves.

Then the Earl of Ferguson told the story of a piano search
years before Billy had joined the band. With two other men in the
car and barely an hour east of St. Louis, when the puzzle of a
chord progression struck with the force of a deep stomach cramp.
Spotting one light shining in the wilderness, a small neon sign
shining over a door, he ordered the car stopped. Trotting up,
Earl noticed the sign blink off. He banged on the door, the
hinges straining from each blow. Nobody turned off a sign in his
face. The door swung open and up stepped an evil-looking, red-
haired farmer in overalls, a man big enough to fill the doorway.

"I said to this giant, 'Quick, I got to get on your piano.' Not
'I got to find your toilet' or 'I got to use your phone,' but 'I got
to use your piano." He shook his head as he laughed now.

55   "That giant rocked on his heels like I had punched him
square in the chest. He left just enough room for me to squeeze
in and sure enough there was a raggedy piano in the corner of
his place.

"P.M. had enough sense to offer to buy some of the man's good whiskey while I'm sitting there playing and trying to figure out the good chord. P.M. always did have good common sense. Most folks try to remember what just happened, but Past already on what's happening next. I'm forgetting you never knew P.M. The guys called him Past Midnight because he was so dark-skinned. The shadow of a shadow. Next thing, they calling him Past, then one day Rabbit showed up calling him P.M., and it stuck. His real name was Wiley Reed, and he was one of the best alto players in the world."

He paused now, glanced out his side window. "Anyway, he showed him class that night. The giant steady looking around suspicious-like at first. I mean, he didn't know us from Adam, didn't know how many more of us was waiting outside to rush in and turn out the joint. But he loosened up and took his mess of keys out and go to his cabinet. I'm just playing away because this is the greatest song of my life, don't care if it is in some country roadhouse way out in Plumb Nelly. I'm cussing, too, Billy, because this song is giving me fits, do you hear me? It just wouldn't let me go. All I wanted was to make it through the bridge. I figured the rest would come soon as I'm back in the car.

"Well, P.M. and the man making small talk, and Leon trying to get slick on everybody and tipping over to get him a few packs of Old Golds. I'm checking all this, see, and closing in on something solid and oh-so-sweet and hearing the big guy go on and on about getting home because his wife already thinking he's sniffing around the new waitress—I remember that part clear as I'm sitting here—when, boom! Leon open up the closet, a mop and a jug of moonshine fell out and this woman inside trying to button up her blouse. She gives a scream like she done seen the boogieman. All hell commence to break loose. Next thing you know Leon backing off and telling the woman he ain't meant no harm, just trying to get some cigarettes, he lie. Big Boy running over and telling me we got to take our whiskey and go, song or no song. I look up and two white guys running down the steps from just over our heads, one of them holding some cards in his hands. The other one run to the telephone like he reporting a robbery. I mean from the outside it's just a little-bitty place on the side of the road but inside all kinds of shit going on. Well, I found the chords I wanted, did a quick run-through and called out to the fellows to haul ass. If some man's wife or some woman's man don't come in there shooting up the place, then the sheriff might raid the place for all-night gambling. Either way, we lose."

Earl was laughing now. A light rain had started to fall just as he ended his tale. The windshield wipers clicked rhythmically, the bump of the road seemed a grace note: *Bachoo-choo, bachoo-choo.*

60 "Never know when you get the tune down right. Go too early and you pluck it raw. Go too late and you got rotten fruit." Earl coughed. "Don't go at all and you put a bad hurt on yourself."

From across the highway, a rabbit darted toward them, then cut away. Earl had turned the car just slightly before straightening it without letting up on the accelerator.

"Almost had us one dead rabbit."

Billy did not answer. He was tapping his pencil on the tablet. Up ahead and to the east they would discover the electric glow of Columbus. Beyond that they would have three more hours before Cleveland and breakfast at the Majestic Hotel on Carnegie Avenue. There might be a new singer or two waiting to try out with the band. Who knows? Somebody—another Billy or Sassy Sarah—might get lucky and ride back with them to New York, her life changed forever. Some young woman, prettier than she would ever know, would otherwise be serving up beef stew or spareribs in some tiny smoky place on Cedar Avenue, notes running through her head or thoughts of a sickly mother and two children she and her husband were trying to feed. How many times Billy and Earl had seen it, how many times they had heard the hope there, the sweat moustaches sprouting, the need to escape the routine nights. It was common ground. They had all been there, falling to sleep in clothes that smelled of cigarette smoke, the world a place of slow mornings with traffic starting and a door slamming, a baby crying and an "oh, goddam, one more funky morning, but I'm alive to see it through anyhow."

There was a bump beneath the car. "You clipped something for sure that time, sportey-odey."

65   "All kinds of stuff out here at night," Earl said. "They like the warm road. Coons, possums, snakes, cows."

"Cows?"

"Yeah, cows." Billy had lit a cigarette. Earl tapped the end of the fresh one he had just placed in his mouth, and Billy reached to light it. "Thanks. Don't tell me you done forgot that cow we nicked on the road to Saratoga Springs."

Yes, yes, Billy remembered. "Cow must have thought we was the Midnight Special, much noise as I was making trying to scare him off the road. Probably just out to get him a little side action in the next field." The car had knocked it to one knee before it struggled back up and, in the rearview mirror, slipped into the darkness.

They were quiet for long moments. After music, after hours, different thoughts could struggle to life. If there was an uneasiness earlier, swift terror could strike them in the darkest hours before dawn. They could grow suddenly uneasy in the silences. They could sense it together like a bone-deep chill starting. For now, Billy pushed the wing shut on his side, rolled his window up another inch.

70   In a small town just west of Columbus, they passed a cafe, the lone light in that stretch. A man behind the counter—white apron, white T-shirt—was scrubbing the counter and talking with a customer. He stopped his work to make a point, head moving from side to side. The customer nodded. Another man stood over a table at the window, dunking a donut. With his free hand, he waved as the car passed. Surprised, Earl honked once, then turned to glance back.

"That back there reminds me of something."

"Huh?"

"That man right back there waving. You didn't see him? Standing back there, waving at us and probably every car coming through here this late."

"Don't tell me you want to get some food," Billy said. "Hell, Earl, I thought those chicken sandwiches and pound cake . . ."

75   "No, no. That ain't what I'm thinking. Had a guy in the band by the name of Boonie years go, way before you joined the band. Boonie could play him some mean trombone. I'm here to tell you. Fact, he could play trumpet and cornet, too. Probably

would have played the tuba, if I would have asked him to. Like you, he was the master of horns. Anyway, something happened—could have been bad gin or something else nobody will ever know about. He just snapped, and they found him one morning standing on a corner cussing at folks and swearing up and down that he was the Governor of Africa. They took him to the jail-house first, then the crazy house. They didn't keep him there long, six, seven months maybe.

"I went up to see him, way out in the country, Billy, you know where they put those places. Well, just past the gate was this man, and he waved at me when I first came in, and, while I was walking around with Boonie, he waved a couple more times. At first, I thought he was just part of the staff because he was all over the place. But then I noticed he's wearing the same kind of clothes as Boonie. And he keeps smiling, you know? By the time I left, he was back out by the gate and waving again. It didn't take me long to figure out that all he had to do was wave at whatever was new and moving by. Like that man back there waving at the night."

Billy only glanced at him, then looked back to his notebook. Earl shook his head and chuckled. "Governor of Africa, can you beat that? Boonie was lucky, though; I mean, the way he wound up. He never got his chops back after he got out. He worked around a little, then finally left the Life. He got a foundry job and raised his family in Detroit. Others ain't been so lucky."

Earl glanced ahead to more lights, showing up through the rain. He knew some who entered the hospitals, never to emerge. And many, too many, died before the age of 50. Just last March, young "Bird" Parker had died in New York, not yet 35. He whose notes surprised like shooting stars. Playing this music could be as risky as working in a steel mill or coal mine. But what were the choices? What could he do about it, leader of some? Perhaps only show them a lesson or two through his example. Now he did limit himself to one large and long drink per night—one part scotch and three parts water—from an oversized coffee mug. Soon he would cut down on his cigarettes. Beyond that he let the rules pronounce the purpose: you needed a clear head and a sound body to play the music he lived for.

Their talk of work and women—the incomplete song still a bright ribbon over their heads—pulled them well beyond the glow of Columbus. Coffee and sandwiches finished, they were down to three cigarettes each and figured there was nothing open between Columbus and Cleveland. Billy took over at the wheel. Twenty miles or so north of Columbus, they neared a car in trouble at the side of the road. The hood was up and in the swath of front headlights was a man—very young, thin, white—kneeling at the back tire.

80   "Keep going, Billy. That cracker'll get help."

Billy slowed. "Well, Earl, it won't hurt . . ."

Earl stared at him, hard. "You getting soft-hearted on me? That boy could be the Klan, see? You remember what happened to the Purnell band down in Tennessee just last month? Huh, remember that stuff? Got beat up by a bunch of rednecks, one of them getting his nose broke, and they still winding up in jail for disturbing the peace and impersonating a band? No, let him get help from his own kind."

Billy pulled the car off the road. "He's just a kid, Earl."

"You go without me, then." He watched Billy leave, then quickly felt under his seat.

85   Earl could hear him ask, "Need a hand?"

"Sure do," the boy said loudly. "If you got a jack on you, we can do this in no time."

Beneath his seat in the Dynaflow, Earl had found the gun wrapped in a towel. He opened the glove compartment and placed it inside, unwrapping the towel and leaving the small door open. He began to hum the new song slowly, softly, watching his friend, smiling Billy, trusting Billy, help a stranger.

Billy brought the jack from their trunk and set it up. He could smell alcohol on the boy, and, straightening up, he saw a girl in the car sip from a flask. Neither could have been older than eighteen. She was trying to hum something, missing, then tried again.

"Dumb me out here without a jack, I swear," the boy said. Billy only nodded as they set the jack under the frame.

90   The boy called the girl out of the car, and she stood apart shyly, both hands holding up the collar of her light coat.

"Your friend back there under the weather?" the boy asked.

"He just don't need the exercise," Billy said. "How about her? She feeling all right?"

The boy looked up in surprise, then he smiled. "No, she all right. She don't need no exercise either." He leaned closer to Billy as they pulled off the wheel and started to set the spare. "'Course, me and her just about exercised out." Then he laughed. "Whoo-ee!"

The tire was on now, and the boy was tightening the lugs. "Pretty nice car you got back there. You a undertaker or a preacher?"

95   "No, neither one. I'm a musician."

The boy whistled low. "Musicians make enough for a car like that? I need to learn me some music. You get to travel a lot and see them big-city women and all like that?"

"Sure do."

The boy glanced at the girl and said loudly. "'Course, a man could go all over the world and never find a woman sweet as my Josie there."

Her hair needed a brush, her dress was wrinkled, and her shoes were old and runover. She was plain and drunk. In the morning she might be in the choir of a tiny church and by evening making biscuits to the staccato of radio news broadcasts. Billy was folding up the jack and turning away.

100   "Ain't she about the prettiest doggone thing a man could ever see?"

"I know how you feel, sport. I got one just as sweet back in New York."

Billy walked away and waved good-bye with his back turned. He slammed the trunk closed, then settled behind the wheel. He pulled the car back onto the highway.

Earl was whistling. "Feel better?" he asked, not looking up.

"What's that for?" Billy pointed to the gun.

105   "I thought about cleaning it. Ain't been cleaned in a year." Then: "My daddy told me once that it takes more than a smile and a good heart to get through this world. Told me sometimes you can reach out a helping hand and get it chopped off."

Billy was shivering. "Hide it, Earl. Please."

"Okay, okay. Look, while you were playing the Good Samaritan with Jethro back there, I finished the song. Listen up, youngblood."

Earl hummed through the opening key, stretching the note, then moved through the bright afternoon of the melody, repeated the line in the thinning light of its early evening. The song soon lifted to the bridge, a vivid golden stairstep on which to linger briefly. Then the return to the opening line that suggested new possibilities: the smell of a pine forest after a rain, a meadow, too, a deer or two frozen on one edge. There was a street, glistening, a small oil slick catching dull rainbows and a stranger's laughter like a bright coin spinning at their feet. Yes, all of that.

The small and proud woman walking, her hips working against yellow wool, had been lost to Earl. She would return, surely, to move through another song, walking to a different rhythm. For now, she had brought Earl excited to Billy's first thoughts. Provided a spirit. Together, they hummed the song through, speeding it up, slowing.

110   Each time, they tried different harmonies—the bass stronger here, the trombones higher there. Most of the parts had been worked through by the time they noticed the hills near Medina taking shape.

"Got it," Billy said, finally. He slapped the wheel with relief.

"It's nice," Earl said.

"Think the people will like it?" Billy asked.

Earl yawned and looked out the window. Maybe he could get twenty minutes or so of sleep before they touched the edges of the city. "You worry too much, Billy. 'Course they gone like it. They got no choice. We did the best we could. We'll run through it this afternoon, do it again in Pittsburgh, and maybe have it ready by the time we hit Philly. Can't you just hear Big City's solo already?" He settled back, eyes closed.

115   Cars, trees, corn fields just harvested were explosions of dull colors. Signs placed one hundred feet apart, a shaving cream ad, suddenly claimed Billy's attention. *The big blue tube's / Just like Louise / You get a thrill / From every squeeze.* He laughed aloud, then started

whistling as the car roared into a stretch of light fog. Billy leaned forward, his head almost touching the windshield. He stiffened.

"Earl, wake up. I got something to tell you."

"Let it slide. Tell me over grits and coffee." Earl kept his eyes closed.

"No, it can't wait. It happened back there in Dayton. I just now remembered. You know on that second break? Well, I stepped outside to get a little air, take a smoke, you understand. A couple folk stroll past and tell me how much they like our playing, so I'm talking with them awhile and then I see this woman—short with a red wig and she standing off to the side. She look up every now and then like she want to come over and say something. But she wait until nobody's around and she walk over real quick-like. Something about her made me think about a bird hopping, then resting, hopping some more. She told me she really like the music, like some of the songs really get a hold of her. . . ."

Earl opened one eye. "Yeah, and she just want to take a cute little man like you home to make music to her all the time."

"No, no, no. Nothing like that, but you better believe I was hoping for some action."

Forehead still to the windshield, Billy fumbled for words, worked a hand like he was flagging down a car. "No, she's smiling but not smiling, if you know what I mean. We talk about a lot of things, then she gets down to the thing she really wanted to talk about, I figure. She told me about her baby. She told me about hearing her baby screaming one day and she rush from her ironing and found him in the next room bleeding. He fell on a stick or glass or something, cut his belly, and blood going every which way. Said her son's belly was thin, like a balloon, but not going down when it's poked. She put her hand there, she said, and could feel each beat of the heart. Every time the heart beat, more blood would spurt out between her fingers. She screamed for help, screamed for her neighbors next door, just screamed and screamed. Blood was all over her, too, she said, but she never saw that until later. All she could do is tell her child not to die and press on that thin belly. And pray and pray, even after he in the ambulance. She told me that baby was all she got in this world."

Billy shook his head slowly. "What could I say to all that? Here I go outside for some fresh air and a draw or two on my Lucky Strikes. She brings me this story when I want to know whether my shoes are shined, my front still holding up, or whether some big-legged woman want to pull me home with her. I touched her on the shoulder, was all I could do. She told me the baby lived, and she smiled this dopey smile. Then she left."

Earl's eyes were closed. He waved his hand as if shooing a fly from his forehead. "It's the music we play, Billy. It opens people up, makes them give up secrets. Better than whiskey or dope for that. It don't kill you, and you can't piss it away. You can whistle it the next day in new places. You can loan it to strangers, and they thank you for it."

Then he shrugged. "It's what keeps us going all night."

Sitting back, fog thinning, Billy nodded and started back whistling. Before long they would sight the giant mills pumping smoke into the grey morning. At Lakewood Billy might swing closer to the grey and glassy Erie. They would pick up speed and head toward the eastside, through a world raging to light outside their windows. Finally, they would gain Carnegie Avenue and weave their way among the early church traffic. They would find the Majestic Hotel, breakfast, and attempt to sleep, two wizards before the band.

Kate Braverman

Kate Braverman is the author of *Hurricane Warning, Lithium for Medea, Palm Latitudes,* and *Squandering the Blue.*

Desert Blues

EVERYTHING WAS COLD AND BLUE ALL THE TIME. There were no longer any increments or divisions. Diana Barrington was surprised by how much she missed them, lines and frontiers, clocks and dates and the debris of convention that she, a poet, had insisted on divesting herself of. Now there was only the icy blue, Baltic blue agony. She felt as if fierce angular waves rose and broke behind her face.

"Why don't we take your psychotic episode across state lines?" Carlotta McKay asked. It was an undifferentiated drained blue afternoon in the flats of Hollywood. The air seemed comprised of failed neon and exiled particles without name. Outside, palms stood in a faded blue stasis like the culmination of centuries of brutal indifference.

It occurred to Diana Barrington that she liked the way her best friend talked about crossing state lines. There was a charge to her words and a sense of blue, of course, because everything was blue. Still, something in Carlotta's voice contained a specific intonation of the amoral. A blue flash of Rimbaud, perhaps, smuggling contraband.

"We could take your nervous breakdown on vacation," Carlotta McKay, her best friend and blood sister, was saying. She was staring at her. "Give your nervous breakdown a break. What do you say?"

5 Diana Barrington formed a miniature blue OK with her lips but her mouth remained sealed shut. Speech was an evolutionary development that had not yet been perfected for her, lips and tongue in predictable cooperation, reliable vocal cords. Diana tried again. She listened for a sound and there was none. Somewhere, blue fins dipped into bands of aquamarine water, a lagoon just past sunset where the tropics wind down, breathless after dynasties of orchids, hurricanes and syphilis. Somewhere, something ambiguous began to swim.

OK, Diana Barrington thought, OK, let's do it. She wanted to say this but lacked the capacity to push the blue sounds out. They were like stones off shore, constantly engraved by waves and the blue motion. There are only these blue repetitions, after all, Diana realized. Was it possible that from these cohesions hierarchies emerged and in eons of crushed blue glass finally concepts of up and down, east and west? Was it simply an inevitability that morality invent itself, the whisper of good and bad just behind a blue shoulder.

"Are you saying yes?" Carlotta McKay demanded. She had been pacing in Brazilian red stiletto heels. She stopped abruptly and brought her pale and dramatically rouged face inordinately close to Diana's. "Blink once for yes," she instructed.

These are the antique corridors, Diana realized, the blue convolutions where grace resides. Here we turn like planets, born and dying alone, isolated by our own light years. Here we take the leap into pure blue, the discovery of faith, horizons and sculpture. This is where we light the candle and blow the flames out.

Diana Barrington blinked. The action seemed stunning and singular, almost the distillation of all previous methods of discrimination, judgment and their resolution. It had the complexity and subtlety of whale migration or ballet. And it was blue.

10   "You were cold yesterday. Are you still cold?" Carlotta McKay inquired. Carlotta stared at her eyes.

Diana Barrington forced herself to blink. In the pale distance, in the blue of debauchery and exhaustion, Carlotta appeared enormous and clear and oddly magnified. She might have been a recently displaced iceberg. She approached with a field of blanket in her arms. She bent down and wrapped a quilt around Diana's shoulders.

"You'll be warm in Nevada," Carlotta told her. "It'll be at least 110."

One hundred and ten, Diana Barrington longed to repeat. One hundred and ten severely pointed assertions, but of what? There are only the blue gradations, after all, breaking at your feet like the ten thousand fingers in the imploring hands of a newly formed blue deity. There is only the arrested dusk, after all, and the onrush of the soft blue glistening vagaries, the sanctioned hours and the way one rubs one's mouth.

"You can't just sit on the kitchen floor shivering," Carlotta decided. "Not for six weeks. Mercury, Nevada, will cure you."

15   "OK," Diana managed, pushing symbols out of the void of her mouth. "Good," she found the ability to say, developed the method, the sequence of things, the parameters, the invention of syllables and language. Diana leaned back against the cool enamel walls of her kitchen, drained. She might have fallen asleep but Carlotta was pacing near her, the garish high heels almost grazing her where she sat wrapped in a quilt on the floor.

"You'll have to get to the Federal Building. You'll have to take a shower, wash your hair, find a sleeping bag, pack food. You'll need a flashlight and a canteen. You'll have to make an effort. You'll have to do the rudiments or I'll think you're too sick for this adventure," Carlotta was saying.

Carlotta was studying the gold dial of her wrist watch. The watch came from France. Diana could remember this. The band was made from the skin of some vanishing species of bird or reptile. Was it possible that the dial of her best friend's watch was somehow connected to a temperature matrix? Did this have something to do with the one hundred and ten blue assertions? Were time and climate also a continuum?

"You're going to have to make the effort," Carlotta was telling her, pacing in her incredibly red and sharp spike heels. "I'll bottom line you. Pack an overnight bag or I'm going to call the paramedics."

Call them, Diana Barrington thought. I'm too sick for this.

20 "Stand up or I'm dialing," Carlotta McKay said.

Diana stood up. Carlotta McKay was doing something. She was writing down the elements in the required procedure. Each item was given a distinct blue number. She would have to take a shower, put on lipstick, assemble objects in a canvas bag and drive her car down Sunset Boulevard to Westwood. She would park in the lot behind the Federal Building. Carlotta would find her and help her. Carlotta would sit next to her and read poetry out loud for her. Diana would have to make this effort or Carlotta McKay was going to telephone the police.

"Will you do this?" Carlotta asked, voice soft. Carlotta was staring into the blue grid of her eyes, searching for the implications of communication. "Will you do this for me?"

Circular blue, Diana Barrington was thinking, the way water casts a spell across eons of liquid. The way the sea stalls, enchanted. And Kauai, where the Pacific is a slow drugged and electric blue beyond blue of all the distilled clarities. How you return to it like opium. No time has passed. All is forgiven.

"I'm tired of holding my breath," Carlotta McKay informed her.

25 There are only the varieties of blue enticement, Diana was thinking. Storms coalescing beneath turquoise. The succession of blue approximations and their cumulative subterfuge. The way we call the random definitions sanctuaries. The way the air is naked when you wear ritual plumeria. The way clouds with intoxicated edges like mirrors or frames are ceaselessly passing. After the architectures of fever, you can say something.

Carlotta's face was an assemblage of slow blue symmetries. A long time passed before Diana could blink.

THEY WERE MOVING FAST THROUGH A DARK BLUE-NESS, through the lie of night. Outside the window, the moon was absolutely full, an astonished white. Diana Barrington began to shiver. They were crossing the desert, like Moses and Buddha. They were supplicants without candles. And she would never be warm enough.

"Do you remember where we are going? Or why?" Carlotta asked her.

A blue flash of Rimbaud. A frontier with its provinces still and gutted. It was always a disappointing season. The carnival came, pitched its torn tent, a woman walked a rope above sawdust. The air was an unusual blue, as if prayers had risen from deserted wharves where the idols went blind. The voices of the devout mingled in the paralyzed blue air, torturing it with radiance and handfuls of small flames.

30   "Do you remember the demonstration?" Carlotta was searching her face. She seemed annoyed.

Diana shook her head, no. There had been a man in the front of the bus. He had done something but his presence was inconsequential. If he had recited a poem or a psalm or juggled fruits or listed the names of stars and planets, saints or healing plants, she would have remembered. There had been a man less than a comma in the ocean, a fluid subtraction in the infinite blue text.

"It is a non-violence demonstration," Carlotta was saying. Carlotta brought her face close to Diana's. "Civil disobedience. We are going to Mercury, Nevada. We are going to shut down the nuclear facility. We may get arrested. We are going to make a statement. Can you remember this?"

Diana shook her head, no.

"You know, it's like you are your own nuclear winter," Carlotta mused. "shivering and delirious simultaneously. Your face is ashen. Your pupils are dilated. Are you hallucinating? Is everything still blue?"

35   You got that right, Diana wanted to say, but couldn't. And then, as if a border in her inexplicable violet interior had been crossed, Diana Barrington recognized that she could speak again. It was the brief blue thaw she was learning to live between.

"Do you think Sartre was right?" Diana asked.

"That hell is other people?" Carlotta said. "Definitely."

"And Shelley? Was Shelley right?" Diana Barrington wanted to know this.

"That prophecy is an attribute of poetry, not vice versa?"
Carlotta was staring into her eyes.

40   "Yes. Exactly," Diana said. She felt breathless. There was so
much unusual blueness. It seemed archaic, raw and elegant. It was
the blue of certain beads and pottery: the blue that has been
birthed by a kiln. The blue at the conclusion of a ritual of blood
and intimacy. It was the sort of blue that lingered in rooms where
the names of gods were called out in adoration. Even Carlotta's
eyes seemed moist and blue.

      "Yes. Shelley was right," Carlotta said.

      "Do you think Pound was right?" Diana pushed a blue flame
into the fire of the many-tiered blue night.

      "That you owe your audience nothing?" Carlotta asked.
"Yes. Absolutely. Or one cannot but pander. Is this a quiz?"

      "Yes," Diana replied.

45   Diana listened to the sound of her yes. It was sudden and
crisp, almost audacious. It might be an intimation of autumnal
configurations, structures in the regions of fallen leaves. It
occurred to her that the desert floor was clear as a kind of mirror.
It might be possible to articulate the universe visually. Or one
could stand on the dark stones and look directly into one's heart.

      "You're forming sentences again," Carlotta noted. "Look at
your mind. Your first words are a quiz." There was something
unpleasant in Carlotta's voice.

      Diana said, "Yes."

      "Is this a desert quiz or a generic survival quiz?" Carlotta
seemed amused.

      "Yes," Diana answered.

50   It was a sharp blue like a slap at the resurgence of the blue
channel, the waves, the relentless ocean of language and experience and disappointment. The places where we are born and
drown, Diana thought, in the blue variances where there are
no directions, no harbors, no one to ring the bells. Steeples
have not yet been invented. The people of the region spend
their days sleeping. Later, they will drink the indigenous alcohol made from perverse fruits and sing songs of no consequence. In nine months, a crop of lean babies will be born
blue and still.

"Your face is quite incredible," Carlotta revealed. "You're on the verge of becoming linguistically impaired again. I can see it coming. Ray Charles could see it coming."

"Yes," Diana managed. She was very cold.

"You have articulate moments. Then is passes and you're frozen again. It's fascinating. Also, you've got a major tic below your right eye now. The entire side of your face is affected. Did you know that? And you're shivering again," Carlotta told her.

"Yes."

55 "Do you think you'll be drooling soon?" Carlotta asked. "I don't want you to embarrass me with people I may be jailed with."

Carlotta seemed to be waiting for Diana to extract a reply of some kind, some practical blue form, perhaps, like a species of precocious amoeba. She tried to blink and found that she could not.

Diana Barrington wanted to tell Carlotta about the quality of the blue. She thought of the blue enormities, infiltrating her conventions with wild birds and fluid dialects that flow from blue mouths and skies with masked clouds and volcanoes and stars and complicated rituals of tenderness in blue rain. It is my fortieth year and I have come to know distance and blueness. At least I know that, Diana thought. All other geography is false.

After a time, which was informed by blue at the edges and blue grids on which the nuances came and went, Diana Barrington realized that Carlotta McKay was no longer staring at her. In fact, Carlotta was now looking out of the bus window, at the immaculate almost-black of the desert and the moon, which was somehow even fuller and a more aggrieved white, a blanched and discarded accomplice.

Diana was considering the implications of the white moon in the fields of night sky when she became aware of a disturbance Carlotta was causing. Carlotta was swaying in her bus seat and snapping her fingers. There was something terrible about this. Carlotta was making the sacred prayed-upon air of the desert night turn neurotic and sordid. Carlotta was adjusting her Walkman radio, pushing the earphones deeper into her ears and turning the volume up. "I just grew, tangled up in blue," Carlotta McKay sang, aggressively out of tune.

60   There are forms even in madness, Diana recognized. Even when the self is revealed as tundra, even in the severe and incalculable, the remote arctic of a ravaged interior. Even where the borders have banished themselves and the increments are a mere suggestion of eternities inscribed in blue glass, even then there are structures which are appropriate and those which are not. There is bruised and then there is tawdry, Diana decided. And the line must be drawn.

      Diana felt desperate and exposed in her seamless avenues of solitude. She looked at Carlotta and felt the distance between them. Somewhere, the horizon expanded extravagant into an exquisite malignancy. The possibilities were exposed, like the one million blue matches of all your imagined orphans.

      Diana Barrington leaned closer to her best friend. She tapped Carlotta on the shoulder. As Carlotta turned, Diana reached out and gracefully, in one motion, removed the earphones from her best friend's ears. Then her fingers unsnapped the radio from the clip at Carlotta's neck. Then Diana let the machine fall through her fingers, out the open window, onto the desert floor where it bounced like a hard blue aching flower.

      "It's an era before music, I presume," Carlotta said. She seemed resigned. After a silence in which land masses created themselves and were sculpted by winds, Carlotta began rummaging in her canvas overnight bag. She extracted croissants, apples, a block of chocolate and cheese. She forced slabs of food into Diana's hands.

      "Eat," Carlotta instructed.

65   Diana began to eat. It was always this way, eating at the full moon when the planet turned hungry and festive. It was necessary to eat. Soon they would play the drums until their fingers bled. The desert floor was a series of blue rudiments, primitive assertions that would later evolve into issues of distinction, of destiny and free will. There would be the choreography of blue resonances, perhaps, nothing more. Or a blue echo, fading of course, and the soft impression left by one blue mouth.

      "Do you want me to read Paz to you?" Carlotta asked, taking out a book from her canvas bag. "In Spanish?"

      Diana blinked. Read the part where he sits down to write in a noon the size of time, she thought. Where outside there are the ruins of afternoon.

"Do you remember where we are going? Or why?" Carlotta asked. The desert was a cool dark blue elegance, a remembrance of tile and beads and mosaics, the continuous blue of a drum across the full moon sand.

Diana shook her head, no.

70 "To close down the nuclear plant? To make a statement? Try to remember," Carlotta said with feeling. Then she began to read.

The Paz words were blue in the almost black of the desert. And the millennium was coming. It was almost here. Now. Diana tilted her face toward the moon, which was an anguish of light in the borderless fields of stars. This is where the wind is born. This is where they fashion direction. This is where they keep the sails.

Diana opened her mouth to speak but no sound found its way out. She wanted to explain to Carlotta that it was simply a question of blue elements and their uncertain paths, their bizarre and accidental resolution. Or perhaps blue atoms and their combinations. What about the cobalt blue of Carlotta McKay's breast cancer treatments? Wasn't that the subliminal intuition, the catalyst, the reason they had come? What blue called to them and why respond? Diana Barrington knew. It was the infected blue of acid rain and nuclear winter and cancer treatments and all things where the violated interiors have turned blue, leaking and contagious.

Diana Barrington was considering the permutations of damaged blue when the bus stopped in north Las Vegas. From the window, she could see the Las Vegas strip in a meaningless distance, impossible to calculate. The air seemed alien and hostile. The bus had stopped in a casino parking lot. It was a blue pause, like a blue comma in the ocean. Was it supposed to mean something?

"Stand up," Carlotta said. "Pick up your bags and walk off the bus."

75 Diana stood up. She picked up her bags. Carlotta was wearing tight Bermuda shorts and garishly over-decorated cowboy boots. It looked as if her boots were studded with rhinestone bullets. The air in her face was hot and shocked. It was like kissing the wrong person and getting caught. Diana realized there were many other people, dozens, perhaps more. They had also been on the bus.

Someone holding a clipboard and wearing a whistle around his neck was saying something. If it had been significant, if it was a stanza from Neruda, if it had been the details from a page in an anonymous diary truly and wholly written and spoken, Diana Barrington would have recognized this and remembered.

When Carlotta began walking, she followed. There were other people wearing Bermuda shorts and Walkman radios and carrying canvas overnight bags, bed rolls and guitars. No one else had rhinestone bullets on their boots. They were crossing a deserted ashy street. They filed into a large shabby structure that seemed to be abandoned. There was a quality of dense silence.

"It's a church," Carlotta told her. "We sleep here."

Diana felt breathless. Of course, after the struggle in the desert, after the purification by heat, there is always this asylum, the blessed place, where we are anointed.

80   Diana blinked. She followed Carlotta into an enormous cool room. Hundreds of small mounds littered the floor. She tripped over one, lost her balance and fell across another. The mounds were oddly pliant, soft, and she suddenly realized, possibly verbal.

"Jesus, you're stepping all over people," Carlotta whispered. Her voice was a harsh charged blue.

Diana blinked.

"Can't you see? It's people, sleeping. People from other buses, from other cities. Jesus, I can't go on with this," Carlotta admitted. She had stopped near the altar. She had spread out her sleeping bag. Now she unrolled Diana's.

"Just lay down and go to sleep." Carlotta glanced at her watch. "The bus leaves again in three hours."

85   Diana got into her sleeping bag. Carlotta was staring at her.

"Take your shoes off first," Carlotta said. She sounded disgusted.

Diana blinked. She took off her shoes. She got back into her sleeping bag. The sanctuary was cold and impersonal. One wall was composed of a blue stained glass. The configuration was angular and precise. It was a distillation of remote afternoons spent selecting names for daughters, giving these daughters the names of qualities and jewels, Grace and Faith, Ruby and Jade. It was the blue of prophets and heretics, of the place where abasement and silence and wind mate and are comprehended as a molecular structure.

Diana closed her eyes. She thought of the way the ocean looks one hour east of Oahu, when Borneo and Fiji are cousins. She knew she could go there, into the blue dynasties littering the flesh of the Pacific like children. This reef, this matrix, this turquoise interpretation. Or bluer. The blue of all the accommodations.

This is how we live, Diana thought, between these vertical blue intuitions, where Jesus and Buddha walk along avenues of blue glass and burning flowers. And names and divisions have been shed as inadequate. There are only a few random syllables in the universe and they are whispered, holy, holy, holy, holy, blue, blue, blue.

90 IN THE MORNING, ON THE BUS, THE SUN IS ALMOST UNBEARABLE. There is an intensity in the sky above her that Diana is attempting to ignore. It is not blue so it is insignificant. She says, "Can we sleep there again?"

"No," Carlotta replies immediately. "We go back to L.A. after the demonstration. If we're not in jail. I'm afraid St. James of the Fried Cactus or whatever it was happens for you only once, like birth and death. Try to make the best of it."

They are aiming themselves east, farther into the desert. The land is increasingly hot, sparse, insomniac and fearful. Here the stones dream their blue dreams but do not believe them, Diana is thinking. Perhaps they are fierce dramas informed by lethal intoxications, a violet abscess of grief, the delirium of mourning, of walls, of all the lost tokens. You can't tell these dreams at breakfast.

"We're going to make a statement," Carlotta is saying, perhaps to herself. "Do you remember?"

Diana says, "Yes."

95 She thinks, this is how we part the sixteen walls. We do it with our fingers. We walk on the sand that burns. We give our flesh for this. We are walking on the burning blue sand, above the perpetual and unceasing drumming. We are opening and closing the millennia of our slow mouths. We are saying up and down, good and bad, right and wrong, yes and no under the

clouds and the avenues of asters winding through all the frailties and timid blue places.

"I want to ask you something," Carlotta says. She reaches over and removes Diana's aviator sunglasses. Then she removes her own. Their eyes are very close. "I've got a few questions. Before you coalesce or disintegrate, and it's a toss-up, you could do either. Do you know that?"

"Yes."

"I have several questions," Carlotta begins.

"It is always a noon the size of time. It's a matter of blue and its modalities. Prophecy is an aspect of poetry. Hell is other people. You owe your audience nothing. You are your brother's keeper, always. Jesus saves. Buddha saves. Moses saves." Diana feels her voice. It is steady.

100   "I want to know what it's like," Carlotta says.

"It's nothing like we thought. Ophelia doesn't play here. You can't sing by the river. There are no rivers or songs here. It's not an abundance but an absence. You don't need your French sunglasses or your tropical wardrobe." Diana is staring at Carlotta now. "You won't be taking photographs or sending postcards. There are no beaches, no mail service."

"Are you going to come back?" Carlotta's voice is soft now.

"I don't know," Diana admits.

"Is there grace and redemption?" Carlotta suddenly asks.

105   Diana laughs. "Always."

"What about my cancer?" Carlotta is staring into her eyes.

Madness. Revelation. The archetypal blue pathways between the nothing. The continuum of knowing. Asylum after struggle. The evolution of an identity suffocating in blueness. Diana looks at Carlotta. There are a billion blue variables between them.

"They got it all. No resurgence. You are clean," Diana replies.

The bus stops. Outside, on the minimalist floor of the desert, where even the rocks seem singular and doomed, thousands of women, children and men are forming irregular eddies. They are holding paper signs and long paper and cloth banners. Beyond them, beside the line of the fence, hundreds of uniformed police stand shoulder to shoulder. Diana Barrington knows what they are doing. They are guarding the nuclear facility at Mercury, Nevada.

110   After the obsessions, the absences, the shadows from candles on the avenues of bougainvillea and sunken galleons, after the atrocities of blue, we invent these barbed wire lines so we may cross them. We do this in the desert where Buddha walked. We step down from buses into the arms of police with weapons. We do this because we are haunted and sick by the thought of the violet horror of nuclear winter, because of the chill, its permanence. We are born for this, Diana is thinking.

      They are standing on the desert now. There are no abstractions. The sand beneath her feet is hot. She can feel her body now and perhaps that is significant. She can feel the sand. The sun. The sun on her back, her face, stinging. And she is not shivering.

      "If you're arrested and can't speak, I'll say you're a performance artist. I'll say you've taken a vow of silence. You won't speak until there is world peace," Carlotta tells her.

      Diana blinks. She is thinking that it would be good to not speak until the blue issues have been resolved, with their pale violet injuries and afternoons of disappointment. And silence through the nights of the pitch blue haunting.

      "I'm afraid," Carlotta says.

115   They are walking toward the fence. The line of police is longer, closer. You can see their weapons where the sun glances off metal. They wear garments of brown and green. They seem specific to the desert, better adapted. You can almost see yourself reflected in the black voids of their sunglasses.

      "Don't be afraid," Diana says. "I'll protect you."

      "You? You're a poet. It would look terrific on your resume," Carlotta sneered. "If I'm arrested, I could lose my license. I'm an attorney. What about me?" Carlotta's eyes seemed wide open, tight and wild.

      It's OK, Diana is thinking. After the insurrections of blue glass, after the deformities of air to invent a mouth, after the distressed molecules, you say yes or no. This is the only blue intoxicant, the one seduction we are certain we remember. This is why the journey begins and ends in acres of arrested blue intensities. This is why we inhabit rooms and landscapes, why we create harbor lights in autumn and all the virescent things, even the ambiguous plaza and whispered dialects. There is only this,

Diana Barrington is thinking as they approach the perimeter of the nuclear facility at Mercury, Nevada. There is only this topography of the heart, with its liquid channels like rivers of solitude, the rivers of an unnamed world waiting for love, for definition, for release, for the final blue rain where the borders dissolve.

Diana takes her best friend's hand. She is beginning to remember. They are walking across sand now. She opens her mouth. "No more Nukes," she shouts.

120 "Are you certain?" Carlotta is looking at her. Carlotta's face is extremely pale. They could reach out and touch the police.

"Yes," Diana replies. Then, loud, "No more Nukes."

The sun is directly over her head now. It is a deliberate configuration. The sun is a presence, perhaps another fact in the blue, another entity. This is something she can think about later. There is now and there is later. There is her hand and the hand of her friend. There is the glare, the sun, the metal. There is this walking across wooden boards, this passing through the wire that once was a fence. There is the holding of Carlotta's hand and how many are in this line holding hands, holding banners and signs. They are walking into the ruined blue gash where they manufacture the diseased molecules and atoms and they are saying no. There are things blue and things other and how now and finally she is no longer cold.

T. Coraghessan Boyle

T. Coraghessan Boyle's stories have appeared in several magazines. Some of his novels are *Water Music, Budding Prospects, World's End*, winner of the 1988 PEN/Faulkner Award, and *East Is East*. His books of short stories include *Descent of Man, Greasy Lake*, and *If the River Was Whiskey*.

Carnal Knowledge

I'D NEVER REALLY THOUGHT MUCH ABOUT MEAT. It was there in the supermarket in a plastic wrapper; it came between slices of bread with mayo and mustard and a dill pickle on the side; it sputtered and smoked on the grill till somebody flipped it over, and then it appeared on the plate, between the baked potato and the julienned carrots, neatly crosshatched and floating in a puddle of red juice. Beef, mutton, pork, venison, dripping burgers and greasy ribs, it was all the same to me—food, the body's fuel, something to savor a moment on the tongue before the digestive system went to work on it. Which is not to say I was totally unconscious of the deeper implications: Every once in a while, I'd eat at home—a quartered chicken, a package of Shake 'N Bake, Stove Top Stuffing and frozen peas, and as I hacked away at the stippled yellow skin and pink flesh of the sanitized bird, I'd wonder at the darkish bits of organ clinging to the ribs—what was that, liver? Kidney?—but in the end, it didn't make me any less fond of Kentucky Fried or Chicken McNuggets. I'd seen those ads in the magazines, too, the ones that showed the veal calves penned up in their own waste, their limbs atrophied and their veins so pumped full of antibiotics they couldn't control their bowels, but when I took a date to Anna Maria's, I could never resist the veal scaloppine.

And then I met Alena Jorgensen.

It was a year ago, two weeks before Thanksgiving—I remember the date because it was my birthday, my 30th, and I'd called in sick and gone to the beach to warm my face, read a book and feel a little sorry for myself. The Santa Anas were blowing and it was clear all the way to Catalina, but there was an edge to the air, a scent of winter, and as far as I could see in either direction, I had the beach pretty much to myself. I found a sheltered spot in a tumble of boulders, spread a blanket and settled down to attack a pastrami on rye I'd brought along for nourishment. Then turned to my book—a comfortingly apocalyptic tract about the demise of the planet—and let the sun warm me as I read about the denuding of the rain forest, the poisoning of the atmosphere and the swift, silent eradication of species. Gulls coasted by overhead. I saw the distant glint of jetliners.

I must have dozed, my head thrown back, the book spread open in my lap, because the next thing I remember, a strange dog was hovering over me and the sun had dipped behind the rocks. The dog was big, wild-haired, with one staring blue eye, and it just looked at me, ears slightly cocked, as if it expected a Milk-Bone or something. I was startled—not that I don't like dogs, but here was this woolly thing poking its snout in my face— and I guess I must have made some sort of defensive gesture, because the dog staggered back a step and froze. Even in the confusion of the moment, I could see that there was something wrong with this dog, an unsteadiness, a gimp, a wobble to its legs. I felt a mixture of pity and revulsion—it had been hit by a car, was that it?—when all at once, I became aware of a wetness on the breast of my windbreaker and an unmistakable odor rose to my nostrils: I'd been pissed on.

5   Pissed on. As I lay there unsuspecting, enjoying the sun, the beach, the solitude, this stupid beast had lifted its leg and used me as a *pissoir*—and now it was poised there on the edge of the blanket as if it expected a reward. A sudden rage seized me. I came up off the blanket with a curse, and it was only then that a dim apprehension seemed to seep into the dog's other eye, the brown one, and it lurched back and fell on its face, just out of reach. And then it lurched and fell again, bobbing and weaving across the sand like a seal out of water. I was on my feet now, murderous, glad to see that the thing was hobbled—it would simplify my task of running it down and beating it to death.

"ALF!" A VOICE CALLED, and as the dog floundered in the sand, I turned and saw Alena Jorgensen poised on the boulder behind me. I don't want to make too much of the moment, don't want to mythologize it or clutter the scene with allusions to Aphrodite rising from the waves or accepting the golden apple from Paris, but she was a pretty impressive sight. Bare-legged, fluid, as tall and uncompromising as her Nordic ancestors and dressed in a Gore-Tex bikini and hooded sweat shirt unzipped to the waist, she blew me away. Piss-spattered and stupefied, I could only gape up at her.

"You bad boy," she said, scolding, "you get out of there." She glanced from the dog to me and back again. "Oh, you bad boy, what have you done?" she demanded, and I was ready to admit to anything, but it was the dog she was addressing, and it flopped over in the sand as if it had been shot. Alena skipped lightly down from the rock, and in the next moment, before I could protest, she was rubbing at the stain on my windbreaker with the wadded-up hem of her sweat shirt.

I tried to stop her—"It's all right," I said. "It's nothing," as if dogs routinely pissed on my wardrobe—but she wouldn't hear of it.

"No," she said, rubbing, her hair flying in my face, the naked skin of her thigh pressed unself-consciously to my own, "no, this is terrible, I'm so embarrassed. Alf, you bad boy. I'll clean it for you, I will, it's the least—oh, look at that, it's stained right through to your T-shirt "

10   I could smell her, the mousse she used in her hair, a lilac soap or perfume, the salt-sweet odor of her sweat—she'd been jogging, that was it. I murmured something about taking it to the cleaner's myself.

She stopped rubbing and straightened up. She was my height, maybe even a fraction taller, and her eyes were slightly mismatched, like the dog's: a deep earnest blue in the right iris, shading to sea-green and turquoise in the left. We were so close we might have been dancing. "Tell you what," she said, and her face lit up with a smile. "Since you're so nice about the whole thing, and most people wouldn't be, even if they knew what poor Alf had been through, why don't you let me wash it for you—and the T-shirt, too?"

I was a little disconcerted at this point—I was the one who'd been pissed on, after all—but my anger was gone. I felt weight-less, adrift, like a piece of fluff floating on the breeze. "Listen," I said, and for the moment, I couldn't look her in the eye, "I don't want to put you to any trouble. . . ."

"I'm ten minutes up the beach, and I've got a washer and drier. Come on, it's no trouble at all. Or do you have plans? I mean, I could just pay for the cleaner's, if you want. . . ."

I was between relationships—the person I'd been seeing off and on for the past year wouldn't even return my calls—and my plans consisted of taking in a solitary late-afternoon movie as a birthday treat, then heading over to my mother's for dinner and the cake with candles. My aunt Irene would be there, and so would my grandmother. They would exclaim over how big I was and how handsome, and then they would begin to contrast my present self with my previous, more diminutive incarnations and finally work themselves up to a spate of reminiscence that would continue unabated till my mother drove them home. And then, if I was lucky, I'd go out to a singles bar and make the acquain-tance of a divorced computer programmer in her mid-30s with three kids and bad breath.

15   I shrugged. "Plans? No, not really. I mean, nothing in particular."

ALENA WAS HOUSE-SITTING A ONE-ROOM BUNGA-
LOW that rose stumplike from the sand, no more than 50 feet
from the tide line. There were trees in the yard behind it and
the place was sandwiched between glass fortresses with
crenelated decks, whipping flags and great hulking concrete
pylons. Sitting on the couch inside, you could feel the full
reverberation of each wave hitting the shore, a slow, steady
pulse that forever defined the place for me. Alena gave me a
faded UC Davis sweat shirt that nearly fit, sprayed stain remover
on my T-shirt and windbreaker and in a single fluid motion
flipped down the lid of the washer and extracted two beers from
the refrigerator beside it.

There was an awkward moment as she settled into the chair
opposite me and we concentrated on our beers. I didn't know
what to say. I was disoriented, giddy, still struggling to grasp
what had happened. Fifteen minutes earlier, I'd been dozing
on the beach, alone on my birthday, feeling sorry for myself,
and now I was ensconced in a cozy beach house, in the presence
of Alena Jorgensen and her spill of naked leg, drinking a beer.
"So what do you do?" she said, setting her beer down on the
coffee table.

I was grateful for the question; too grateful, maybe. I
described to her at length how dull my job was, nearly ten years
with the same agency, writing ad copy, my brain gone numb with
disuse. I was somewhere in the middle of a blow-by-blow
account of our current campaign for a Ghanian vodka distilled
from calabash husks when she said, "I know what you mean," and
told me she'd dropped out of veterinary school herself. "After I
saw what they did to the animals. I mean, can you see neutering
a dog just for our convenience, just because it's easier for us if
they don't have a sex life?" Her voice grew hot. "It's the same old
story, species fascism at its worst."

Alf was lying at my feet, grunting softly and looking up
mournfully out of his staring blue eye, as blameless a creature as
ever lived. I made a small noise of agreement and then focused
on Alf. "And your dog," I said, "he's arthritic? Or is it hip dysplasia or what?" I was pleased with myself for the question—aside
from tapeworm, hip dysplasia was the only veterinary term I

could dredge up from the memory bank, and I could see Alf's problems ran deeper than worms.

20   Alena looked angry suddenly. "Don't I wish," she said. She paused to draw a bitter breath. "There's nothing wrong with Alf that wasn't inflicted on him. They tortured him, maimed him, mutilated him."

"Tortured him?" I echoed, feeling the indignation rise in me—this beautiful girl, this innocent beast. "Who?"

Alena leaned forward and there was real hate in her eyes. She mentioned a prominent shoe company—spat out the name, actually. It was an ordinary name, a familiar one, and it hung in the air between us, suddenly sinister. Alf had been a part of an experiment to market booties for dogs—suede, cordovan, patent leather, the works. The dogs were made to pace a treadmill in their booties to assess wear; Alf was part of the control group.

"Control group?" I could feel the hair rising on the back of my neck.

"They used eighty-grit sandpaper on the treads to accelerate the process." Alena shot a glance out the window to where the surf pounded the shore; she bit her lip. "Alf was one of the dogs without booties."

25   I was stunned. I wanted to get up and comfort her, but I might as well have been grafted to the chair. "I don't believe it," I said. "How could anybody—?"

"Believe it," she said. She studied me for a moment, then crossed the room to dig through a cardboard box in the corner. If I was moved by the emotion she'd called up, I was moved even more by the sight of her bending over the box in her Gore-Tex bikini; I clung to the edge of the chair as if it were a plunging roller coaster. A moment later, she dropped a dozen file folders in my lap. The uppermost bore the name of the shoe company, and it was crammed with news clippings, several pages of a diary relating to plant operations and workers' shifts at the Grand Rapids facility and a floor plan of the laboratories. The folders beneath it were inscribed with the names of cosmetics firms, biomedical-research centers, furriers, tanners, meat packers. Alena perched on the edge of the coffee table and watched as I shuffled through them.

"You know the Draize Test?"

I gave her a blank look.

"They inject chemicals into rabbits' eyes to see how much it'll take before they go blind. The rabbits are in cages, thousands of them, and they take a needle and jab it into their eyes—and you know why, you know in the name of what great humanitarian cause this is going on, even as we speak?"

30   I didn't know. The surf pounded at my feet. I glanced at Alf and then back into her angry eyes.

"Mascara, that's what. Mascara. They torture countless thousands of rabbits so women can look like sluts."

I thought the characterization a bit harsh, but when I studied her pale lashes and tight lipstickless mouth, I saw that she meant it. At any rate, the notion set her off, and she launched into a two-hour lecture, gesturing with her flawless hands, quoting figures, digging through her files for the odd photo of legless mice or morphine-addicted gerbils. She told me how she'd rescued Alf herself, raiding the laboratory with six other members of the Animal Liberation Front, the militant group in honor of which Alf had been named. At first, she'd been content to write letters and carry placards, but now, with the lives of so many animals at stake, she'd turned to more direct action: harassment, vandalism, sabotage. She described how she'd spiked trees with Earth-First!-ers in Oregon, cut miles of barbed-wire fence on cattle ranches in Nevada, destroyed records in biomedical-research labs up and down the coast and insinuated herself between the hunters and the bighorn sheep in the mountains of Arizona. I could only nod and exclaim, smile ruefully and whistle in a low "Holy cow!" sort of way. Finally, she paused to level her unsettling eyes on me. "You know what Isaac Bashevis Singer said?"

We were on our third beer. The sun was gone. I didn't have a clue.

"Every day is Auschwitz for the animals."

35   I looked down into the amber aperture of my beer bottle and nodded my head sadly. The drier had stopped an hour and a half ago. I wondered if she'd go out to dinner with me, and what she would eat if she did. "Uh, I was wondering," I said, "if . . . if you might want to go out for something to eat—"

Alf chose that moment to heave himself up from the floor
and urinate on the wall behind me. My dinner proposal hung in
the balance as Alena shot up off the edge of the table to scold
him and then gently usher him out the door. "Poor Alf," she
said sighing, turning back to me with a shrug. "But listen, I'm
sorry if I talked your head off—I didn't mean to, but it's rare to
find somebody on your own wave length."

She smiled. *On your own wave length:* The words illuminated me,
excited me, sent up a tremor I could feel all the way down in the
deepest nodes of my reproductive tract. "So how about dinner?"
I persisted. Restaurants were running through my head—would
it have to be a veggie? Could there be a whiff of grilled flesh in
the air? Curdled goat's milk and tabouleh, tofu, lentil soup,
sprouts: *Every day is Auschwitz for the animals.* "No place with meat, of
course."

She just looked at me.

"I mean, I don't eat meat myself," I lied, "or actually, not
anymore"—since the pastrami sandwich, that is—"but I don't
really know anyplace that . . ." I trailed off lamely.

40   "I'm a vegan," she said.

After two hours of blind bunnies, butchered calves and
mutilated pups, I couldn't resist the joke. "I'm from Venus
myself."

She laughed, but I could see she didn't find it all that funny.
Vegans didn't eat meat or fish, she explained, or milk or cheese
or eggs, and they didn't wear wool or leather—or fur, of course.

"Of course," I said. We were both standing there, hovering
over the coffee table. I was beginning to feel a little foolish.

"Why don't we just eat here," she said.

45   THE DEEP THROB OF THE OCEAN SEEMED TO SETTLE
IN MY BONES as we lay there in bed that night, Alena and I,
and I learned all about the fluency of her limbs and the sweetness of her vegetable tongue. Alf sprawled on the floor beneath
us, wheezing and groaning in his sleep, and I blessed him for his
incontinence and his doggy stupidity. Something was happening
to me—I could feel it in the way the boards shifted under me, feel

it with each beat of the surf—and I was ready to go along with it. In the morning, I called in sick again.

Alena was watching me from bed as I dialed the office and described how the flu had migrated from my head to my gut and beyond, and there was a look in her eye that told me I would spend the rest of the day right there beside her, peeling grapes and dropping them one by one between her parted and expectant lips. I was wrong. Half an hour later, after a breakfast of brewer's yeast and what appeared to be some sort of bark marinated in yogurt, I found myself marching up and down the sidewalk in front of a fur emporium in Beverly Hills, waving a placard that read HOW DOES IT FEEL TO WEAR A CORPSE? in letters that dripped like blood.

It was a shock. I'd seen protest marches on TV, antiwar rallies and civil rights demonstrations and all that, but I'd never warmed my heels on the pavement or chanted slogans or felt the naked stick in my hand. There were maybe 40 of us in all, mostly women, and we waved our placards at passing cars and blocked traffic on the sidewalk. One woman had smeared her face and hands with cold cream steeped in Red #3, and Alena had found a ratty mink stole somewhere—the kind that features whole animals sewed together, snout to tail, their miniature limbs dangling—and she'd taken a can of crimson spray paint to their muzzles so that they looked freshly killed. She brandished this grisly banner on a stick high above her head, whooping like a savage and chanting, "Fur is death, fur is death," over and over again till it became a mantra for the crowd. The day was unseasonably warm, the Jaguars glinted in the sun and the palms nodded in the breeze, and no one but for a single tight-lipped salesman glowering from behind the store's immaculate windows paid the slightest bit of attention to us.

I marched out there on the sidewalk—feeling exposed and conspicuous but marching nonetheless—for Alena's sake and for the sake of the foxes and the martens and all the rest, and for my own sake, too: With each step I took, I could feel my consciousness expanding like a balloon, the breath of saintliness seeping steadily into me. Up to this point, I'd worn suede and leather like anybody else—ankle boots and Air Jordans, a bombardier jacket I'd had since high school. If I'd drawn the line with fur, it was only because I'd never had any use for it. If I'd lived in the Yukon—and sometimes, drowsing through a meeting at work, I found myself fantasizing about it—I would have worn fur, no compunction, no second thoughts.

But not anymore. Now I was a protester, a placard waver, now I was fighting for the right of every last weasel and lynx to grow old and die gracefully, now I was Alena Jorgensen's lover and a force to be reckoned with. Of course, my feet hurt and I was running sweat and praying that no one from work would drive by and see me there on the sidewalk with my crazy cohorts and denunciatory sign.

50   We marched for hours, back and forth, till I thought we'd wear a groove in the pavement. We chanted and jeered and nobody so much as looked at us twice. We could have been Hare Krishnas, bums, anti-abortionists or lepers, what did it matter? To the rest of the world, to the uninitiated masses to whose sorry number I'd belonged just 24 hours earlier, we were invisible. I was hungry, tired, discouraged. Alena was ignoring me. Even the woman in redface was slowing down, her chant a hoarse whisper that was sucked up and obliterated in the roar of traffic. And then, as the afternoon faded toward rush hour, a wizened silvery old woman who might have been an aging star or a star's mother or even the first dimly remembered wife of a studio exec got out of a long white car at the curb and strode fearlessly toward us. Despite the heat—it must have been 80 degrees at this point—she was wearing an ankle-length silver-fox coat, a bristling shouldery wafting mass of peltry that must have decimated every burrow on the tundra. It was the moment we'd been waiting for.

A cry went up, shrill and ululating, and we converged on the lone old woman like a Cheyenne war party scouring the plains. The man beside me went down on all fours and howled like a dog, Alena slashed the air with her limp mink and blood sang in my ears. "Murderer!" I screamed, getting into it. "Torturer! Nazi!" The strings in my neck were tight. I didn't know what I was saying. The crowd gibbered. The placards danced. I was so close to the old woman I could smell her—her perfume, a whiff of moth balls from the coat—and it intoxicated me, maddened me, and I stepped in front of her and blocked her path with all the seething militant bulk of my 185 pounds of sinew and muscle.

I never saw the chauffeur. Alena told me afterward that he was a former kickboxing champion who's been banned from the sport for excessive brutality. The first blow seemed to drop from above, a shell lobbed from deep within enemy territory; the others came at me like a windmill churning in a storm. Someone screamed. I remember focusing on the flawless rigid pleats of the chauffeur's trousers, and things got a bit hazy.

I woke to the dull thump of the surf slamming at the shore and the touch of Alena's lips on my own. I felt as if I'd been broken on the wheel, dismantled and put back together again. "Lie still," she said, and her tongue moved across my swollen cheek. Stricken, I could only drag my head across the pillow and gaze into the depths of her parti-colored eyes. "You're one of us now," she whispered.

Next morning, I didn't even bother to call in sick.

55   BY THE END OF THE WEEK, I'd recovered enough to crave meat, for which I felt deeply ashamed, and to wear out a pair of vinyl huaraches on the picket line. Together, and with various coalitions of antivivisectionists, militant vegans and cat lovers, Alena and I tramped a hundred miles of sidewalk, spray-painted inflammatory slogans across the windows of supermarkets and burger stands, denounced tanners, furriers, poulterers and sausage makers and somehow found time to break up a cockfight in Pacoima. It was exhilarating, heady, dangerous. If I'd been disconnected in the past, I was plugged in now. I felt righteous— for the first time in my life, I had a cause—I had Alena, Alena above all. She fascinated me, fixated me, made me feel like a tomcat leaping in and out of second-story windows, oblivious to the free fall and the picket fence below. There was her beauty, of course, a triumph of evolution and the happy interchange of genes going all the way back to the cave men, but it was more than that—it was her commitment to animals, to the righting of wrongs, to morality that made her irresistible. Was it love? The

term is something I've always had difficulty with, but I suppose it was. Sure it was. Love, pure and simple. I had it, it had me.

"You know what?" Alena said one night as she stood over the miniature stove, searing tofu in oil and garlic. We'd spent the afternoon demonstrating out in front of a *tortilla* factory that used rendered animal fat as a congealing agent, after which we'd been chased three blocks by an assistant manager at Von's who objected to Alena's spray-painting MEAT IS DEATH over the specials in the front window. I was giddy with the adolescent joy of it. I sank into the couch with a beer and watched Alf limp across the floor to fling himself down and lick at a suspicious spot on the floor. The surf boomed like thunder.

"What?" I said.

"Thanksgiving's coming."

I let it ride a moment, wondering if I should invite Alena to my mother's for a big basted bird stuffed with canned oysters and buttered bread crumbs, and then realized it probably wouldn't be such a great idea. I said nothing.

60   She glanced over her shoulder. "The animals don't have a whole lot to be thankful for, that's for sure. It's just an excuse for the meat industry to butcher a couple million turkeys, is all it is." She paused; hot safflower oil popped in the pan. "I think it's time for a little road trip," she said. "Can we take your car?"

"Sure, but where are we going?"

She gave me her *Gioconda* smile. "To liberate some turkeys."

IN THE MORNING, I CALLED MY BOSS to tell him I had pancreatic cancer and wouldn't be in for a while, then we threw some things into the car, helped Alf scrabble into the back seat and headed up Route Five for the San Joaquin Valley. We drove for three hours through a fog so dense the windows might as well have been packed with cotton. Alena was secretive, but I could see she was excited. I knew only that we were on our way to rendezvous with a certain "Rolfe," a longtime friend of hers and a big name in the world of ecotage and animal rights, after which we would commit some desperate and illegal act for which the turkeys would be eternally grateful.

There was a truck stalled in front of the sign for our exit at Calpurnia Springs, and I had to brake hard and jerk the wheel around twice to keep the tires on the pavement. Alena came up out of her seat and Alf slammed into the armrest like a sack of meal, but we made it. A few minutes later, we were gliding through the ghostly vacancy of the town itself, lights drifting past in a nimbus of fog, glowing pink, yellow and white, and then there was only the blacktop road and the pale void that engulfed it. We'd gone ten miles or so when Alena instructed me to slow down and began to study the right-hand shoulder with a keen, unwavering eye.

65   The earth breathed in and out. I squinted hard into the soft drifting glow of the headlights. "There, there!" she cried and I swung the wheel to the right and suddenly we were lurching along a pitted dirt road that rose up from the blacktop like a goat path worn into the side of a mountain. Five minutes later, Alf sat up in the back seat and began to whine, and then a crude unpainted shack began to detach itself from the vagueness around us.

Rolfe met us on the porch. He was tall and leathery, in his 50s, I guessed, with a shock of hair and rutted features that brought Samuel Beckett to mind. He was wearing gum boots and jeans and a faded lumberjack shirt that looked as if it had been washed a hundred times. Alf took a quick pee against the side of the house, then fumbled up the steps to roll over and fawn at Rolfe's feet.

"Rolfe!" Alena called, and there was too much animation in her voice, too much familiarity, for my taste. She took the steps in a bound and threw herself into his arms. I watched them kiss, and it wasn't a fatherly-daughterly sort of kiss, not at all. It was a kiss with some meaning behind it, and I didn't like it. Rolfe, I thought: What kind of name is that?

"Rolfe," Alena gasped, still a little breathless from bouncing up the steps like a cheerleader. "I'd like you to meet Jim."

This was my signal. I ascended the porch steps and held out my hand. Rolfe gave me a look out of the hooded depths of his eyes and then took my hand in a hard callused grip, the grip of the wood splitter, the fence mender, the liberator of hothouse turkeys and laboratory mice. "A pleasure," he said, and his voice rasped like sandpaper.

70   There was a fire going inside, and Alena and I sat before it and warmed our hands while Alf whined and sniffed and Rolfe served Red Zinger tea in Japanese cups the size of thimbles. Alena hadn't stopped chattering since we stepped through the door, and Rolfe came right back at her in his woodsy rasp, the two of them exchanging names and news and gossip as if they were talking in code. I studied the reproductions of teal and widgeon that hung from the peeling walls, noticed the case of Heinz vegetarian beans in the corner and the half gallon of Jack Daniel's on the mantel. Finally, after the third cup of tea, Alena settled back in her chair—a huge old Salvation Army sort of thing with a soiled antimacassar—and said, "So what's the plan?"

Rolfe gave me another look, a quick predatory darting of the eyes, as if he weren't sure I could be trusted, and then turned back to Alena. "Hedda Gabler's Range-Fed Turkey Ranch," he said. "And no, I don't find the name cute, not at all." He looked at me now, a long steady assay. "They grind up the heads for cat food, and the neck, the organs and the rest, that they wrap up in paper and stuff back in the body cavity like it was a war atrocity or something. Whatever did a turkey go and do to us to deserve a fate like that?"

The question was rhetorical, even if it seemed to have been aimed at me, and I made no response other than to compose my face in a look that wedded grief, outrage and resolve. I was thinking of all the turkeys I'd sent to their doom, of the plucked wishbones, the pope's noses and the crisp browned skin I used to relish as a kid. It brought a lump to my throat, and something more: I realized I was hungry.

"Ben Franklin wanted to make them a national symbol," Alena chimed in, "did you know that? But the meat eaters won out."

"Fifty thousand birds," Rolfe said, glancing at Alena and bringing his incendiary gaze back to rest on me. "I have information they're going to start slaughtering them tomorrow for the fresh-not-frozen market."

75   "Yuppie poultry." Alena's voice was drenched in disgust.

For a moment, no one spoke. I became aware of the crackling of the fire. The fog pressed at the windows. It was getting dark.

"You can see the place from the highway," Rolfe said finally, "but the only access is through Calpurnia Springs. It's about twenty miles—twenty-two point three, to be exact."

Alena's eyes were bright. She was gazing at Rolfe as if he'd just dropped down from heaven. I felt something heave in my stomach.

"We strike tonight."

80 ROLFE INSISTED THAT WE TAKE MY CAR—"Everybody around here knows my pickup, and I can't take any chances on a little operation like this"—but we did mask the plates, front and back, with an inch-thick smear of mud. We blackened our faces like commandos and collected our tools from the shed out back—tin snips, crowbars and two five-gallon cans of gasoline. "Gasoline?" I said, trying the heft of the can.

Rolfe gave me a crazy look. "To create a diversion," he said. Alf, for obvious reasons, stayed behind in the shack.

If the fog had been thick in daylight, it was impermeable now; the sky collapsed upon the earth. It took hold of the headlights and threw them back at me till my eyes began to water from the effort of keeping the car on the road. But for the ruts and bumps, we might have been floating in space. Alena sat up front between Rolfe and me, curiously silent. Rolfe didn't have much to say, either, save for the occasional grunted command: "Hang a right here"; "Hard left"; "Easy, easy." I thought about meat and jail and the heroic proportions to which I was about to swell in Alena's eyes and what I intended to do to her when we finally got to bed. It was two A.M. by the dashboard clock.

"OK," Rolfe said, and his voice came at me so suddenly it startled me, "pull over here—and kill the lights."

We stepped out into the hush of night and eased the doors shut behind us. I couldn't see a thing, but I could hear the not-so-distant hiss of traffic on the highway, and another sound, too, muffled and indistinct, the gentle, unconscious suspiration of thousands of my fellow creatures. And I could smell them, a seething rancid odor of feces and feathers and naked scaly feet; it crawled down my throat and burned my nostrils. "Whew," I said in a whisper, "I can smell them."

85   Rolfe and Alena were vague presences at my side. Rolfe flipped open the trunk and in the next moment, I felt the heft of a crowbar and a pair of tin snips in my hand. "Listen, you, Jim," he whispered, taking me by the wrist in his iron grip and leading me half a dozen steps forward. "Feel this?"

I felt a grid of wire, which he promptly cut: *snip, snip, snip.*

"This is their enclosure—they're out there in the day, scratching around in the dirt. You get lost, you follow this wire. Now, you're going to take a section out of this side, Alena's got the west side and I've got the south. Once that's done, I signal with the flashlight and we bust open the doors to the turkey houses—they're these big low white buildings; you'll see them when we get close—and flush the birds out. Don't worry about me or Alena. Just worry about getting as many birds out as you can."

I was worried. Worried about everything, from some half-crazed farmer with a shotgun or an AK-47, or whatever they carried these days, to losing Alena in the fog to the turkeys themselves—how big were they? Were they violent? They had claws and beaks, didn't they? And how were they going to feel about me bursting into their bedroom in the middle of the night?

"And when the gas cans go up, you high-tail it back to the car, got it?"

90   I could hear the turkeys tossing in their sleep. A truck shifted gears out on the highway. "I think so," I whispered.

"And one more thing—be sure to leave the keys in the ignition."

This gave me a pause. "But—?"

"The getaway." Alena was so close I could feel her breath on my ear. "I mean, we don't want to be fumbling around for keys when all hell is breaking loose out there, do we?"

I eased open the door and reinserted the key in the ignition, even though the automatic buzzer warned me against it. "OK," I murmured, but they were already gone, soaked up in the shadows and the mist. At this point, my heart was hammering so loudly I could barely hear the rustling of the turkeys. This is crazy, I told myself, it's hurtful and wrong, not to mention illegal. Spray-painting slogans was one thing, but this was something else altogether. I thought of the turkey farmer asleep in his bed, an entrepreneur working to make America strong, a man with a wife and kids and a mortgage . . . but then I thought of all those innocent turkeys consigned to death, and finally I thought of Alena, long-legged and loving, and the way she came to me out of the darkness of the bathroom and the boom of the surf. I took the tin snips to the wire.

95   I must have been at it half an hour, 45 minutes, gradually working my way toward the big white sheds that had begun to emerge from the gloom up ahead, when I saw Rolfe's flashlight blinking off to the left. This was my signal to head to the nearest shed, snap off the padlock with my crowbar, fling open the doors and herd a bunch of cranky, suspicious gobblers out into the night. It was now or never, I looked twice around me and then broke for the nearest shed in an awkward crouching gait. The turkeys must have sensed that something was up—from behind the long white windowless wall there arose a watchful gabbling, a soughing of feathers that fanned up like a breeze in the treetops. *Hold on, you toms and hens,* I thought, *freedom is at hand. A* jerk of the wrist and the padlock fell to the ground. Blood pounding in my ears, I took hold of the door and jerked it open with a great dull booming reverberation—and suddenly, there they were, turkeys, thousands upon thousands of them, cloaked in white feathers under a string of dim yellow bulbs. The light glinted in their reptilian eyes. Somewhere a dog began to bark.

    I steeled myself and sprang through the door with a shout, whirling the crowbar over my head. "All right!" I boomed, and the echo gave it back to me a hundred times over. "This is it! Turkeys, on your feet!" Nothing. No response. But for the whisper of rustling feathers and the alertly cocked heads, they might have been sculptures, throw pillows, they might as well have been dead and butchered and served up with yams and onions and all the trimmings. The barking of the dog went up a notch. I thought I heard voices.

The turkeys crouched on the concrete floor, wave upon wave of them, stupid and immovable; they perched in the rafters, on shelves and platforms, huddled in wooden stalls. Desperate, I rushed into the front rank of them, swinging my crowbar, stamping my feet and howling like the wishbone plucker I once was. That did it. There was a shriek from the nearest bird and the others took it up till an unholy racket filled the place, and now they were moving, tumbling down from their perches, flapping their wings in a storm of dried excrement and pecked-over grain, pouring across the concrete floor till it vanished beneath them. Encouraged, I screamed again—"Yeeeeeee-ha—ha-ha-ha!"—and beat at the aluminum walls with the crowbar as the turkeys shot through the doorway into the night.

It was then that the black mouth of the doorway erupted with light and the *ka-boom!* of the gas cans sent a tremor through the earth. *Run!* a voice screamed in my head, and the adrenaline kicked in and all of a sudden, I was scrambling for the door in a hurricane of turkeys. They were everywhere, flapping their wings, gobbling and screeching, loosing their bowels in panic. Something hit the back of my legs and all at once I was down among them, on the floor, in the dirt and feathers and wet turkey shit. I was a roadbed, a turkey expressway. Their claws dug at my back, my shoulders, the crown of my head. Panicked now, choking on the feathers and dust and worse, I fought to my feet as the big screeching birds launched themselves around me and I staggered out into the barnyard. "There! Who's that there?" a voice roared, and I was off and running.

What can I say? I vaulted turkeys, kicked them aside like so many footballs, slashed and tore at them as they sailed through the air. I ran till my lungs felt as if they were burning right through my chest, disoriented, bewildered, terrified of the shotgun blast I was sure would cut me down at any moment. Behind me the fire raged and lit the fog till it glowed blood-red and hellish. But where was the fence? And where the car?

100 I got control of my feet then and stood stock-still in a flurry of turkeys, squinting into a wall of fog. Was that it? Was that the car over there? At that moment, I heard an engine start up somewhere behind me—a familiar engine with a familiar

coughing gurgle in the throat of the carburetor—and then the lights blinked on briefly 300 yards away. I heard the engine race and listened, helpless, as the car roared off in the opposite direction. I stood there a moment longer, forlorn and forsaken, and then I ran blindly off into the night, putting the fire, the shouts and the barking and the incessant mindless squawking of the turkeys as far behind me as I could.

WHEN DAWN FINALLY BROKE, it was only just perceptibly, so thick was the fog. I'd made my way to a blacktop road—which road and where it led I didn't know—and sat crouched and shivering in a clump of weeds just off the shoulder. Alena wouldn't desert me, I was sure of that—she loved me, as I loved her; needed me, as I needed her—and I was sure she'd be cruising along the back roads looking for me. My pride was wounded, of course, and if I never laid eyes on Rolfe again I felt I wouldn't be missing much, but at least I hadn't been drilled full of shot, savaged by farm dogs or pecked to death by irate turkeys. I was sore all over, my shin throbbed where I'd slammed into something substantial while vaulting through the night, there were feathers in my hair and my face and arms were a mosaic of cuts and scratches and long trailing fissures of dirt. I'd been sitting there for what seemed like hours, cursing Rolfe, developing suspicions about Alena and unflattering theories about environmentalists in general, when finally I heard the familiar slurp and roar of my car cutting through the mist ahead of me.

Rolfe was driving, his face impassive. I flung myself into the road like a tattered beggar, waving my arms over my head and giving vent to my joy, and he very nearly ran me down. Alena was out of the car before it stopped, wrapping me up in her arms, and then she was bundling me into the back seat with Alf and we were on our way back to the hideaway. "What happened?" she cried, as if she couldn't have guessed. "Where were you? We waited as long as we could."

I was feeling sulky, betrayed, feeling as if I were owed a whole lot more than a perfunctory hug and a string of insipid questions. Still, as I told my tale, I began to warm to it—they'd got away in the car with the heater going, and I'd stayed behind to fight the turkeys, the farmers and the elements, too, and if that weren't heroic, I'd like to know what was. I looked into Alena's admiring eyes and pictured Rolfe's shack, a nip or two from the bottle of Jack Daniel's, maybe a peanut-butter-and-tofu sandwich and then the bed, with Alena in it. Rolfe said nothing.

Back at Rolfe's, I took a shower and scrubbed the turkey droppings from my pores, then helped myself to the bourbon. It was ten in the morning and the house was dark—if the world had ever been without fog, there was no sign of it here. When Rolfe stepped out onto the porch to fetch an armload of firewood, I pulled Alena down into my lap. "Hey," she murmured, "I thought you were an invalid."

105   She was wearing a pair of too-tight jeans and an oversized sweater with nothing underneath it. I slipped my hand inside the sweater and found something to hold on to. "Invalid?" I said, nuzzling at her sleeve. "Hell, I'm a turkey liberator, an ecoguerrilla, a friend of the animals and the environment, too."

She laughed, but she pushed herself up and crossed the room to stare out the occluded window. "Listen, Jim," she said, "what we did last night was great, really great, but it's just the beginning." Alf looked up at her expectantly. I heard Rolfe fumbling around on the porch, the thump of wood on wood. She turned around to face me now. "What I mean is, Rolfe wants me to go up to Wyoming for a little bit, just outside Yellowstone—"

Me? Rolfe wants me? There was no invitation in that, no plurality, no acknowledgment of all we'd done and meant to each other. "For what?" I said. "What do you mean?"

"There's this grizzly—a pair of them, actually—and they've been raiding places outside the park. One of them made off with the mayor's Doberman the other night and the people are up in arms. We—I mean, Rolfe and me and some other people from the old Bolt Weevils in Minnesota?—we're going to go up there and make sure the Park Service—or the local yahoos—don't eliminate them. The bears, I mean."

My tone was corrosive. "You and Rolfe?"

110   "There's nothing between us, if that's what you're thinking—this has to do with animals, that's all."

"Like us?"

She shook her head slowly. "Not like us, no. We're the plague on this planet, don't you know that?"

Suddenly, I was angry. Seething. Here I'd crouched in the bushes all night covered in turkey crap, and now I was part of a plague. I was on my feet. "No, I don't know that."

She gave me a look that let me know it didn't matter, that she was already gone, that her agenda, at least for the moment, didn't include me and there was no use arguing about it. "Look," she said, her voice dropping as Rolfe slammed back through the door with a load of wood, "I'll see you in L.A. in a month or so, OK?" She gave me an apologetic smile. "Water the plants for me?"

115   AN HOUR LATER, I WAS ON THE ROAD AGAIN. I'd helped Rolfe stack the wood beside the fireplace, allowed Alena to brush my lips with a goodbye kiss, and then stood there on the porch while Rolfe locked up, lifted Alf into the bed of his pickup and rumbled down the rutted dirt road with Alena at his side. I watched till their brake lights dissolved in the drifting gray mist, then fired up my car and lurched down the road behind them. *A month or so:* I felt hollow inside. I pictured her with Rolfe, eating yogurt and wheat germ, stopping at motels, wrestling grizzlies and spiking trees. The hollowness opened up, cored me out till I felt as if I'd been plucked and gutted and served up on a platter myself.

I found my way back through Calpurnia Springs without incident—there were no roadblocks, no flashing lights and grim-looking troopers searching trunks and back seats for a tallish 30-year-old ecoterrorist with turkey tracks down his back—but after I turned onto the highway for Los Angeles, I had a shock. Ten miles up the road, my nightmare materialized out of the gloom: red lights everywhere, signal flares and police cars lined up on the shoulder. I was on the very edge of panicking, a beat away from cutting across the meridian and giving them a run for it, when I saw the truck jackknifed up ahead. I slowed to 40, 30, and then hit the brakes. In a moment, I was stalled in a lane of cars and there was something all over the road, ghostly and white in the fog. At first I thought it must have been flung from the truck, rolls of toilet paper or crates of soap powder ruptured on the pavement. It was neither. As I inched closer, the tires creeping now, the pulse of the lights in my face, I saw that the road was coated in feathers, turkey feathers. A storm of them. A blizzard. And more: There was flesh there, too, slick and greasy, a red pulp ground into the surface of the road, thrown up like slush from the tires of the car ahead of me, ground beneath the massive wheels of the truck. Turkeys. Turkeys everywhere.

The car crept forward. I flicked on the windshield wipers, hit the WASHER button, and for a moment, a scrim of diluted blood obscured the windows and the hollowness opened up inside me till I thought it would suck me inside out. Behind me, someone was leaning on his horn. A trooper loomed up out of the gloom, waving me on with the dead yellow eye of his flashlight. I thought of Alena and felt sick. All there was between us had come to this, expectations gone sour, a smear on the road. I wanted to get out and shoot myself, turn myself in, close my eyes and wake up in jail, in a hair shirt, in a strait jacket, anything. It went on. Time passed. Nothing moved. And then, miraculously, a vision began to emerge from behind the smeared glass and the gray belly of the fog, lights glowing golden in the waste. I saw the sign, GAS/FOOD/LODGING, and my hand was on the blinker.

It took me a moment, picturing the place, the generic tile, the false cheer of the lights, the odor of charred flesh hanging heavy on the air, Big Mac, three-piece dark meat, carne asada, cheeseburger. The engine coughed. The lights glowed. I didn't think of Alena then, didn't think of Rolfe or grizzlies or the doomed bleating flocks and herds or of the blind bunnies and cancerous mice—I thought only of the cavern opening inside me and how to fill it. "Meat," and I spoke the word aloud, talking to calm myself as if I'd awakened from a bad dream, "it's only meat."

Reynolds Price

Reynolds Price is the author of several collections of stories including, *The Names and Faces of Heroes* and *Permanent Errors*. Among his many novels are A *Long and Happy Life*, *A Generous Man*, *The Surface of Earth*, and *Kate Vaiden*. He has also published plays, verse, and nonfiction.

Two Useful Visits

BACK THEN YOUR KIN COULD LEAN DOWN ON YOU with the weight of the world and still not quite say "Get yourself up here to see Mary Greet; she's dying fast, and it's your plain duty." So in mid-February in 1960, on the floor of my own despair, I got a postcard from my cousin Anna Palmer. It said "Aunt Mary is sinking fast and speaks of you." I changed my plans for the next Sunday and made the two-hour drive to see her through clear warm weather that lifted a corner at least of my spirits.

When I'd seen her last in August '58, Mary claimed to be "somewhere way past my eighties." And though she'd picked 60 pounds of cotton the day before—a great deal of cotton—the pictures of her I took on that visit show a balding head, eyes opalescent with the film of age, and the fixed stance of an ancient sybil, senior to God. So if she was, say, more than 90 in the pictures, then she might very well have been born a slave. Even in those years of frank segregation, I'd never been able to ask her the truth. My older kin never mentioned slavery, as if it were some much-cherished dead loved one, too painful to summon. And I'd hesitated with Mary Greet from a vague, maybe misplaced courtesy—you seldom ask men if they've been in prison. The time had come though. I had a need now, to understand pain, that licensed the probe. I'd ask her today.

WHEN I PULLED UP BY HER MATCH-BOX HOUSE, she was out in the yard in a straight-backed chair, apparently searching an old hound for ticks. I knew she couldn't see me till I got much closer; so I stood by the car and raised my voice, "Aunt Mary, dogs don't have ticks in the winter."

She didn't look up, and I thought "Now she's deaf." But then she spoke to the dog clearly, "White man claiming it's winter, Saul." And when I walked closer, there in her lap was a rusty can with fat ticks swimming in kerosene. I said "Can you tell who I am?"

Still picking at Saul, Mary said "You who you been every day I knowed you.

I admired her skill at staving me off, but I had to keep teasing. "Am I Sam House?" Sam was my younger brother, then 26.

She finally turned her long face toward me and shaded her eyes, "Fool, you used to be Hilman. Sit down." That far, she was right—the summer loss of my wife and daughter had cored me out at 34; but could her eyes really see that well? She pointed to the sandy ground beneath us. It was good enough for Saul; who was I to decline, on a warm dry day?

I sat and, since she'd called me a fool, I thought "All right, I'll ask her right off." When Saul's next tick hit the bottom of the can, I said "Aunt Mary, were you born a slave?" For the next still minute, I thought I'd struck her.

But next she let out a dry chuckle. She lifted Saul's droopy right ear and leaned down, "Tell him, Saul. *You* know." She faced me again and said "Hilman, you feeling good as you look?"

10   I said "No *ma'am*" but I felt some ease; and for nearly two hours, we sat in the last of that midwinter spring and asked each other aimless questions about our safe past, both dodging the traps of here and now.

This much came clear, from her answers and my memory. Mary cooked for my mother's parents from the week they settled here in 1882. And though she retired before I was born, she was in and out of my grandmother's house all through my childhood. She took the rights accorded her age and always came in through the front door—no knock, just a statement, "It's nothing but *me*." Then she'd head for the kitchen and sit by the sink, a new addition since her days there. Most of my kin ignored her politely. They thought they knew all she had to tell. But early she won my affectionate awe. She treated me like the full-grown man I meant to be, that tart and dead-level, that unforgiving whenever I failed.

One morning when I was maybe ten, she asked me a thing no black person had, "Hil, what you meaning to *be*, down the road?" I said "Aunt Mary, I'm busy right now" and pounded off to start some game. She said "Here, *sir!*" Then in sight of my mother, she said "You turn your back on this old soul, and you'll see a heap of backs turned on you." Mother nodded, and I stayed in place to say I planned to be a doctor; by then it was already my great goal. She said "No sir, you waited too late." Mother smiled behind her, and we mutely agreed—Mary was cracked. But of course she was right; and many more times, when she sounded wild to other bystanders, she thrust straight fingers deep into my quick.

Even this afternoon in 1960, as I stood to leave, having said nothing about my loss, Mary finally said "When you setting up house and making *your* young uns?"

I said "I'm trying to learn from you—you thriving out here with nothing but a hound and doing grand." I'd yet to see any sign of poor health.

15   Saul had loped off an hour ago, but Mary looked for him as though he mattered. Then she found my face again and tried to smile, but her eyes wouldn't light. "Us mean old women, we free-standing trees—don't need no trellis to help us climb.

I estimate you ain't that free." She tried again at the smile, and it worked. There were four good teeth.

I gave her five dollars and drove back home, thinking she'd likely be standing free when I'd thinned down from loneliness and vanished.

BUT LATE NEXT AUGUST, ANNA PALMER PHONED ME. Calls from Anna were rare as blizzards; and before she finished expressing her delicate worries for me—I was known, in the family, to be still "blue"—I thought "Mary's dead." Strictly speaking, I was wrong. Anna said Aunt Mary was on her deathbed and refused to rise. I thought "By the time I drive up there, she'll rise and be out pulling more cotton."

No, Mary was in the same one-room shack she inhabited alone, long before I knew her. All the windows were covered with old cardboard; but there'd never been a lock on the door, so I'd tapped loudly and then stepped into punishing heat. You could have baked bricks in the palms of your hands, but you couldn't have seen an inch ahead till you stood in the heat and let your eyes open. The one oil lamp was full but not lit. And as ever, in all my visits here, there was no human with her. Today there was even no trace of Saul. She was in the far corner on a narrow cot, under three wool blankets; and she seemed asleep or already dead. But as I stepped toward her, her head tried to find me.

Anna had said that she cooked Aunt Mary two meals a day and spoon-fed them to her and that June, Mary's great-great nephew, turned up to watch her every few nights and give her milk; she craved buttermilk. So maybe she weighed a scant 80 pounds, but her scalp was bald as any old man's. And when her mouth gapped open to breathe, I could see that the last four teeth had dissolved. I drew up the chair, "Aunt Mary, it's Hilman." She didn't look up, so I said "Hilman House. You resting easy?"

Then the huge eyes ransacked my face and found nothing. But she found the strength to say a fierce "No."

I thought she meant she didn't recognize me, so I said "—Rosella Hilman's son, that you used to like."

She said "Not so" and waved a spider hand, as if to cancel my presence.

I leaned back. But the hand came on, took the edge of my coat and pulled me down, eight inches from her face.

She whispered "They working me to death, Mr. Phipps."

25   I thought she said Phipps, though later I recalled a long-dead kinsman named Brownlee Fitts. But I said "No, I'm Hilman."

If she'd had her old power, she'd have snapped my neck. But she only nagged at my coat again, "You hear what I say and *help* me, else I be laid out dead at your feet by dark today."

So I said "Mary, where would you rather be?"

She was eager as any child to tell me, "Lord Jesus, in bed. I'm *tired*, man. This last piece of work bout broke my mind—my back broke sometime yesterday." Both hands were out of the cover now, busy with the work old doctors called "picking," a reflex act of failing nerves.

I drew off the blankets, smoothed her bunched nightgown, settled her flat. She was light to move as a locust shell, though the only woman I'd touched in months. I smoothed her pillow, a cast-off towel of Anna's but clean in a linen case. Then I bent and said "Is that any help at all?"

30   She thought a long time and said "No" again but not as hard. And when I'd sat another half hour, trying to think of any-thing under the sun but me and the two I'd lost, I gradually saw that Mary Greet had also gone, from this nearby, with no fur-ther plea, command or moan. No one alive had made me the gift of so much trust, though I knew she'd left both me and the world as a girl again, in pain more hopeless than any of mine.

Madison Smartt Bell

Madison Smartt Bell is the author of two
collections of stories, *Zero db* and *Barking Man*.
Among his several novels are *A Soldier's Joy, Straight
Cut, Waiting for the End of the World, The Washington
Square Ensemble, The Year of Silence,* and *Doctor Sleep.*
He has also published screenplays and verse.

Dragon's Seed

MACKIE LOUDON LIVED ALONE IN A
SMALL HOUSE made of iron and stone on a short street west of
21st Avenue. She had lived there, alone, for a long time. Old ivy
grew in a carpet across her front steps and in her yard the grass
was tall, with volunteer shoots of privet standing in it. The street
was old enough to have a few big trees and the houses were raised
on a high embankment above the sidewalk. It was quiet down the
whole length of her block, almost always very, very quiet.

Indoors, it seemed that inertia ruled, though maybe that was
just a first impression. The front room had once been a parlor,
but now, scattered among the original furnishings, were all of
Mackie Loudon's sculpture tools. There were pole lamps, a
rocker, a couple of armchairs, some fragile little end tables, also
hammers and chisels and files and other devices, and a variety of
sculptures in wood and stone. In former times people had come

from the north to take the sculptures away and sell them, but it was a long time since their visits had stopped. She did not remember the reason or care about it, since she was not in want.

The things she didn't need to use stayed put exactly where they were. In the kitchen, on the gas stove, an iron skillet sat with browning shreds of egg still plastered to it, a relic of the very last time Mackie Loudon had bothered to make herself a hot meal. Asians had moved to a storefront within walking distance of her house, to open a store and cafeteria, and she went there to provender herself with things she never knew the names of. She bought salt plums, and packets of tiny dried fish whose eyes were bigger than their heads, and crocks of buried vegetables plugged with mud. She dumped the empty containers in the sink and when it filled she bagged them up and carried the bag down a rickety outside staircase to a place in the alley from where it would eventually disappear. There was one pot that she used for coffee and that was all. On the windowsill above the sink was an old teacup, its inside covered with a filagree of tiny tannin-colored cracks. Each morning, if the day was fair, a bar of sunlight would find a painted rose on its upper rim, warm it a moment, then pass on.

She wore flowered cotton dresses, knee-length, with no shape, and in winter a man's tweed overcoat. With the light behind her, her legs showed through the fabric of the skirt. They were very slightly bowed, and her shoulders were rather big for a woman, her hands strong. She had a little trouble with arthritis, but not so much she couldn't work. Her features were flat, her skin strong and wrinkly like elephant hide. A few long white hairs flew away from her chin. The rest of her hair was thick and gray, and she hacked it off herself in a rough helmet shape and peered out from underneath its visor. Her right eye was green, her left pale blue and troubled by an unusual sort of tic. Over five or so minutes the eyelid would lower, imperceptibly and inexorably closing itself till it was fully shut, and then quite suddenly fly back open in a startled blue awakening. Because of this, some said that Mackie Louden had the evil eye, and others thought she was a witch, which was not true, although she did hold colloquy with demons.

5   Before the fireplace in the parlor was a five-foot length of a big walnut log, out of which Mackie Loudon was carving a great head of Medusa. For a work stand she used a stone sculpture she'd forgotten, mostly a flat-topped limestone rock, with an ill-defined head and arm of Sisyphus just visible underneath it. She stood on a rotting embroidered ottoman to reach the top of the section of wood, and took her chisels from the mantelpiece where they were lined. The front windows had not been washed in years and what light came through was weak and dingy, but she could see as much as she required to. Her chisels were ordered from New York and each was sharp enough to shave with. She didn't often need to use her mallets; wherever she touched her scoop to its surface the walnut curled away like butter. She carved, the strange eye opened and closed on its off-beat rhythm, and the murmur and mutter of her demons soothed her like a song.

There were two of them, Eliel and Azazael. Each made occasional inconsistent protestations of being good, or evil. Often they quarreled, with each other or with her, and at other times they would cooperate in the interlocking way of opposites. Eliel reported himself to be the spirit of air and Azazael the spirit of darkness. Sometimes they would exchange these roles, or sometimes both would compete to occupy one or the other. They laid conflicting claims to powers of memory and magic, though Mackie Loudon could always point out that there was little enough in the real world they'd ever accomplished on their own.

Azazael was usually hostile to Medusa. *You don't know what you're getting into,* he said. *You're not sure yourself just what you're calling up, or why.*

"The one sure thing is you're a gloomy devil," Mackie Loudon said. But she said it with affection, being so much in control this morning that the demonic bickering was as pleasant to her as a choir. "You've always got the wrong idea," she said to Azazael, "You're my unnecessary demon." She moved the chisel and another pale peel of the outer wood came falling away from its dark core.

MACKIE LOUDON WAS HEADED HOME FROM A FOR-
AGING EXPEDITION, her shoulders pulled down by the two
plastic shopping bags that swung low from the ends of her arms.
Her head was lowered also and she scanned the pavement ahead
of her for anything of interest that might be likely to appear.
A couple of feet above the nape of her neck, Eliel and Azazael
invisibly whirled around each other, swooping and darting like
barn swallows at evening. They were having one of the witless
arguments to which immaterial beings are prone, about whether
or not it was really raining. It was plain enough to Mackie
Loudon that it *was* raining, but not hard enough for her to
bother stopping to take out the extra plastic bag she carried to tie
around her head when it was really raining hard. There were
only a few fat raindrops splattering down, spaced far apart on the
sidewalk.

10   She had almost come to the line of people shuffling into the
matinee at the President Theater when she halted and sank to one
knee to reach for a cloudy blue glass marble wedged in a triangu-
lar chip in the pavement. Just then there was some commotion in
the movie crowd, and she looked up as a little black girl not more
than five ran out into the street weeping and screaming, with a fat
black woman chasing her and flogging her across the shoulders
with a chain dog leash, or so Azazael began to maintain.

Did you see that? hissed Azazael, his voice turning sibilant as it
lowered. On the street a car squealed to a sudden halt, blasted its
horn once and then drove on. The line had reformed itself and
the tail of it dragged slowly into the theater's lobby.

See what? said Eliel. *None of these people look like they saw anything. . . .*
They never see, said Azazael. *That's the way of the world, you know.*

Mackie Loudon grasped the marble with her thumb and
forefinger and held it near her stable eye, but it had lost its lus-
ter. The cloud in it looked no longer like a whirlwind, but a
cataract. She flipped the marble over the curb and watched it roll
through a drain's grating.

15   *Are you deaf and dumb and blind?* Azazael was carping. *Don't you
know what happens to children nowadays?*

"SHUT UP!!" Mackie Loudon cried, as she arose and caught up her bags, "Both of you, now, you just shut up." On the other side of the street an ancient man who'd been dozing in a porch swing snapped his head up to stare at her.

IN THE BEDROOM WAS A LOW BED WITH A SAGGILY SOFT MATTRESS and whenever Mackie Loudon retired she felt it pressing in on all the sides of her like clay. But if she woke in the middle of the night she'd find herself sucked out through a rip in the sky, floating in an inky universal darkness, the stars immeasurably distant from herself and one another, and a long long way below, the blue and green Earth reduced to the size of a teardrop. Somewhere down there her husband, son, and a pair of grandchildren (that she knew of) continued to exist, and she felt wistful for them, or sometimes felt an even deeper pang.

You chose us, sang Eliel and Azazael. Out here, they always joined in a chorus. Out here, she sometimes thought she almost saw them, bright flickerings at the edges of her eyes. *And look, it's even more beautiful than you'd ever hoped it would be.*

"Yes, but it's lonely too," Mackie Loudon said.

You chose us, the demons droned, which was the truth, or near it.

MEDUSA WASN'T GOING WELL; Azazael's objections were gaining ground, or somehow something else was wrong. Mackie Loudon couldn't make out what was the matter, quite. She wandered away from the unfinished carving, and her mind wandered with her, or sometimes strayed. As she passed along the dairy aisle at the A&P, small hands no bigger than insect limbs reached from the milk cartons to pluck at the hairs of her forearm. She wasn't sure just where or why but she suspected it had happened before, similar little tactile intimations grasping at her from brown paper sacks or withered posters stapled to the phone poles.

Oh, you remember, Azazael was teasing her, *you can remember anytime you want.*

"No, I can't," Mackie Loudon said petulantly. Across the aisle, a matron gave her a curt look and pushed her cart along a little faster.

Never mind, Eliel said soothingly. *I'll remember for you. I'll keep it for you till you need it, that's all right.* And it was true that Eliel did remember everything and had forgiven Mackie Loudon for it, long ago.

25   THERE WAS A BOY STANDING IN THE ALLEY when Mackie Loudon set her garbage down, just a little old boy with a brush of pale hair and slate-colored eyes and a small brown scab on his jaw line. He wore shorts and a T-shirt with holes and he stood still as a concrete jockey; only his eyes moved slightly, tracking her. Mackie Loudon straightened up and put her hands on her hips.

"Are you real?" she said to him.

The boy shifted his weight to his other leg. "Why wouldn't I be," he said shortly.

"Hmmph," said Mackie Loudon, and put her head to one side to change her angle on him.

"Lady, your yard sho is a mess," the boy said. "The front yard and the back yard both."

30   "You're too little to cut grass yet awhile," she said. "Lawnmower'd chew you up and spit you out."

"Who's that?" the boy said, and raised his arm to point at the house.

Mackie Loudon's heart clutched up and she whipped around. It was a long time since anyone other than her had looked out of those windows. But all he was pointing to was a plaster bust she'd set on a sill and forgotten so well it was invisible to her now.

"Oh, that's just Paris," she said.

"Funny name," the boy said. *"Real* good-looking feller, though."

35   "He was a fool and don't you forget it," Mackie Loudon said, in a sharper tone.

"Well, who was he then?"

"Question is, who are *you*?"

"Gil mostly just calls me Monkey."

"That's not much name for a person," Mackie Loudon said. "What's your real name, boy?"

40 The child's face clouded over and he looked at the gravel between his feet.

"Won't tell, hey?" Mackie Loudon said. "All right, I'll just call you Preston. You answer to that?"

The boy raised his eyes back to her.

"All right, Preston, you drink milk?"

"Sometime not all the time," Preston said.

45 "You eat cookies, I expect?"

"*All* the time," Preston said, and followed her up the steps into the house. She blew a small dried spider from a water-spotted glass and give him milk, and a lotus seed cake from a white waxed bag of them. Preston looked strangely at the cake's embossed and egg-white polished surface before he took a bite.

"What do you think?" Mackie Loudon said. She had poured an inch of cold coffee into her mug and was eating a lotus-seed cake herself.

"I don't know, but it ain't a cookie," Preston said, and continued to eat.

"It's sweet, though, right? And just one will keep you on your feet all day. And do you know the secret?"

50 "Secret?"

"Got *thousand-year-old egg yolk* in it," Mackie Loudon said. "That's what puts the kick in it for you."

Preston bugged his eyes at her and slid down from his seat. He laid a trail of crumbs into the parlor, where she found him crouched on the desiccated carpet, lifting a corner of the sheet she'd used to veil Medusa.

"Oooooo, *snakes*," said Preston, delighted. Mackie Loudon pulled his hand away so that the sheet fell back.

"Let that alone, it's not done yet," she said. "It's got something wrong with it, I can't tell what."

55 Preston turned a circle in the middle of the room, pointing at heads on the mantel and the bookcases.

"Who's that?" he said. "And that? and that?"

"Just some folks I used to know," Mackie Loudon told him. "But didn't you want me to tell you about Paris?" When Preston nodded, she took a lump of plasticine from an end-table drawer and gave it to him to occupy his hands, which otherwise seemed to wander. Half-consciously he kneaded the clay from one crude shape to another, and his eyes kept roving around the room, but she could tell that he was listening closely. She started with the Judgment of Paris and went on and on. Preston came back on the next morning and within a couple of weeks she'd started them into the Trojan war. By first frost they were on their way with the Odyssey.

The demons kept silent while Preston was there, and were quieter than usual even after he'd left. Azazael did a little griping about how the boy was wasting her time, but he had nothing to say with any real bite to it. Eliel was rather withdrawn, since he was much occupied with the task of observing Gil through Mackie Loudon's eyes and storing up in memory all he saw.

Preston lived with Gil in a house right next to Mackie Loudon's house. The paint was peeling off the clapboard in long curly strips, and on the front door was a red-and-blue decal of a skull cloven by a zigzag lightning bolt. The windows, painted shut for a decade, were blacked out day and night with dirty sheets, behind which strange bluish lights were sometimes seen to flash in one room or another. There was no woman living there, though every so often one would visit, and sometimes little gangs of other scroungy children would appear and remain for a day or several, though the only one there permanently was Preston.

60   Gil himself was tall and stooped, with thinning black hair and not much chin. He affected motorcycle garb, though it didn't suit him.

He was thin as from some wasting disease, and the boots and black leather and studded armbands hung slackly from him like the plumage of some mangy kind of buzzard. He drove a newly-customized black van with its rear windows cut in the shape of card-deck spades. He never seemed to go out to work, but he dealt in prodigious quantities of mail, getting and sending rafts of big brown cartons. Mackie Loudon would have thought he trafficked in drugs or other bulkier contraband, if she cared to think about it at all, but all these notions had been assumed by Eliel, ever since the first time Gil had come to her door to fetch Preston. "Come out, Monk," he said through the mail slot, his voice whiny and insinuating. "Time to come along with Gil . . ." and she and the demons had seen the thousand tiny gates behind Preston's lips and eyes slide shut.

PRESTON LOVED THE ILIAD, the Odyssey, he loved the story of Perseus and the Gorgon, though he flinched a little at Diana and Acteon, but he didn't want to hear one word of Jason and the Argonauts. Indeed, at the first mention of the name a wracking change came over him, as if he'd been . . . possessed. He paled, he shook, he formed a fist of sharp white knuckles and smashed the little plasticine figure Mackie Loudon had made to represent the hero. Then he was out the back door and running pell mell down the alley.

Azazael was back in a flash. *What did I tell you?* he suggested. *There's something in this set-up that is really really queer.*

"Children take these fits sometimes," Mackie Loudon said, for Azazael's remark was only typical of the weak and cloudy innuendos he'd been uttering through that fall. She turned to Eliel for confirmation, but for some reason Eliel didn't seem to be around.

65   PRESTON DIDN'T COME BACK FOR A WEEK OR MORE, but on the fifth day Gil came by to fetch him just the same. Mackie Loudon surprised herself by opening the door. Gil stood on the lower step, fidgeting with a dog's training collar, the links purling from hand to hand in a way that obscurely put her in mind of something disagreeable.

"The Monkey with you?" Gil said.

"That's no name for a human child," Mackie Loudon said. "And no, I hadn't seen him in a long time."

Gil nodded but didn't shift himself. He stretched the chain taut, its end rings strung on his middle fingers, then shut it between the palms of his hands.

"Didn't know you had a dog," Mackie Loudon said.

70   "Hee hee," said Gil. The fronts of his yellowing teeth were graven in black.

"Does that boy belong to you?"

Gil smiled again with his rotten teeth. "Yes, I believe you could say that," he said. "His skinny little butt is mine." He tossed the clump of chain and caught it with a jingle. "Old woman, I wouldn't suggest you meddle," he said, and turned to look back toward the street. "Nobody cares what goes on around here." He withdrew down the weedy walk, his feet slipping loosely in the outsize boots. Loathingly, she followed him a little way, and when she stopped to look about her she saw that what he said was true. The houses on the block were held by knaves or madmen, or by no one. The lawns were dead, the trees were dying, a frigid wind blew garbage down the center of the street. From half the houses, broken windows overlooked her like sockets in a row of hollowed skulls.

ON A COLD BLUE MORNING Preston came to stand in the alley below the house again. For the first time Mackie Loudon noticed he didn't have a winter coat. She had to go and take his hand and lead him, to get him to come in. Though he seemed glad to see her, he wouldn't say a word. He sat in his usual wooden chair in the kitchen and stared at the pendulum swing of his feet.

"Cat got your tongue, has it?" Mackie Loudon said, and placed a yellow bean cake on the table near his hand. She went to the refrigerator for the milk she'd bought the day before, in some demonic premonition of his return, poured a glass and set it by him, took the carton back. In the light of the refrigerator's yellowed bulb she saw the faint blue photograph smeared on the carton's wall, and looked at it, and looked at Preston, and looked at the carton again. A line of blue letters crawled under the picture: Jason Sturges of Birmingham, eight years old and missing since.... She shut the door and leaned on it and breathed before she turned to him.

75   "My God, boy," she said at last. "Do you know who you are?" And though the child didn't answer her, Eliel came back

from wherever he'd been hiding and all at once returned to her the burden of her perception and her memory.

YOU BLEW IT, AZAZAEL SNAPPED AT HER. *You bungled everything, like usual.*

Why couldn't you have just kept still a little longer? Eliel said. *God knows you stayed quiet long enough.* Mackie Loudon didn't answer them. She stalked from room to room, banging into the doorjambs and the furniture. It was a long time since they'd been so angry with her, especially in concert, but she knew that they were justified. Preston, Jason, had bolted from the house the moment she'd asked that stupid question; she hadn't been quick enough to catch him. After that she'd called the police, called them once, called them twice

That was pretty stupid too, Azazael said. *Everything considered, that might have been your worst move yet.* Mackie Loudon whirled on the parlor carpet and clawed one hand through the blank space where his voice came from. The Argonaut's little wooden ship crunched under her shoe; she booted its doomsaying figurehead into a corner. She went to her window and thumbed back a corner of the blind. Across the way, Gil's house hulked in the gathering twilight. It had taken the police all day and many calls to come, *all for nothing,* Eliel snapped. She had watched them come up to the porch and confer with Gil for a minute or two in the doorway and then leave.

"God damn," said Mackie Loudon, and let the blind fall back. She walked to the room's center and whipped the sheet off her Medusa. *What's the point?* said Azazael. She regarded the wooden expression of the broad blank face. The blunt heads of the snakes were blind because she'd never made their eyes. No *power there,* Eliel said sadly.

Mackie Loudon flung the chisel that had come into her hand; it stuck between Medusa's eyes and sagged. She was on Gil's board-sprung porch, pounding so heavily on the door that she almost fell forward when he snatched it from under her hand.

"The meddling old bat," Gil said contemplatively. "The *crazy* old bat, as the cops would say."

"Where's that boy?" Mackie Loudon said.

Gil raised one hand directly above the bald spot on his head and snapped his fingers once.

"Gone," he said. He made a plopping sound with his loose lips. "You understand, he just had to go."

85   "What did—"

"*Never you mind,*" Gil said, and his face hardened. He stepped across the doorsill and shoved her in the chest with the butt end of his palm. His arm was weak and reedy-looking, but somehow it sent her staggering a long way back, down the porch steps into the littered yard. A slow fine drizzle sifted into her hair from the dark sky.

"I *told* you not to meddle," Gil said, and gave her another skinny little shove. "What good do you think it did anybody? The *police* say I should let them know if you *harass* me." He went on talking and pushing but Mackie Loudon wasn't really listening anymore. She was wondering what had happened to her strength. Her arms had always been powerful but now she couldn't seem to lift them, she couldn't speak a single word, and her legs seemed ready to give way and dump her on the matted grass and mud.

"I'm telling you, old bat," Gil said. "You want to stop messing in my business altogether." He gave her a two-handed shove and she went over the edge of the embankment. She tumbled down and cracked the back of her head on the sidewalk, hard enough to jumble her vision briefly, though it didn't knock her out. She lay with her left hand hanging off the curbstone, knuckles down. The rain fell into the corners of her open eyes. The quarreling demonic voices spiraled up and up away from her, until they'd left her all alone in the silence of a vacuum, empty even of a single thought. Two or three people passed her by before anyone bothered to try and pick her up.

"OH MACKIE, MACKIE," Nurse Margaret said from the height of her burnt-clay six-foot-two. Her hair was pinned back so tight under the white cap that it seemed to pull her sorrowing eyes even wider. "You last left here, you were talking so loud and walking so proud, I hoped to never see you back." Under Mackie Loudon's nose she shook two pills, one fire-engine-red, one robin's-egg-blue, but Mackie Loudon would not take her medication. She would not use her skills in craft class. She would not go to therapy group, she would not interact with anyone. She would not even speak a word. She would not. She would not.

90 WITH THE DEMONS GONE THE INTERIOR SILENCE WAS DEEP INDEED, but Mackie Loudon was not aware of it. Human voices were distant and as completely unintelligible as the noise of the crickets in the grass. She let herself be herded from point to point on the ward, moving like an exhumed corpse made to simulate animation by a programmed sequence of electric shocks. She sat on a sprung couch in the dayroom and moved no more than a ledge of rock. All on its own her left eye opened and shut its lizard lid. An orderly pushed a mop before her, up and down, up and down. Behind her was the slap of playing cards and a mumble of voices blended into the static that came from the untuned TV. The season's changes appeared on the shatter-proof glass of the front window as if projected on a screen.

"MACKIE LOU! MACKIE LOU!" She heard, but it had been a long time since she'd recognized her name or any variation on it. A bluish plume of flame flashed up toward the darkened ceiling and went out. She sat up suddenly and turned. Two beds away in the long row, Little Wilbur was springing up and down on his mattress. Normally they tied him in, how had he got loose? But everything that happened next was even more improbable.

"Mackie Lou! Watch me, watch me, Mackie Lou!" Little Wilbur stopped his simian bounce, squirted a stream of lighter fluid into his mouth, and blew sharply across a match he'd struck. Another compact fireball rolled in midair toward the doorway, illuminating the trio of orderlies who came near to

knocking each other down in their haste to pin Little Wilbur to
the floor and stuff his arms into restraints and haul him kicking
and shouting from the room.

"Watch me, Mackie Lou!" But the demonic voices drowned
him out. Azazael and Eliel were back, furiously arguing over the
implications of what they'd seen, yammering so fast she couldn't
follow them. They jabbered at incomprehensible speed, but
after an hour, when they'd come to some agreement, they slowed
down and turned to her again.

We've got a notion for you, said Eliel. *We've thought of a way for you to
solve your problem.*

95 Mackie Loudon gave her head a long sad shake against the
pillow. "You're not even real," she said.

You know better, said Azazael.

"Well. But you can't *do* anything."

Maybe not, said Eliel, *But watch us show you how to do it.*

"All right," she said. "At least I'll hear you out," and she listened meekly and attentively until almost dawn. As usual she got
up with the others, shuffled in a line of others to receive the
breakfast tray. But once they'd been sent into the day room, she
called for Nurse Margaret and asked for her pills and began one
more of her miraculously swift recoveries.

100 IT WAS SPRING WHEN MACKIE LOUDON WAS RELEASED
and the weeds were knee-deep in her yard, but in the house nothing was much changed. She did a meager bit of dusting, then
plucked the chisel from between Medusa's eyes, licked her thumb
and moistened the wounded wood. After a long considering
moment, she went to the bedroom and snatched a big mirror
loose from the closet door and propped it on a parlor chair. The
reflection reversed all her movements, making her tend to cut
herself as she worked. It took the rest of the day to get the hang of
it, and she stayed up with it through the night, but by next morning it was done and she wasn't even tired yet.

She taped her cuts and made herself a breakfast of dried
mushrooms and dried minnows, drank a pot of coffee, had a
spoon or two of pickled vegetables. She found her bottle of

linseed oil and gave the finished carving a light anointment, then covered it once more with the sheet. When she closed her eyes and concentrated she felt her strong pulse striking tiny hammer blows; she felt the Gorgon visage pushing out on her brow as if embossed upon a shield. With care she brushed her hair down over her forehead, and went out.

In the shed that faced the alley there was a lawnmower, which, though rusted looked as if it would probably run. She dragged it around to the front yard, then carried a gas can down to a filling station two blocks over and had it filled. At a neighboring hardware store she bought a three-foot crowbar, and came home with this awkwardly balanced load. She was cutting the front lawn when Gil came out and did a double take.

"Well if it ain't the old bat back," he said, shouting over the noise of the engine. Mackie Loudon gave him a cheerful wave and went on with her mowing. Cut ends of the tough privet stumps whirred around her head. Gil stared, and shook his head, and went down to his van. When its hind end had turned a corner, Mackie Loudon shut the mower off and went in her front door and out the back, collecting the crowbar on the way. One good jab and pry was good enough to break the flimsy lock on Gil's back door. She went in and softly shut the door behind her.

In Gil's front room a video camera watched her from the gloom, like an insect eye extended on a stalk. A light flick from the crowbar's tip shattered the lens into fine glass dust. She went throughout the whole house that way, smashing the cameras and enlargers, gouging out the works of the projectors and video decks with the hooked end of the crowbar. She didn't look at the tapes or the films, but she couldn't help seeing the big still prints, which showed children with children, children with grownups, children with assorted animals, a few children being tortured and killed.

105   *They sowed bones,* said Eliel, and Azazael answered, *They'll have their harvest.*

She didn't have long to wait for Gil, not much more than the time it took her to prepare. There was a two-gallon bucket under his sink which she took empty to her house and brought back full. She dipped herself a ration in a mug and set it on a chair arm. Gil's key was turning in the lock; she stooped and hoisted the bucket. His eyes slid greasily around the wreck of his equipment, and he made a quick move toward her, but once she tossed the bucket on him he stopped, perplexed, and sniffed. She took the butane lighter from the patch pocket on her skirt and with her other hand pulled back her hair to reveal the Gorgon. Gil's hands had just come up in supplication when he was turned to stone. She took a good swig from the mug and flicked the lighter's little wheel. A long bright tongue of fire stretched out and drew him wholly in.

IT WAS A WINDLESS DAY AND THE HOUSE BURNED ALL ALONE, flames rising vertically into the cloudless blue sky. The firemen came, the police came, they blocked off either end of the street and soaked the roofs of nearby houses, but there was nothing of the burning house to save. The people came out of houses that were not yet abandoned and stood on the sidewalks with folded arms and grimly watched it burn. Mackie Loudon stood in her half-cut yard, leaning on the mower for support. Her other arm was tightly wrapped around herself, because in spite of the spring weather and the fire's harsh heat she was feeling very cold. She waited to be taken into custody, but no one seemed to notice her at all, and when the fire had fallen into its own embers, she went into her house and shut the door.

Alice Schell

Alice Schell's first published short story is reprinted here; she is now at work on a cycle of stories.

Slamming On Pig's Misery

EVVIE TIGHTENED HER THIGHS and clenched her buttocks. Everything snapped shut. Her jaws stiffened. Her eyelids tensed, squeezing out the fading afternoon light. Inside her mittens her fingernails cut small wounds in her palms. Even her toes, her scalp, were poised hard as she waited for the snorts of edgy laughs. She finally forced her eyes open. Through the screen of her lashes she saw her plaid coat only half buttoned, saw the gooseflesh of her brown thighs, her cotton drawers down around her knees in thirty-degree weather.

Bean and his twin brother Joe Boy stared at the scant patch between Evvie's legs, Joe Boy looking as if he wanted to run. *"Hairs!"* he breathed coarsely, casting a frightened glance at his brother.

"Hush your mouth," Bean said. He straightened up and peered into Evvie's shut face, his voice a low whine. "How are we supposed to get a look if you don't spread yourself out?"

Evvie clamped her thighs tighter, setting her teeth against her lower lip, biting back the taste of shame. Bean took off his mittens, which were covered with crystals of snow, and tried to stick his finger into the small cleft between Evvie's legs. She hit him sharply with her right fist, landing a blow beneath one eye that sent him flailing onto the icy ground.

5   Joe Boy started to cry. Bean struggled and huffed to get back on his feet. "Aw, Evvie, you *said*, you *promised. . . .*"

Evvie jerked at her mittens, fumbling to pull up her drawers. Her voice came out high and ragged: "I *promised* a look, and you weren't supposed to touch me ever, ever, ever!"

Bean pinched his lips together, sullen, "Well, just for that, Evvie, you can only have one ride, not two."

Evvie held her breath, the old surge of helplessness swelling up inside her like dangerous rising waters. She tried not to shout: "If I don't get my two rides, Bean Stoner, I'll tell."

Bean let out a thin, shaky giggle, "If you tell, you're just telling on yourself. And everyone will know what you've been doing since Shuckle's took back your sled!"

10   He glared at her, triumphant, but there was a glaze of terror in his eyes. His mama would take the strap to him if she ever found out what he was up to. But it wasn't just a whipping he was afraid of. He was scared of Evvie, too; he thought she was crazy. Everyone on the Row thought she was crazy. Bean's mother had seen her in the middle of the night: standing out in the snow right out in the back yard, staring up at the town clock. And other people had timed her: over an hour in the outhouse. What could she be doing in there all that time?

Evvie gazed at Bean for a moment, at a loss, then she hit him again, breathing harshly through her mouth as if she couldn't take in enough air, or take it in fast enough. When she tried to bring her lips together, her jaws danced spasmodically. She knew she'd bitten the inside of her cheek only when her tongue touched the salty ooze in her flesh. She whirled at Joe Boy as if the sudden pain was his fault, slapping him off his haunches where he'd just leaned forward to see what she meant to trade for the use of Bean's new Flexible Flyer.

Now Bean and Joe Boy were both choking on tears. Just like ten-year-olds, Evvie thought. She gulped the frigid air.

"Where's the sled?" she demanded. Bean waved his mittened fist toward a clump of ice-covered bushes, then sank back into the snow, avoiding his brother's eyes.

The tightness in Evvie's chest, the feeling of being roped and knotted, began to ease as soon as she found the sled. She had discovered when she was only nine years old, the year she had leapt from the swing just when it reached its highest point, that there was nothing like the fierce liberty of sledding, nothing at all. You stood at the top of a long, deep hill, so high up that you couldn't see where it ended, the bottom lost somewhere on the floor of a steep white canyon. You closed your mouth on your fear, you chewed and tasted it and then spat it out. You let yourself drop, one with the sled, plummeting down, down, pins of sleet stinging your face. You were threshed bare by the wind, cut loose from your body, suspended in air that was cold and free. She picked up the sled and walked to the top of Pig's Misery—the most dangerous sledding spot in New Sharon, maybe in all of Meade County.

A steep hill for sledding, it dropped at a forty-five-degree angle from a wide plateau at the north end of Mr. Barron's sprawling estate. The place was a menace even on foot—an obstacle course of trees, rocks, thorny bushes and sudden deep fissures in the earth. It had seen dozens of sledding accidents; one of them had left Mose Burhannan with a body he would never feel, frozen from the chin down.

15   No one knew for sure how the hill had earned its sinister name. Deacon Holme said that the plateau at the top of Pig's Misery had been a hog butchering site many years ago when the Barron family kept its own cold storage house. At the butcher shop, when Mr. Gipe opened the door to the ice room, Evvie had glimpsed headless hog bodies, stiff, raw, hanging by their hind legs. She'd shut her eyes too late: she saw the hogs, squealing and bleeding, helpless.

Now, after her brief struggle with Bean, Evvie held the Flexible Flyer loosely, moving back as far as she could to the rear of the plateau. She needed plenty of room to run, gripping the sled aslant her body, slamming down on it just as she reached the edge of the hill, exploding in a headlong plunge down the scarred and pitted face of Pig's Misery.

In the watery, late-afternoon light, Evvie barely saw the black shapes that loomed in her path as she blazed through the packed snow. She already knew the landscape. She had learned it over many patient months, in hard daylight, when she could see the rocks and gnarled roots of trees and unexpected drops in the earth. She had plotted a path from the top to the bottom, where the hill ended abruptly, intersected by the long driveway which curved from the wide stone-arched entrance of the estate up to Mr. Barron's mansion a half-mile away.

Evvie retraced her route through the flat stretch of ground on the far side of the driveway and trudged to the top of Pig's Misery, breathing the scent of new snow in the air. The last light had drained from the sky by the time she reached the plateau. Bean and Joe Boy watched her from a distance, wary, impatient, slapping their hands against their thighs and stamping their feet up and down to keep warm. Bean shouted at her: "You just better hurry up, Evvie!"

Joe Boy echoed: "Yeah, you just better hurry up!"

20   Evvie deadened her ears to their voices and gripped the sled. She burned with anticipation, her body leaping forward and into the second ride—running, slamming, hurtling through the early winter twilight, skimming the earth, down past the driveway and into the tree-barricaded ground beyond.

The second ride was better than the first—colder, freer. When it was over she slowly climbed Pig's Misery and, wordless, handed the sled to Bean. He snatched the sled and ran with his brother, yelling as they zigzagged through the snow: "You're a crazy person, Evvie Tooms!"

Evvie winced. "I am not!" She stared at the two boys as they ran in the gathering dusk, watching them until they turned at the Row. She shouted again: "I am not!"

Her throat was hoarse. She felt suddenly lethargic. Shaking the snow from her mittens, she thrust her hands into her coat sleeves like a muff and stood gazing at the sprinkles of light that had gradually appeared in the windows of homes on the Row. From Pig's Misery she could see the entire street, including her house and those next to it, eerily awash in the light of the town clock. She lived in Old Row, in one of the two-room houses that originally had given the Row its name—six adjoining wood dwellings, unpainted, each hardly more than a narrow corridor with a bedroom atop a kitchen, all sharing a single long tin roof. A parallel row of outhouses ran along the edge of their common back yard.

Old Row looked especially cramped and desolate because it sat in the shadow of Town Council Hall, the rear of which, through some miscalculation in planning, was thrust right up against the meager back yard of the houses. Poised in an ornate turret on the roof of Council Hall was the stony light into the rear windows of every house in Old Row. Most folks shuttered their bedroom windows against the light with dark green blinds. Not Evvie's father. He would open the blind at night so that the clockface stared right into the bedroom, a harsh floodlight that burned away the shadows in every corner of the room. To Evvie, the clockface was not a face at all, but a blank lidless eye that watched everything.

25   A sifting snow had begun to fall. Evvie thought about her sled, now back on the shelf at Schuckle's Big Store in Dorsey. When she had first set eyes on the sled two months ago, she had looked away from it, afraid. It was a gift for her eleventh birthday. She had wanted the sled more than anything, even more than a trip to the carnival in Dorsey, where the girl with spangled wings walked in the air.

But when Papa had set the sled against the wall in the kitchen, her throat grew crowded. She didn't want a gift from Papa. When he gave her things, she wanted to run. In the summer, he had brought home a game of jacks for her. She'd left the jacks on the kitchen table and darted to the outhouse, where she sat on the gritty uneven flooring, her back against the loosely bolted door. She was still there as darkness fell.

When Papa forced open the door, Evvie half arose, stumbling backwards onto one of the lidded seats as he held a lantern to her face. She stood pinned by his look. He said nothing, only stared at her—a long look, narrow and still, as if he saw her through the sight of his hunting rifle. She heard her heartbeat in her ears.

Except for those occasional long looks, Papa hardly ever glanced at her. It was that way with Mama, too. They seldom looked at her or at each other, they hardly ever spoke, except for the little chips and pieces of talk that fell to the bottom of a well of dense silence: Fetch the kerosene jug. Get some more corncobs. From Mama: Bring me my Bible, Evva Lena.

When Evvie was still in third grade, she often awoke at night to the rasp of bedsprings from the room above her, a dull pounding somewhere in the walls, in the floor; her mother's voice, a sketched wire: "Please . . . Jesus have mercy!" The sound was everywhere. Instead of covering her ears, Evvie pressed her blanket tight against her eyes, trying to stop the pictures that came like an invasion from somewhere inside her. She breathed so fast her chest shook.

30   Her father would often cut the silence in the house by saying to Evvie, "Go on upstairs, girl." Sometimes he waited until Mama was out of the house; other times she was standing right there in the kitchen, or sitting by the stove with her Bible, trying to still the tremor in her hands, her eyes lost behind her reading glasses. And Evvie would go. She never cried. She had learned to push down her tears, to turn them back. They seemed to originate not in her eyes but in her throat. From there she would force them down into her chest, a brimming reservoir that left her congested, always filled up, afraid of drowning from the inside.

On the day Papa brought the new sled home, she had looked away from it, then back again. It was propped against the wall near the back door, where a dazzling winter sun played on its shellacked surface, bright as a mirror. She shut her eyes. Behind her eyelids an afterimage throbbed, the words SNOW BIRD in splotches of red, green, gold.

Papa stood looking out of the front window, only half turned in her direction. He held his body loose, his hands in his back pockets; a small muscle twitched along the side of his jaw as he shifted his tobacco from one cheek to the other. Evvie touched the Snow Bird, pulled away, touched it again. After a long, heavy moment, she had seized the sled, clutching it like a shield.

She stored the sled under the old davenport that served as her bed, pushed against one wall of the kitchen opposite the stairway. The bed was set away from the curtainless rear window and was partly screened by the stove, so that the full glare of the clock's eye never reached her.

When Papa and Mama were upstairs at night in bed, Evvie lay in that strange twilight, sometimes hugging herself as if to keep warm. She let her upper body dangle over the side of her bed, looking under it to reassure herself that the sled was in its special place. The blood would rush to her head, suffusing her face with heat, leaving her dizzy with longing: she waited for snow.

35 By the middle of December, a bitter winter had invaded the town, but there was no snow. Wind and ice storms tore the tar paper roofing off houses, destroyed trees. One of the ice storms brought down the mulberry tree in back of the A.M.E. church. Water froze in the pipes. Folks on the Row ran out of fuel, and the story went around that Rufus Beal's family down the street had chopped up and burned their old reed organ in the kitchen stove.

Rumors rustled along the Row like furtive wind: some colored men were caught stealing coal from the railroad yard. But no one was ever sure who it was that got caught, or if the thievery had every really happened. Evvie heard people talking about it in low voices when she went down to Heiser's for kerosene. "That wasn't Peter they caught down there in the yard, was it?" "Naw." "Was it Bolts?" "Naw." "Well then, who was it?"

The frigid spell dragged on. The town was beaten into numbness. Still there was no snow. At the end of the month Evvie's sled disappeared from its place under her bed. When she came home from school one day and looked for the sled, Papa and Mama were silent. Mama was at the stove, melting lard in a skillet, thick slices of scrapple on a plate in one hand. Her father was at the back door, using the ice pick to wedge newspaper into the cracks around the door.

Evvie knelt next to the davenport. When she saw that the sled was gone, she dropped to her hands and knees, staring at the empty space and sweeping it with her hand as if the sled were a miniature toy, a marble that had rolled into a corner; she would surely be able to fetch it from its hiding place if she groped long enough. She swept and swept, her one small whimper lost in the sizzling noise of frying scrapple and the dull chuck-chuck of

Papa's hammer as he tacked oilcloth over the crumpled newspapers around the door.

Evvie learned from Bean what had happened. He sought her out, prancing up to her in the schoolyard. "Haw, Evvie! Where's your new sled, Evvie? Looks like the man from Schuckle's came and took it back, hey, Evvie!"

40   Joe Boy mimicked his brother. "Looks like the man from Schuckle's came and took it back, hey, Evvie!"

It finally snowed on New Year's Day. Evvie looked at the snow with cinder-dry eyes. She wondered: if it had snowed earlier, if she'd had a chance to go sledding, would Schuckle's have repossessed a used sled? The snow continued, wiping out the boundaries that marked where the Row left off and the rest of New Sharon began, shrouding the town with a veil of spectral whiteness.

The sledding on Pig's Misery, what there was of it, seemed sharper, rasher than usual in the dense new snow. Every day after school Evvie walked up to the hill to watch. Others had come to watch, too, especially kids like Bean and Joe Boy who were too scared to do anything but coast on level ground in the schoolyard. Bean's new sled looked as though it had never been used.

AFTER BEAN AND JOE BOY WENT HOME, Evvie waited on Pig's Misery until it was nearly dark. Then, faltering, she started home too, once in a while lingering to scoop up a handful of snow in her mittens, tossing it into the air, where it danced and cascaded down on her upturned face. She made her way slowly, using one foot like a brush to form long, unbroken patterns in the snow. She finally stood in front of her house. Through the frost-glazed window she saw the weak glow from the kerosene lamp on the table.

When Evvie turned the knob of the front door, which opened into the kitchen, she smelled blood. She pulled back, afraid that she would see her mother bleeding, her father standing over her with his belt. But it was not her mother's blood she smelled. Evvie looked at Papa's hands, stained red up to his wrists. He had been skinning rabbits. Hunting illegally again, out of season. The frail carcasses of the rabbits floated in a galvanized tub of brick-colored water.

45   Her parents stood close to the stove. They'd had a habit of standing next to the stove to keep warm, and they stood there now even though it gave off hardly a spark of heat. Evvie glanced at the grate, where the ashes had already turned white, and at the empty coal bucket next to the chimney. Her mother, humming a gospel song under her breath, absently stirred a pan of hominy that looked cold and glutinous.

Evvie took off her coat and hung it on the back door, avoiding the mirror over the Victrola cabinet where they kept the washbasin. She reached into the cabinet for the washrag and wiped the dampness from her face, eyes still turned away from the glass. She used to look at herself in that mirror, trying to discover the secret fault in her that caused Papa and Mama to be always looking away from her, always staring at something on the other side of the room, at something outside the window. After a while Evvie stopped looking at herself in any mirror, turning away from her reflection in passing windows, even in the blade of a knife.

She sat at the kitchen table and pulled off her dripping galoshes, then with the floor rag carefully wiped up the pool of dirty water that had dribbled from her boots onto the linoleum. Mama came to the table with a plate of hominy, some biscuits still in the baking tin; she slid the can of syrup toward Evvie.

Evvie pried off the lid and spread a thin layer of syrup on the biscuits. She took small, nervous bites, like a sick person who is afraid the food won't stay down. She labored to breathe as she listened to the tense edge of Mama's voice singing "Jesus Is All the World to Me."

When Evvie finished eating, she noiselessly lay her fork on the empty plate. She sat with her knees and feet pressed hard against each other, elbows jammed close to her sides. She felt too big, too visible.

50   "Ten take away one is nine. . . ." Silently, she began to play the game she had made up in Miss Brubaker's class after she'd learned to do subtraction: "Nine take away one is eight, eight take away one is seven, seven take away one is six. . . ." And then: "Evvie, take away

toes is nine, Evvie take away feet is eight, Evvie take away legs is seven . . . Evvie, take away face is one, Evvie take away . . ."

Silence, as Mama scraped the leftover hominy into a Mason jar and put it in the icebox. Wiping her hands on the sides of her apron, she took the scoop from the coal bucket and started to remove the cold ashes from the grate.

Then her father spoke to Evvie without looking at her. "Get on upstairs, girl." She glanced at her mother's averted face, one cheek still mottled with old bruises.

Mama said, "Mind your papa, Evva Lena."

Evvie tried to swallow past the small fist of dread that squeezed her throat. She moved up the stairs, Papa behind her. They stepped into the bed-room, dark except for a thread of white light around the edges of the drawn window blind. Papa pulled sharply on the blind so that it snapped up with a loud crack. Light from the town clock flooded the room, where all around them, their clothes—Mama's, Papa's, her own—hung from nails driven into the walls, bunched empty shapes that crowded the narrow room, shrinking it down to a space that could not hold much more than the bed, Mama's rocking chair, the legless chest of drawers.

55   Evvie walked stiff-footed to her parents' bed and stared from the window at the row of outhouses, unreal in the glimmer of the big clock. In the silence every sound leapt up, magnified. She heard the swish of Papa's belt as he pulled it from the loops of his trousers; as he hung up the belt, the tiny click of the buckle scraping against the nail on the door. She could not look at him, but she knew that the glinting clockface silvered his nakedness with a patina of icy light.

The mattress tilted to one side when he dropped his weight onto the bed. She smelled rabbit blood on his hands, sticky against her face as he pulled her toward him. He let her go as she sank to her knees. Evvie closed her eyes, her gaze turned inward where she saw the town clock explode in shards of glass, petrifying them with eruptions of freezing light.

Downstairs in the kitchen, her mother kept singing in a low tight voice, "Jesus is all the world to me, my life, my joy, my all. . . . He is my friend, from day to day, without Him I would fall. . . ."

In the back yard that night, long after the Row had drifted into sleep, Evvie packed her mouth with snow and stood outside in the cold until numbness crept over her like a second skin and she stopped feeling anything at all.

EVVIE STOOD AT THE TOP OF PIG'S MISERY. It was snowing again as she watched the curling driveway at the foot of the hill. She had learned Mr. Barron's schedule so well that there was no longer any need to check the town clock. His Packard limousine, driven by Seth Price, always turned into the driveway after sunset, exactly as the clock chimed the first stroke of five. There would be snow-misted beams from the headlights of the car as it moved through the early dusk.

60   She had already made her bargain with Bean, right after school. "Well, do you want to?" His eyes glistened. She saw that he was afraid, that he was greedy. She wanted to hit him. "Well, *do* you?"

Bean stepped away from her, holding his sled awkwardly behind him. He wet his lip, dried it on the cuff of his sleeve. Then, with a sly, calculating look: "I don't know, Evvie."

She swallowed hard. She reached into her coat pocket and drew out a dingy, blue-flowered handkerchief, knotted at one end. Pulling off her mittens and holding them in her teeth, she undid the knot and removed a nickel and two pennies. She stuffed her mittens into one pocket and held the money toward Bean. "I have seven cents." The words came out half strangled. She watched him as he considered the coins. He looked away.

Then with sudden, spiteful firmness he announced, "Not until you admit you're a crazy person."

Evvie stared, shaken. She whispered. "I am *not a* crazy person!"

65   Bean set his lips. "Not until you admit you're a crazy person."

"No," she said.

Their eyes locked, and for a moment Bean's quivering mouth made her believe he would give up. But he persisted. She began to fear that she wouldn't get to use the sled after all. "You're a crazy person. Mama said so."

"No."

"Say it."

70 "No."

"All right for you, Evvie. . . ."

"No."

In the snow-hushed stillness they heard shouts and laughter from the sledders on the far side of Pig's Misery. Bean looked at her doggedly. "Not until you admit you're a crazy person."

Evvie's fist balled up inside her mittens. She gazed toward the Row, toward her house. Bean's voice seemed to drift toward her from a great distance: "You're not getting any rides, Evvie. Not until you admit you're . . ."

75 She stared past him. In a barely audible voice, clotted like the voice of someone who has just emerged from sleep, who has not spoken for a long time, she whispered, "I'm a crazy person."

Bean blinked at her, hesitant. Then he grabbed the money, jeering a little as he backed away. "You better not forget what else you owe me, either!" He was slipping and sliding, almost stumbling in the snow to get away from her.

Evvie shot back at him, tears scalding her throat: "*This* time, don't bring your stupid brother!"

Bean was already halfway down the hill. He shrieked at her in a high, tremulous voice: "You're only getting one ride, Evvie Tooms!"

EVVIE WAITED, HOLDING THE SLED UPRIGHT, its red runners planted in the snow. Standing at the top of Pig's Misery, watching smoke coil lazily out of some of the chimneys on the Row, seeing no smoke coming from her own house, she waited. Above her, the late afternoon sky, distant and white, took on a cold radiance. The snow had the look of ash as it drifted down in a fine powdery screen. She turned her gaze toward the south end of town.

80 In the distance, Mr. Barron's Packard moved slowly up Main Street and through the square. No other cars were on the road. The limousine paused at the stop sign in front of the post office, and Evvie knew, without looking at the clock, that it must be

three minutes to five. The car moved forward, past Council Hall, down past the Methodist church and up the hill where the lane into the Meredith Academy grounds began. Another pause for a stop sign, around the corner near the white cemetery. The car skidded slightly toward the cemetery fence, straightened itself. A long line of bare trees sheathed in ice. At last, in stately slow motion, the turn into the driveway of the Barron estate.

Evvie stood poised at the top of Pig's Misery, holding the sled aslant her body. The town clock began its deep chime. Five o'clock. She shivered. The unbidden images came fast, stuttering, flashing like an untended reel at the end of the picture show.

Five o'clock. At the sound of the hammer striking the bell, she streaks forward like wind-whipped fire, slamming the Flexible Flyer onto a snow-burdened earth that seems to leap up at her with the force of granite.

The chiming of the clock is lost in the rush of the wind, and the trees and rocks of Pig's Misery blur past her as she steers the sled toward the headlights on the Packard. She careens through the glittering landscape with such exactness that even she is caught by surprise when the Packard suddenly rears up in front of her, a black wall of steel dappled with chrome.

As she swings into the path of the car, its headlights slide wildly from side to side in a yellowish arc, like searchlights cut from their moorings.

85   Her body shudders and snaps as dark water floods her throat, rushes into her nostrils, streams from her eyes. The Flexible Flyer splinters beneath her and falls away in a hail of bright fragments, but she continues to glide, fighting the wind, fighting the pull of the earth, at last lifted up and soaring over the town under the power of her own shattered wings.

Terry Bisson

Terry Bisson published two stories in *The Isaac Asimov Science Fiction Magazine* in 1990; "Bears Discover Fire" has been nominated for a Nebula Award and included in an anthology of the year's best science fiction. In 1986, his novel *Talking Man* was a nominee for the World Fantasy Award. He has published several other novels including, *Wyrldmaker* and *Fire on the Mountain,* and a biography of Nat Turner.

Bears Discover Fire

I WAS DRIVING WITH MY BROTHER, the preacher, and my nephew, the preacher's son, on I-65 just north of Bowling Green when we got a flat. It was Sunday night and we had been to visit Mother at the Home. We were in my car. The flat caused what you might call knowing groans since, as the old-fashioned one in my family (so they tell me), I fix my own tires, and my brother is always telling me to get radials and quit buying old tires.

But if you know how to mount and fix tires yourself, you can pick them up for almost nothing.

Since it was a left rear tire, I pulled over left, onto the median grass. The way my Caddy stumbled to a stop, I figured the tire was ruined. "I guess there's no need asking if you have any of that *FlatFix* in the trunk," said Wallace.

"Here, son, hold the light," I said to Wallace Jr. He's old enough to want to help and not old enough (yet) to think he knows it all. If I'd married and had kids, he's the kind I'd have wanted.

5   An old Caddy has a big trunk that tends to fill up like a shed. Mine's a '56. Wallace was wearing his Sunday shirt, so he didn't offer to help while I pulled magazines, fishing tackle, wooden tool box, some old clothes, a comealong wrapped in a grass sack, and a tobacco sprayer out of the way, looking for my jack. The spare looked a little soft.

The light went out. "Shake it, son," I said.

It went back on. The bumper jack was long gone, but I carry a little 1/4 ton hydraulic. I finally found it under Mother's old *Southern Livings*, 1978–1986. I had been meaning to drop them at the dump. If Wallace hadn't been along, I'd have let Wallace Jr. position the jack under the axle, but I got on my knees and did it myself. There's nothing wrong with a boy learning to change a tire. Even if you're not going to fix and mount them, you're still going to have to change a few in this life. The light went off again before I had the wheel off the ground. I was surprised at how dark the night was already. It was late October and beginning to get cool. "Shake it again, son," I said.

It went back on but it was weak. Flickery.

"With radials you just don't *have* flats," Wallace explained in that voice he uses when he's talking to a number of people at once; in this case, Wallace Jr. and myself. "And even when you do, you just squirt them with this stuff called *FlatFix* and you just drive on. $3.95 the can."

10   "Uncle Bobby can fix a tire hisself," said Wallace Jr., out of loyalty I presume.

"Himself," I said from halfway under the car. If it was up to Wallace, the boy would talk like what Mother used to call "a helock from the gorges of the mountains." But drive on radials.

"Shake that light again," I said. It was about gone. I spun the lugs off into the hubcap and pulled the wheel. The tire had blown out along the sidewall. "Won't be fixing this one," I said. Not that I cared. I have a pile as tall as a man out by the barn.

The light went out again, then came back better than ever as I was fitting the spare over the lugs. "Much better," I said. There was a flood of dim orange flickery light. But when I turned to find the lug nuts, I was surprised to see that the flashlight the boy was holding was dead. The light was coming from two bears at the edge of the trees, holding torches. They were big, three-hundred pounders, standing about five feet tall. Wallace Jr. and his father had seen them and were standing perfectly still. It's best not to alarm bears.

I fished the lug nuts out of the hubcap and spun them on. I usually like to put a little oil on them, but this time I let it go. I reached under the car and let the jack down and pulled it out. I was relieved to see that the spare was high enough to drive on. I put the jack and lug wrench and the flat into the trunk. Instead of replacing the hubcap, I put it in there too. All this time, the bears never made a move. They just held the torches up, whether out of curiosity or helpfulness, there was no way of knowing. It looked like there may have been more bears behind them, in the trees.

15   Opening three doors at once, we got into the car and drove off. Wallace was the first to speak. "Looks like bears have discovered fire," he said.

WHEN WE FIRST TOOK MOTHER TO THE HOME, almost four years (forty-seven months) ago, she told Wallace and me she was ready to die. "Don't worry about me, boys," she whispered, pulling us both down so the nurse wouldn't hear. "I've drove a million miles and I'm ready to pass over to the other shore. I won't have long to linger here." She drove a consolidated school bus for thirty-nine years. Later, after Wallace left, she told me about her dream. A bunch of doctors were sitting around in a circle discussing her case. One said, "We've done all we can for her, boys, let's let her go." They all turned their hands up and smiled. When she didn't die that fall, she seemed disappointed, though as spring came she forgot about it, as old people will.

In addition to taking Wallace and Wallace Jr. to see Mother on Sunday nights, I go myself on Tuesdays and Thursdays. I usually find her sitting in front of the TV, even though she doesn't ing down.

"What's this I hear about bears discovering fire?" she said on
Tuesday. "It's true," I told her as I combed her long white hair
with the shell comb Wallace had bought her from Florida.
Monday there had been a story in the Louisville *Courier-Journal,*
and Tuesday one on NBC or CBS Nightly News. People were
seeing bears all over the state, and in Virginia as well. They had
quit hibernating, and were apparently planning to spend the
winter in the medians of the interstates. There have always been
bears in the mountains of Virginia, but not here in western
Kentucky, not for almost a hundred years. The last one was
killed when Mother was a girl. The theory in the *Courier-Journal*
was that they were following I-65 down from the forests of
Michigan and Canada, but one old man from Allen County
(interviewed on nationwide TV) said that there had always been
a few bears left back in the hills, and they had come out to join
the others now that they had discovered fire.

"They don't hibernate any more," I said. "They make a fire
and keep it going all winter."

20   "I declare," Mother said. "What'll they think of next!" The
nurse came to take her tobacco away, which is the signal for
bedtime.

EVERY OCTOBER, WALLACE JR. STAYS WITH ME while his
parents go to camp. I realize how backward that sounds, but
there it is. My brother is a minister (House of the Righteous
Way, Reformed), but he makes two thirds of his living in real
estate. He and Elizabeth go to a Christian Success Retreat in
South Carolina, where people from all over the country practice
selling things to one another. I know what it's like not because
they've ever bothered to tell me, but because I've seen the
Revolving Equity Success Plan ads late at night on TV.

The schoolbus let Wallace Jr. off at my house on Wednesday,
the day they left. The boy doesn't have to pack much of a bag
when he stays with me. He has his own room here. As the eldest
of our family, I hung onto the old home place near Smiths

Grove. It's getting run down, but Wallace Jr. and I don't mind. He has his own room in Bowling Green, too, but since Wallace and Elizabeth move to a different house every three months (part of the Plan), he keeps his .22 and his comics, the stuff that's important to a boy his age, in his room here at the home place. It's the room his dad and I used to share.

Wallace Jr. is twelve. I found him sitting on the back porch that overlooks the interstate when I got home from work. I sell crop insurance.

After I changed clothes, I showed him how to break the bead on a tire two ways, with a hammer and by backing a car over it. Like making sorghum, fixing tires by hand is a dying art. The boy caught on fast, though. "Tomorrow I'll show you how to mount your tire with the hammer and a tire iron," I said.

25   "What I wish is I could see the bears," he said. He was looking across the field to I-65, where the northbound lanes cut off the corner of our field. From the house at night, sometimes the traffic sounds like a waterfall.

"Can't see their fire in the daytime," I said. "But wait till tonight." That night CBS or NBC (I forget which is which) did a special on the bears, which were becoming a story of nationwide interest. They were seen in Kentucky, West Virginia, Missouri, Illinois (southern), and, of course, Virginia. There have always been bears in Virginia. Some characters there were even talking about hunting them. A scientist said they were heading into the states where there is some snow but not too much, and where there is enough timber in the medians for firewood. He had gone in with a video camera, but his shots were just blurry figures sitting around a fire. Another scientist said the bears were attracted by the berries on a new bush that grew only in the medians of the interstates. He claimed this berry was the first new species in recent history, brought about by the mixing of seeds along the highway. He ate one on TV, making a face, and called it a "newberry." A climatic ecologist said that the warm winters (there was no snow last winter in Nashville, and only one flurry in Louisville) had changed the bears' hibernation cycle, and now they were able to remember things from year to year. "Bears may have discovered fire centuries ago," he said, "but forgot it." Another theory was that they had discovered (or remembered) fire when Yellowstone burned, several years ago.

The TV showed more guys talking about bears than it showed bears, and Wallace Jr. and I lost interest. After the supper dishes were done I took the boy out behind the house and down to our fence. Across the interstate and through the trees, we could see the light of the bears' fire. Wallace Jr. wanted to go back to the house and get his .22 and go shoot one, and I explained why that would be wrong. "Besides," I said, "a .22 wouldn't do much more to a bear than make it mad."

"Besides," I added, "It's illegal to hunt in the medians."

THE ONLY TRICK TO MOUNTING A TIRE BY HAND, once you have beaten or pried it onto the rim, is setting the bead. You do this by setting the tire upright, sitting on it, and bouncing it up and down between your legs while the air goes in. When the bead sets on the rim, it makes a satisfying "pop." On Thursday, I kept Wallace Jr. home from school and showed him how to do this until he got it right. Then we climbed our fence and crossed the field to get a look at the bears.

In northern Virginia, according to "Good Morning America," the bears were keeping their fires going all day long. Here in western Kentucky, though, it was still warm for late October and they only stayed around the fires at night. Where they went and what they did in the daytime, I don't know. Maybe they were watching from the newberry bushes as Wallace Jr. and I climbed the government fence and crossed the northbound lanes. I carried an axe and Wallace Jr. brought his .22, not because he wanted to kill a bear but because a boy likes to carry some kind of a gun. The median was all tangled with brush and vines under the maples, oaks, and sycamores. Even though we were only a hundred yards from the house, I had never been there, and neither had anyone else that I knew of. It was like a created country. We found a path in the center and followed it down across a slow, short stream that flowed out of one grate and into another. The tracks in the gray mud were the first bear signs we saw. There was a musty but not really unpleasant smell. In a clearing under a big hollow beech, where the fire had been, we found nothing but ashes. Logs were drawn up in a rough circle and the smell was stronger. I stirred the ashes and found enough coals left to start a new flame, so I banked them back the way they had been left.

I cut a little firewood and stacked it to one side, just to be neighborly.

Maybe the bears were watching us from the bushes even then. There's no way to know. I tasted one of the newberries and spit it out. It was so sweet it was sour, just the sort of thing you would imagine a bear would like.

THAT EVENING AFTER SUPPER, I ASKED WALLACE JR. if he might want to go with me to visit Mother. I wasn't surprised when he said "yes." Kids have more consideration than folks give them credit for. We found her sitting on the concrete front porch of the Home, watching the cars go by on I-65. The nurse said she had been agitated all day. I wasn't surprised by that, either. Every fall as the leaves change, she gets restless, maybe the word is hopeful, again. I brought her into the dayroom and combed her long white hair. "Nothing but bears on TV anymore," the nurse complained, flipping the channels. Wallace Jr. picked up the remote after the nurse left, and we watched a CBS or NBC Special Report about some hunters in Virginia who had gotten their houses torched. The TV interviewed a hunter and his wife whose $117,500 Shenandoah Valley home had burned. She blamed the bears. He didn't blame the bears, but he was suing for compensation from the state since he had a valid hunting license. The state hunting commissioner came on and said that possession of a hunting license didn't prohibit (enjoin, I think, was the word he used) *the hunted* from striking back. I thought that was a pretty liberal view for a state commissioner. Of course, he had a vested interest in not paying off. I'm not a hunter myself.

"Don't bother coming on Sunday," Mother told Wallace Jr. with a wink. "I've drove a million miles and I've got one hand on the gate." I'm used to her saying stuff like that, especially in the

fall, but I was afraid it would upset the boy. In fact, he looked
worried after we left and I asked him what was wrong.

35   "How could she have drove a million miles?" he asked. She
had told him 48 miles a day for 39 years, and he had worked it
out on his calculator to be 336,960 miles.

"Have *driven*," I said. "And it's forty-eight in the morning
and forty-eight in the afternoon. Plus there were the football
trips. Plus, old folks exaggerate a little." Mother was the first
woman school bus driver in the state. She did it every day and
raised a family, too. Dad just farmed.

I USUALLY GET OFF THE INTERSTATE AT SMITHS
GROVE, but that night I drove north all the way to Horse Cave
and doubled back so Wallace Jr. and I could see the bears' fires.
There were not as many as you would think from the TV—one
every six or seven miles, hidden back in a clump of trees or
under a rocky ledge. Probably they look for water as well as wood.
Wallace Jr. wanted to stop, but it's against the law to stop on the
interstate and I was afraid the state police would run us off.

There was a card from Wallace in the mailbox. He and
Elizabeth were doing fine and having a wonderful time. Not a word
about Wallace Jr., but the boy didn't seem to mind. Like most kids
his age, he doesn't really enjoy going places with his parents.

ON SATURDAY AFTERNOON, THE HOME CALLED MY
OFFICE (Burley Belt Drought & Hail) and left word that
Mother was gone. I was on the road. I work Saturdays. It's the
only day a lot of part-time farmers are home. My heart literally
skipped a beat when I called in and got the message, but only a
beat. I had long been prepared. "It's a blessing," I said when I
got the nurse on the phone.

40   "You don't understand," the nurse said. "Not *passed* away,
gone. *Ran* away, gone. Your mother has escaped." Mother had
gone through the door at the end of the corridor when no one was
looking, wedging the door with her comb and taking a bedspread
which belonged to the Home. What about her tobacco? I asked.

It was gone. That was a sure sign she was planning to stay away. I was in Franklin, and it took me less than an hour to get to the Home on I-65. The nurse told me that Mother had been acting more and more confused lately. Of course they are going to say that. We looked around the grounds, which is only an acre with no trees between the interstate and a soybean field. Then they had me leave a message at the Sheriff's office. I would have to keep paying for her care until she was officially listed as Missing, which would be Monday.

It was dark by the time I got back to the house, and Wallace Jr. was fixing supper. This just involves opening a few cans, already selected and grouped together with a rubber band. I told him his grandmother had gone, and he nodded, saying, "She told us she would be." I called Florida and left a message. There was nothing more to be done. I sat down and tried to watch TV, but there was nothing on. Then, I looked out the back door, and saw the fire-light twinkling through the trees across the northbound lane of I-65, and realized I just might know where to find her.

IT WAS DEFINITELY GETTING COLDER, so I got my jacket. I told the boy to wait by the phone in case the Sheriff called, but when I looked back, halfway across the field, there he was behind me. He didn't have a jacket. I let him catch up. He was carrying his .22, and I made him leave it leaning against our fence. It was harder climbing the government fence in the dark, at my age, than it had been in the daylight. I am sixty-one. The highway was busy with cars heading south and trucks heading north.

Crossing the shoulder, I got my pants cuffs wet on the long grass, already wet with dew. It is actually bluegrass.

The first few feet into the trees it was pitch black and the boy grabbed my hand. Then it got lighter. At first I thought it was the moon, but it was the high beams shining like moonlight into the treetops, allowing Wallace Jr. and me to pick our way through the brush. We soon found the path and its familiar bear smell.

I was wary of approaching the bears at night. If we stayed on the path we might run into one in the dark, but if we went

234 | Terry Bisson

through the bushes we might be seen as intruders. I wondered if maybe we shouldn't have brought the gun.

We stayed on the path. The light seemed to drip down from the canopy of the woods like rain. The going was easy, especially if we didn't try to look at the path but let our feet find their own way.

Then through the trees I saw their fire.

THE FIRE WAS MOSTLY OF SYCAMORE AND BEECH BRANCHES, the kind of fire that puts out very little heat or light and lots of smoke. The bears hadn't learned the ins and outs of wood yet. They did okay at tending it, though. A large cinnamon brown northern-looking bear was poking the fire with a stick, adding a branch now and then from a pile at his side. The others sat around in a loose circle on the logs. Most were smaller black or honey bears, one was a mother with cubs. Some were eating berries from a hubcap. Not eating, but just watching the fire, my mother sat among them with the bedspread from the Home around her shoulders.

If the bears noticed us, they didn't let on. Mother patted a spot right next to her on the log and I sat down. A bear moved over to let Wallace Jr. sit on her other side.

50   The bear smell is rank but not unpleasant, once you get used to it. It's not like a barn smell, but wilder. I leaned over to whisper something to Mother and she shook her head. *It would be rude to whisper around these creatures that don't possess the power of speech,* she let me know without speaking. Wallace Jr. was silent too. Mother shared the bedspread with us and we sat for what seemed hours, looking into the fire.

The big bear tended the fire, breaking up the dry branches by holding one end and stepping on them, like people do. He was good at keeping it going at the same level. Another bear poked the fire from time to time, but the others left it alone. It looked like only a few of the bears knew how to use fire, and were carrying the others along. But isn't that how it is with everything? Every once in a while, a smaller bear walked into the circle of firelight with an armload of wood and dropped it onto the pile. Median wood has a silvery cast, like driftwood.

Wallace Jr. isn't fidgety like a lot of kids. I found it pleasant to sit and stare into the fire. I took a little piece of Mother's *Red Man*, though I don't generally chew. It was no different from visiting her at the Home, only more interesting, because of the bears. There were about eight or ten of them. Inside the fire itself, things weren't so dull, either: little dramas were being played out as fiery chambers were created and then destroyed in a crashing of sparks. My imagination ran wild. I looked around the circle at the bears and wondered what they saw. Some had their eyes closed. Though they were gathered together, their spirits still seemed solitary, as if each bear was sitting alone in front of its own fire.

The hubcap came around and we all took some newberries. I don't know about Mother, but I just pretended to eat mine. Wallace Jr. made a face and spit his out. When he went to sleep, I wrapped the bedspread around all three of us. It was getting colder and we were not provided, like the bears, with fur. I was ready to go home, but not Mother. She pointed up toward the canopy of trees, where a light was spreading, and then pointed to herself. Did she think it was angels approaching from on high? It was only the high beams of some southbound truck, but she seemed mighty pleased. Holding her hand, I felt it grow colder and colder in mine.

WALLACE JR. WOKE ME UP BY TAPPING ON MY KNEE. It was past dawn, and his grandmother had died sitting on the log between us. The fire was banked up and the bears were gone and someone was crashing straight through the woods, ignoring the path. It was Wallace. Two state troopers were right behind him. He was wearing a white shirt, and I realized it was Sunday morning. Underneath his sadness on learning of Mother's death, he looked peeved.

55   The troopers were sniffing the air and nodding. The bear smell was still strong. Wallace and I wrapped Mother in the bedspread and started with her body back out to the highway. The troopers stayed behind and scattered the bears' ashes and flung their firewood away into the brushes. It seemed a petty thing to

do. They were like bears themselves, each one solitary in his own uniform.

There was Wallace's Olds 98 on the median, with its radial tires looking squashed on the grass. In front of it there was a police car with a trooper standing beside it, and behind it a funeral home hearse, also an Olds 98.

"First report we've had of them bothering old folks," the trooper said to Wallace. "That's not hardly what happened at all," I said, but nobody asked me to explain. They have their own procedures. Two men in suits got out of the hearse and opened the rear door. That to me was the point at which Mother departed this life. After we put her in, I put my arms around the boy. He was shivering even though it wasn't that cold. Sometimes death will do that, especially at dawn, with the police around and the grass wet, even when it comes as a friend.

We stood for a minute watching the cars pass. "It's a blessing," Wallace said. It's surprising how much traffic there is at 6:22 A.M.

THAT AFTERNOON, I WENT BACK TO THE MEDIAN and cut a little firewood to replace what the troopers had flung away. I could see the fire through the trees that night.

60   I went back two nights later, after the funeral. The fire was going and it was the same bunch of bears, as far as I could tell. I sat around with them a while but it seemed to make them nervous, so I went home. I had taken a handful of newberries from the hubcap, and on Sunday I went with the boy and arranged them on Mother's grave. I tried again, but it's no use, you can't eat them.

Unless you're a bear.

Rick Bass

Rick Bass is the author of *The Watch, The Deer Pasture, Oil Notes: A Narrative, Wild to the Heart,* and *Winter: Notes from Montana.* His stories have been reprinted in *The Best American Short Stories, O. Henry Prize* annuals, *Editor's Choice,* and *New Stories from the South.*

Fires

SOME YEARS THE HEAT COMES IN APRIL. There is always wind in April, but with luck, there is warmth, too. There is usually a drought, so that the fields are dry, and the wind is from the south. Everyone in the valley moves their seedlings from the indoors to the outdoors, into their old barns-turned-into greenhouses. Root crops are what do best up here. The soil is rich from all the many fires, and potatoes from this valley taste like candy. Carrots pull free of the dark earth and taste like crisp sun. I like to cook with onions. Strawberries do well, too, if they're kept watered.

The snow line has moved up out of the valley by April, up into the woods, and even on up above the woods, disappearing, except for the smallest remote oval patches of it, and the snowshoe hares, gaunt but still white, move down out of the snow as it retreats to get to the gardens' fresh berries and the green growing grasses; but you can see the hares coming a mile away, coming after your berries—hopping through the green-and-gold sun-filled woods, as white and pure as Persian cats, hopping over brown logs, coming down the centuries-old game trails of black earth.

The rabbits come straight for my outside garden like zombies, relentless, and I sit on the back porch and sight in on them. But because they are too beautiful to kill in great numbers, I shoot only one every month or so, just to warn them. I clean the one I shoot and fry it in a skillet with onions and half a piece of bacon.

Sometimes at night I'll get up and look out the window and see the rabbits out in the garden, nibbling at whatever's available, but also standing around the greenhouse, all around it, just *aching* to get in: several of them digging at the earth around it, trying to tunnel in—dirt flying all through the air—while others of them just sit there at the doorway, waiting.

5 The hares are only snow-white like that for a few weeks, after the snow is gone; then they begin to lose the white fur—or rather, they do not lose it, but it begins to turn brown, like leaves decaying, so that they are mottled for a while, during the change, but then finally they are completely brown, and safe again, with the snows gone. But for those few weeks when they are still white, the rabbits sit out in my garden like white boulders. I haven't had a woman living with me in a long time now. Whenever one does move in with me, it feels as if I've tricked her, have caught her in a trap: as if the gate has been closed behind her and she doesn't yet realize it. It's very remote up here.

ONE SUMMER, MY FRIEND TOM'S SISTER CAME UP here to spend the summer with Tom and his wife, Nancy, and to train at altitude. Her name was Glenda, and she was a runner from Washington, and that was all she did, was run. Glenda was very good, and she had run in races in Italy, in France, and in Switzerland. She told everyone when she got up here that this was the most beautiful place that she had ever seen, told all these rough loggers and their hard wives this, and we all believed her. Very few of us had ever been anywhere else to be able to question her.

We would all sit out at the picnic tables in front of the saloon, ten or twelve of us at a time, half the town, and watch the river. Ducks and geese, heading back north, stopped in our valley to breed, to build nests, and to raise their young. Ravens, with their wings and backs shining greasy in the sun, were always flying across the valley, from one side of the mountains to the other. Anyone who needed to make a little money could always do so in April by planting seedlings for the Forest Service, and it was always a time of relaxation because of that fact, a time of no tempers, only loose happiness. I did not need much money, in April or in any other month, and I would often sit out at the picnic table with Glenda and Tom and Nancy and drink beer. Glenda would never drink more than two. She had yellow hair that was cut short, and lake-blue eyes, a pale face, and a big grin, not unlike Tom's, that belied her seriousness, though now that she is gone, I think I remember her always being able to grin *because* of her seriousness. I certainly don't understand why it seems that way to me now. Like the rest of us, Glenda has no worries, not in April, and certainly not later on in the summer. She had only to run.

I never saw Glenda in the fall, which was when she left; I don't know if she ever smiled like that when she got back to Washington or not. She was separated from her boyfriend, who lived in California, and she didn't seem to miss him, didn't ever seem to think about him.

The planters burned the slopes they had cut the previous summer and fall, before planting the seedlings, and in the afternoons there would be a sweet-smelling haze that started about halfway up the valley walls and rose into the highest mountains and then spilled over them, moving north into Canada, riding on the south winds. The fires' haze never settled in our valley but would hang just above us, on the days it was there, turning all the sunlight a beautiful, smoky blue and making things when seen across the valley—a barn in another pasture, or a fence line—seem much farther away than they really were. It made things seem softer, too.

There was a long, zippered scar on the inside of Glenda's knee that started just above her ankle and went all the way up inside her leg to mid-thigh. She had injured the knee when she was seventeen, long before the days of arthroscopic surgery, and she'd had to have the knee rebuilt the old-fashioned way, with blades and scissors, but the scar only seemed to make her legs, both of them, look even more beautiful, the part that was not scarred, and even the scar had a graceful curve to it as it ran such a long distance up her leg.

Glenda wore green nylon shorts and a small white shirt when she ran, and a headband. Her running shoes were dirty white, the color of the road dust during the drought.

"I'm thirty-two, and have six or seven more good years of running," she said whenever anyone asked her what her plans were, and why she ran so much, and why she had come to our valley to run. Mostly, it was the men who sat around with us in front of the saloon, watching the river, watching the spring winds, and just being glad with the rest of us that winter was over. I do not think the women liked Glenda very much, except for Nancy.

It was not very well understood in the valley what a great runner Glenda was.

I think it gave Glenda pleasure that it wasn't.

15 "I WOULD LIKE FOR YOU TO FOLLOW GLENDA ON THE BICYCLE," Tom said the first time I met her. Tom had invited me over for dinner—Glenda had gotten into the valley the day before, though we had all known that she was coming for weeks beforehand, and we had been waiting for her.

"There's money available from her sponsor to pay you for it," Tom said, handing me some money, or trying to, finally putting it in my shirt pocket. He had been drinking, and seemed as happy as I had seen him in a long time. He called her "Glen" instead of "Glenda" sometimes—and after putting the money in my pocket, he put an arm around Nancy, who looked embarrassed for me, and the other arm around Glenda, who did not, and so I had to keep the money, which was not that much, anyway.

"You just ride along behind her, with a pistol"—Tom had a pistol holstered on his belt, a big pistol, and he took it off and handed it to me—"and you make sure nothing happens to her, the way it did to that Ocherson woman."

The Ocherson woman had been visiting friends and had been walking home, but had never made it: a bear had evidently charged out of the willows along the river road and had dragged her back across the river. It was in the spring when she disappeared, and everyone thought she had run away; and her husband had even gone around all summer making a fool out of himself by talking badly about her, and then hunters found her in the fall, right before the first snow. There were always bear stories in any valley, but we thought ours was the worst, because it was the most recent, and because it had been a woman.

"It'll be good exercise for me," I said to Tom, and then I said to Glenda, "Do you run fast?"

20 IT WASN'T A BAD JOB. I was able to keep up with her most of the time, and we started early in the mornings. Some days Glenda would run a few miles, very fast, and other days it seemed she was going to run forever. There was hardly ever any traffic— not a single car or truck—and I'd daydream as I rode along behind her.

We'd leave the meadows out in front of Tom's place and head up the South Fork road, up into the woods, toward the summit, going past my cabin. The sun would be burning brightly by the time we neared the summit, and we'd be up into the haze from the planting fires, and everything would be foggy and old-looking, as if we had gone back in time—as if we were living in a time when things had really *happened,* when things still mattered and not everything had been decided yet.

Glenda would be sweating so hard from running the summit that her shirt and shorts would be drenched, her hair damp and sticking to the side of her face, and the sweat would wet her socks and even her tennis shoes. But she was always saying that the people she would be racing against would be training even harder than she was.

There were lakes up past the summit and the air was cooler; on the north slopes the lakes still had thin crusts of ice over them, crusts that thawed out, barely, each afternoon, but that froze again each night, and what Glenda liked to do after she'd reached the summit—her face as bright as if sunburned, and her wrists limp and loose, sometimes wavering a little in her stride, finally, so great was the heat, and her exhaustion—was to leave the road and run down the game trail leading to the lakes—tripping, stumbling, running downhill again; and I would have to throw the bike down and hurry after her—and pulling her shirt off, she would run out into the shallows of the first lake, her feet breaking through the thin ice, and then she would sit down in the cold water, like some animal chased there by hounds.

"It feels good," she said, the first time she did that, and she leaned her head back on the ice behind her, the ice she had not broken through, and she spread her arms out across the ice as if she were resting on a crucifix, and she looked up at the haze in the sky, with nothing above us, for we were above the tree line.

25 "Come over here," she said. "Come feel this."

I waded out into the pond, following her trail through the ice, and sat down next to her.

She took my hand and put it on her chest.

What I felt in there was like nothing I had ever imagined: it was like lifting up the hood of a car that is still running, with all the cables and belts and fan blades still running. I wanted to take my hand away; I wanted to get her to a doctor I wondered if she was going to die, and if I would be responsible. I wanted to pull my hand away, but she made me keep it there, and gradually the drumming slowed, became steadier, and still she made me keep my hand there, until we could both feel the water's coldness. Then we got out—I had to help her up, because her injured knee was stiff—and we laid our clothes out on rocks to dry in the sun, and we lay out on flat rocks ourselves and let the wind and sun dry us as well. She said that she had come to the mountains to run because it would strengthen her knee. But there was something that made me believe that that was not the reason, and not the truth, though I cannot tell you what other reason there might have been.

We went into the lake every hot day, after her run, and there was always the thinnest sheet of ice, back in the shadows. It felt wonderful; and lying out in the sun afterward was wonderful, too. After we had dried, our hair smelled like the smoke from the fires in the valley below. Sometimes I thought that Glenda might be dying, and had come here to live her last days, to run in country of great beauty.

30   AFTER WE WERE DRY, we walked back, and as we went back over the crest of the summit and started down toward the valley, we would slowly come out of the haze, and would be able to see all of the valley below us, green and soft, with the slow wind of the Yaak River crawling through the middle of it, and on the north wall of the valley, midway up the slopes, the ragged fires would be burning, with wavering lines and shifting walls of smoke rising from behind the trees, sheets of smoke rising straight into the sky.

The temptation to get on the bike and just coast all the way down was always strong, but I knew what my job was, we both did, and it was the time when the bears were coming out of hibernation, when everything was, and the safety of the winter was not to be confused with the seriousness of summer, with the way things were changing.

Sometimes, walking back, we could come upon ruffed grouse—males—courting and fanning in the middle of the road, spinning and doing their little dance, their throat sacs inflated bright and red, pulsing, and the grouse would not want to let us past—they would stamp their feet and spin in mad little circles, trying to block where it was we were going, trying to protect some certain small area they had staked out for themselves. Glenda seemed to stiffen whenever we came upon the fanning males, and shrieked when they rushed at her ankles, making as if to peck her.

We would stop back by my cabin for lunch, on the way back into the valley. I would open all the windows—the sun would have heated all the logs in the house, so that when we came inside there was a rich dry smell, as it is when you have been away from your house for a long time and first come back—but that smell was always there, in my cabin—and we would sit at the breakfast-room table and look out the window, out at the old weedy chicken house I'd never used but which the people who had lived in the cabin before me had built, and we would look at the woods going up onto the mountain behind the chicken house.

I had planted a few wild apple trees in the back yard that spring, and the place that had sold them to me said that these trees would be able to withstand even the coldest winters, though I was not sure I believed it. They were small trees, and it was supposed to be four years before they began bearing fruit, and that sounded to me like such a long time that I had to really think about it before buying them. But I just bought them without really knowing why I was doing it. I also didn't know what would make a person run as much as Glenda did. But I liked riding with her, and having coffee with her after the runs, and I knew I would be sad to see her leave the valley. I think that was what kept up the distance between us, a nice distance, just the right-sized distance—the fact that each of us knew that she was only going to be there a certain amount of time—that she would be there for the rest of May and June, and all through July, and on through most of August, but that then she would be gone. We knew what was going to happen, it was a certainty, and therefore it seemed to take away any danger, any wildness. There was a wonderful sense of control. She drank her coffee black. We would snack on smoked whitefish that I had caught the previous winter.

35   I had a couple of dogs in the back yard. Texas hounds that I'd brought up north with me a few years ago, and I kept them in a pen in the winter so that they wouldn't roam and chase and catch deer, but in the spring and summer the sun felt so thin and good and the hounds were so old that I didn't keep them penned up but instead just let them lie around in the grass, dozing. There was one thing they would chase, though, in the summer. It lived under the chicken house—I don't know what it was; it was dark, and ran too fast for me to ever get a good look at it— and it's also possible that even if I had been able to see it, it would have been some animal that I had never seen before—some rare animal, something from Canada perhaps—maybe something no one had ever seen. Whatever it was—small and dark, with fur, but not shaggy, not a bear cub—it never grew from year to year, but always stayed the same, through it seemed young

somehow, as if it might *someday* grow—anyway, it lived in a burrow under the chicken house, and it excited the dogs terribly. It would come ripping out of the woods, just a fleet dark blur through the woods, headed for the burrow, and the old dogs would be up and baying, right on its tail, but the thing always made it into the burrow just ahead of them.

Glenda and I would sit at the window and watch for it. But it kept no timetable, and there was no telling when it would come, or even if it would. We called it a hedgehog, because that was the closest thing we figured it resembled.

Some nights Glenda would call me on the shortwave radio, would key the mike a few times to make it crackle and wake me up, and then, mysteriously, I would hear her voice in the night, floating in static, as if it were in the night, out with the stars—her voice: "Have you seen the hedgehog?" she would ask, sleepily, but it would only be a radio that was in the dark house with me, not her, not her real voice. "Did you see the hedgehog?" she'd want to know, and I'd wish she were staying with me, I'd wish she were with me at that moment. But it would be no good—Glenda was leaving in August, or September at the latest.

"No," I'd say. "No hedgehog today. Maybe it's gone away." I'd say—though I had thought that again and again, dozen of times, but then I would always see it again, just when I thought I never would.

"How are the dogs?" she'd ask. "How are Homer and Ann?"

40   "They're asleep."

"Good night," she'd say.

"Good night," I would say.

ON THURSDAY NIGHTS, I would always have Tom and Nancy and Glenda over for dinner. Friday was Glenda's day off from running, so that she could drink, could stay up late, and she did not have to worry about any aftereffects the next morning. We would start out drinking at the Dirty Shame, sitting out front watching the river, watching the ducks and geese headed north, and then before dusk we would go back down to my ranch, and Glenda and I would fix dinner while Tom and Nancy sat on the front porch and smoked cigars and watched the elk come out into the dusk in the meadow across the road.

"Where's this famous hedgehog?" Tom would bellow, blowing smoke rings into the night, big, perfect O's, and the elk would lift their heads, chewing the summer grass like cattle, the bulls' antlers glowing with velvet.

45 "In the back yard," Glenda would say, washing the salad, or rinsing off the carrots, or the trout filets. "But you can only see him in the daytime."

"Aww, *bullshit!*" Tom would roar, standing up with his bottle of Jack Daniel's, and he'd take off down the steps, stumbling, and we'd all put down what we were doing and get flashlights and go with him to make sure he was all right, because Tom was a trapper, and it riled him to think there was an animal he did not know, could not trap, could not even see—Tom had tried to trap the hedgehog before but had never caught anything—and Tom did not believe there was any such animal. Out by the chicken coop, Tom would get down on his hands and knees, breathing hard, and we'd crowd all around and try to shine the flashlight into the deep, dusty hole, to see if there might be a patch of fur, the tip of a snout, *anything*—and Tom would be making grunting noises that were, I supposed, designed to make the animal want to come out—but we never saw anything, and it would be cold under all the stars, and we'd be able to see the far-off glows that were the planting fires, burning slowly, even into the night, but which were being held in check by backfires; they were in control.

WE HAD ONE OF THOSE PROPANE FISH FRYERS, and we'd put it out on the front porch and cut the trout into cubes, roll them around in sweet mustard and flour, then drop them in the hot spattering grease. We'd fix more than a hundred of the trout cubes, and there were never any left over. Glenda had a tremendous appetite, eating almost as many as would Tom, and licking her fingers afterward, asking if there were any more. We'd take whatever we were drinking up on the roof—Tom, his Jack Daniel's, and Glenda and I, rum-and-Cokes, and Nancy, vodka—and we'd sit high on the steep roof of my cabin, above the second-story bedroom dormer—Tom sat out on the end of the dormer as if it were a saddle—and Glenda would sit next to me for warmth, as we'd watch the far-off fires of the burns, a flaming orange color as they sawed their way across the mountainside, raging, but contained. Below us, in the back yard, those rabbits that had still not turned brown would begin to come out of the woods, dozens of them, moving in on the greenhouse and then stopping, just lining up all around it, wanting to get into the tender young carrots and the Simpson lettuce. I had put sheets down on the ground out in the back yard to trick them, and we'd laugh as the rabbits moved nervously from sheet to sheet, several of them huddling together on one sheet at a time, thinking they were protected; and, all the time, moving in on the greenhouse.

"Turn back, you bastards!" Tom would shout happily, whenever he saw the rabbits start coming out of the woods in the moonlight, and his shouts would wake the ducks down on the pond, and they would begin clucking to themselves, quacking, and it was a reassuring sound. Nancy made Tom tie a rope around his waist and tie the other end around the chimney in case he fell. But Tom said that he wasn't afraid of anything, and that he was going to live forever.

GLENDA WEIGHED HERSELF BEFORE AND AFTER EACH RUN. I had to remember that I did not want to grow too close to her, as she would be leaving. I only wanted to be her friend. We ran and rode in silence. We never saw any bears. But she was frightened of them, even as the summer went on without us seeing any, and so I always carried the pistol. We had been pale from the long sunless winter, but were beginning to grow brown from lying out by the lake up at the summit. Glenda took long naps after her runs, we both did, Glenda sleeping on my couch, and I'd cover her with a blanket and lie down on the floor next to her, and the sun would pour in through the windows, and there was no world outside our valley. But I could feel my heart pounding.

———

50   IT TURNED DRIER THAN EVER IN AUGUST. The loggers were cutting again. It was always dry and windy, and the fields and meadows turned to crisp hay. Everyone was terrified of sparks, especially the old people, because they'd seen the big fires rush through the valley in the past, moving through like an army—the big fire in 1901, and then the monstrous one, in 1921, that burned up every tree except for the very luckiest ones, so that for years afterward the entire valley was barren and scorched, smoldering—and the wind in our faces was hot, and we went down to the saloon in the early afternoons, after we had stopped off at my cabin, and we'd drink beer.

  Glenda would lie on her back on top of the picnic table and look up at the clouds. She would be going back to Washington in three weeks, and then down to California, she said. We were both as brown as nuts. Almost all the men would be off in the woods, logging. We would have the whole valley to ourselves. Tom and Nancy had been calling us "the lovebirds" in July, trying to get something going, I think, but they stopped in August. She was running harder than ever, really improving, so that I was having trouble keeping up with her near the top of the summit, on the days that Glenda ran it.

  There was no ice left anywhere, no snow, not even in the darkest, coolest parts of the forest, but the lakes and ponds and creeks and rivers were still ice-cold when we leaped into them, hot and heart-hammering; and each time, Glenda made me put my hand on her breast, her heart thumping and jumping around as if about to burst out, until I could finally feel it calming, and then almost stopping, as the lake's cold waters worked on her.

  "Don't you ever leave this place, Joe Barry," she'd say to me as she watched the clouds. "You've got it really good here, Joe Barry."

  I'd be stroking her knee with my fingers, running them along the inside scar, and the wind would be moving her hair around. She would close her eyes after a while, and it was hot, but there would be goose bumps on her legs, on her arms.

55   "No, ma'am, I wouldn't do that," I'd say, and take another swig of beer. "Wild horses couldn't take me away from this place—no, they couldn't."

I'd think about her heart, jumping and flapping around in her small chest like a fish in a footlocker, after those long runs; at the top of the summit, I'd wonder how anything could ever be so *alive*.

THE AFTERNOON THAT SHE SET FIRE TO THE FIELD across the road from my cabin was a still day, windless, and I guess that Glenda thought it was safe, that it would just be a grass fire and would do no harm—and she was right, though I did not know that. I saw her standing out in the middle of the field, lighting matches, bending down and cupping her hands until a small blaze appeared at her feet. Then she came running across the field toward my cabin.

I loved to watch her run. I did not know why she had set the fire, and I was very afraid that it might cross the road and burn up my hay barn, even my cabin—but I was not as frightened as I might have been. It was the day before Glenda was going to leave, and mostly I just was delighted to see her.

She came running up the steps, pounded on my door, and then came inside, breathless, having run a dead sprint all the way. The fire was spreading fast, even without a wind, because the grass was so dry, and red-winged blackbirds were leaping up out of the grass ahead of it, and I could see marsh rabbits and mice scurrying across the road, coming into my yard. An elk bounded across the meadow. There was a lot of smoke. It was late in the afternoon, not quite dusk, but soon would be, and Glenda was pulling me by the hand, taking me back outside and down the steps, back out toward the fire, toward the pond on the far side of the field. It was a large pond, large enough to protect us, I hoped, and we ran hard across the field, with a new wind suddenly picking up, a wind made from the flames, and we got to the pond and kicked our shoes off, pulled off our shirts and jeans, and splashed out into the water, and waited for the flames to get to us and then work their way around us.

60   It was just a grass fire. But the heat was intense as it rushed toward us, blasting our faces with the hot winds.

It was terrifying.

We ducked our heads under the water to cool our drying faces, and splashed water on each other's shoulders. Birds were flying past us, and grasshoppers, and small mice were diving into the pond with us, where hungry trout were rising and snapping at them, swallowing them like corn. It was growing dark and there were flames all around us. We could only wait to see if the grass was going to burn itself up as the fire swept past.

"Please, love," Glenda was saying, and I did not understand at first that she was speaking to me. "Please."

We had moved out into the deepest part of the pond, chest-deep, and kept having to duck beneath the surface because of the heat. Our lips and faces were blistering. Pieces of ash were floating down on the water like snow. It was not until nightfall that the flames died down, just a few orange ones flickering here and there. But all the rest of the small field was black and smoldering, and still too hot for someone with no shoes to walk across.

65   It was cold. I was colder than I had ever been. We held on to each other all night, holding each other tightly, because we were shivering. I thought about luck, about chance. I thought about fears, all the different ones, and the things that could make a person run. She left at daylight, would not let me drive her home, but trotted, instead, heading up the road to Tom's.

That was two years ago. The rabbits have changed, and then changed again: twice.

The hedgehog—I have never seen it again. After all these years, it has left. I wish I knew for sure that was what it had been; I wish I had a name for it.

Will it be back? I do not think so. Why was it here in the first place? I do not know.

Just the same, predictable ways of rabbits—that is all I have left now.

70   Is Glenda still running? It is mid-February. It hurts to remember her. The field across the road lies scorched and black, hidden beneath a cover of snow.

Anya Achtenberg

Anya Achtenberg's story, her first, won the *New Letters* fiction contest. Her two books of poems are *I Knew What the Small Girl Knew* and *The Stone Language*.

Cold Ground

Cold ground was my bed last night and rock was my pillow, too.
BOB MARLEY

SHE WAS SINGING AT THE TOP OF HER LUNGS, bowing and pivoting on one heel and then the other. She threw back her head and drew her right arm up in a precise arc, like a bird with one wing getting ready to fly. She was dressed like a boy, high-tops and all. I watched her over my newspaper in the mornings on my way to work, knowing that if I weren't careful she would notice me, and I wanted to avoid an exchange. She never begged, she just firmly demanded a specific amount, and if refused or ignored, stared at the offender as if they had just lost the opportunity of a lifetime.

In the cold or rainy weather, when eight or ten of them came inside for shelter, she presided over the benches where they sat. They all talked up and back, but she seemed to have the deciding voice on any issue. I never saw her singing to them, and after awhile I realized it was all a big joke. She was not so crazy nor even so drunk that she just lost control and sang in the middle of the rush-hour crowd; she was singing precisely *to* that crowd, and watching them. Some people, and I think she liked those best, looked straight at her and laughed out loud. Others got flustered, and nervously read their papers or stared away from her. Still others were somehow (I was never able to understand it) able to ignore her totally, as if so involved with their own lives that not even such a spectacle could sway their vision from the tasks and pleasures of the day. I think she used to sing extra loudly around them, but gave that up after awhile, they seemed so unshakable.

She wasn't vulnerable like some of the homeless, or so it seemed to me at the time. They stand in the street all day long and hold out their hands, or use styrofoam cups, and plead in those weak little voices, help me, please help me. She wasn't angry either, like the ones who stamp their feet and keep changing direction while they yell warnings and threats. But she was there in the station everyday, and I started to wonder about her.

Watching her made me think about the times when I had no place to go. There were a few years when I spent most of my nights in coffee shops or out in the streets or, with luck, stayed the night on the floor of a friend's apartment. I thought about her when I was washing the dishes. She hadn't washed a dish in a long time. She probably ate out of the garbage, or at a shelter where somebody served her and she got up from the table when she was done. I wondered what she did at night. Sometimes it frightened me to think about it. I wondered how she could close her eyes and go to sleep in the subway station or in an alley where anything could have happened to her. I decided that one night I would follow her to see where she ate, where she went to the bathroom, where she slept. I had never seen her do anything but stand around and sing or talk. Actually, I had seen her sit down only once or twice, and then in the middle of a very animated conversation with a man who held his bag of aluminum cans in his lap.

5   It is so hard to tell you what I saw and what I did. I wish I could just stand up like her and sing in the middle of everything, in the middle of work and everyone rushing home to their families, their lovers, their dinners. I wish I could just stand up and sing at the

top of my lungs, louder than the express barreling through the station, or the local grinding to a halt, opening and filling.

This was around the time when many people in the city's psychiatric wards were being released because there was no room for them inside. This was a time when people were pushing each other off the subway platform into the tracks to be run over by an approaching train. This was a time when language failed me. I was losing the names of things. I couldn't name what people wanted, went to work for or bought; everyday there were new gadgets. I could not name what people wanted from each other. I could not name the parts of the body, or how they worked. I couldn't even make my body open. I stopped feeling pleasure and stopped looking for it.

Even my voice was getting smaller and, as it did, I kept thinking about her singing, how ridiculous she was and yet how she pushed her voice into the air, how she filled the station and no one stopped her. No one made her go away or hurt her; at least I never saw it happen. People acted more like her captive than anything else when she was the one who should have been afraid of them. They were doing her a favor after all, letting her hang around the station.

It was the same all over the city. When I cut through the Port Authority Saturday mornings on my way to work, I saw people lining the walls, some still asleep, others chewing on an old piece of bread or something out of the trash barrels, others just staring. This was their place all night, but early morning the cops would come and chase them all away until rush hour was over. I started to look for her there, but no one sang. I heard only the rumbling of some of them deep in their throats, within the layers of rags like frayed nooses around their necks. The walls held their smell long after the cops cleared the homeless away, the walls around me, in front of me, the stained and bloodied walls.

I get so tired when I think about that time. An hour did not go by when that woman's song did not roll through my head. I couldn't concentrate on anything else, so I started to take long walks again at night, the way I used to do when I didn't have a place to live, or lived with too many people to find any quiet, or there was no heat and I couldn't bear it. I began staying out later, without even cabfare in my pocket to make it the same as it was back then when I had no choice. I thought I would leave things to chance, but nothing happened, nothing changed.

10   That was it, that was one of the things that drove me crazy. I felt like lying down and dying and that bitch was standing up, in her filthy men's clothes, without a place to lay her head. No one would ever want to touch her, except maybe in some alley mixing their smells like animals, and she was standing up and singing.

Most nights I walked up and down Broadway, watching it change from poor to fashionable, from bars to schools. I kept walking and watching the lights change until I began to see their pattern and could time myself, just like a cab driver, to walk street after street at just the right rhythm so I would never have to stop for a light. When morning came and the traffic lights did not stare out of the darkness at me, I went down into the subway to go to work and sat waiting with my newspaper or stood against the side of the newspaper stand to watch her and listen to her sing, and see how she mocked us all.

It became my pattern to nap through my lunch break, then force myself through the rest of the day. One day as usual I ate dinner in the kitchen as the pipes clanged and the family next door went through its noisy preparations. Then all the evening sounds rolled around in my head until I slept. After a few hours I got up and began to walk again through the same streets.

I knew if I followed her I would find something hidden about her. She could not be only what I saw. She could not carry all that she owned with her. Her whole story could not be on her face, or in her song, or in the split and bloody feet of the man she talked to on the bench. I knew that these people were just like everybody else, and if I followed her I would find she had the same things everyone else had, whether filthy or wrapped in a plastic bag, whether in the park under layers of rags or in the dreams that passed through her as she slept, perhaps, in daylight and noise. I knew she was like everyone else when she slept and in the moment when she woke. I knew she could not escape as I could not, although homeless, without locks and keys, without identification. She must have had the same nightmares and the same unclean hands, the same ways of separating herself from others, the same running away and waste of the pure minutes.

Who did she think she was? Someone so different, so special, that just because she had no room to go to and close the door behind her, she had to parade before the rest of us everyday? I knew that if I followed her, something would open inside of me, and I would be able to see and speak, and perhaps sing. Even if she had the same hard and blind, sad and cruel thoughts and ways as we did in her endless patrol of the streets, in her minute by minute search for food and warmth and covering, I knew that if I followed her, something would open and rain, and I would slip in it and be like her, and sing and know.

15   The rain had not let up all night, but I needed to get out of the house. No one saw me leave. There were a few people sitting on the bench in the station, and she stood above them, entertaining them with her song. I stood to the side of the newsstand and watched. At that hour, trains pulled into the station at no predictable interval. I was angry at myself; what was I doing there at that hour? A local's rumblings began far off, and as the train came toward me, I felt very cold. I could see myself at the edge of the platform, I didn't know who might push me, but I felt I could not stop falling. There was time to see the train before it hit me, to be lying on the tracks, to be silent or screaming, to know what was coming, to howl with fear and pain at the severing of myself from myself, to try to hold myself as one body, one mind, to fail, to be split apart, be crushed, to know.

I heard her moving, rustling her paper shopping bags. I knew then that she kept her possessions under a bench in the subway station, at least for the nights of rain. I could see that she owned things, that she hoarded and hid, that she did not stand up completely empty and open to fling her arms apart and sing, a different creature from the rest of us.

I guess it was then that I began to imagine doing things that I had never thought about before. I saw myself at the edge of the platform as the train came closer. I saw her. It would be easy, she did not protect herself, did not sense any danger from me. I looked soft and vulnerable. She smiled at me and dipped into a bow. She rocked up and back on her feet as if nothing could tip her over, no wind, no storm, no hand. Her song flew out, deep and sprawling, and I saw myself push her, and felt the terrible wind, and heard her land in the tracks, and burned in my body as I imagined the train, car after car, scream over her and destroy her form with its sound and its speed. I sunk back behind the newsstand in a damp corner of steel and concrete, trying to stop the pictures in my mind, and listened for her drunken voice to rise whole again from the platform. I saw her rocking up and back with a ridiculous smile on her face, and I was angry and glad and saw the tears that had run into my hands. I felt weak, and cursed her.

I stood there for a long time and stared at the tracks. I stole glances at her but she never saw me. Another train pulled into the station and two cops got out. They talked to the clerk in the token booth for a while, then pushed through the swinging door into the station. She was dozing on the bench, falling over to one side, her bottle in its paper bag wedged between her thighs. One of the cops rapped on the bench with his nightstick. He did not touch her shoulder, nor her forehead. He did not bend to her and speak softly. He pounded on the bench next to her thigh and on the wall over her head, and then she got up, smiling, and bowed low. They told her she couldn't stay there all night and should go to a shelter. She said no and sat back down. "Look," one of them said, "it's stopped raining," and both moved forward as if to force her. She jumped up with her hands raised in the air, and begged them in an exaggerated whine not to shoot. She smiled as if she knew that their bullets could not penetrate. Even if they pumped the bullets from all of the chambers of the guns into her chest, she would still bow and sing, and rock up and back like a tree in a storm, surviving, upright, mighty, and the two of them, spitting out little noises from their firesticks, could do her no harm. They could push her out of the station and she would come right back, she could live right there in the middle of all of us, piss in our streets and eat the food we threw away. She laughed and marched up the stairs with her arms in the air like a captured bank robber. I saw her at the top of the steps outlined against the dim street light. The cops turned to wait for the next train and didn't notice me run up the stairs.

A man was standing on the corner, shivering in the dampness. He watched me pass. The woman walked, looking up at the sky. Her humming swelled. The wind pushed me along behind her. She crossed the avenue and kept walking the side streets until she came to the park that ran alongside the river. I was frightened of the rats but kept on going. I wanted to see her lie down, I wanted to watch her sleep, to see how she covered herself, how she lay alone in darkness near the river and the moonlight, no one to sing to.

20   She moved through one of the arched passageways. I became her shadow. She left the path at a recess between the rocks and the curved cold stone of the passageway. Lumbering around with her laces undone, she gathered some papers and leaves and propped them up like a pillow for a sick friend. She undid her zipper and scratched her belly, rubbed lower down and sighed, and then lay down with some old newspapers across her shoulders. The early light shone on her face, the river ran by and the wind passed over, blowing the leaves about her quiet form. I stood and shivered and watched.

For me, lying alone and exposed to the sky, to its thunder and wind, to its kingdom of clouds well out of reach, was to become very small, to be in danger, to be easily crushed. Often as I lay by the window in my room, I could not close my eyes and face the stream of images that would run through me while I slept. I could not let go of time measured by the clock's dim glow. Sometimes it seemed impossible to live until morning; my heart might keep to its work only if one were awake to tend it like a sacred fire.

But she, in her dirty pants and old sneakers, lying on the harsh ground close to the highway, beneath a few newspapers with their irrelevant scandals fitting themselves to the angles of her body, lay alone and, it seemed, without fear. She slept peacefully under the stars that one cannot see from the lamplit streets. Only at the edge of the city could one begin to see what goes on beyond the numbered streets of the island, and there she slept peacefully while I could barely go on.

With my coat buttoned to my neck and my heavy gloves on, I edged up closer until I could see the way her chest rose and her lip flapped open as she inhaled and exhaled the sweet air of the park. She never saw me. I picked up a rock that lay near my food and flung it at her head, at her sleep, at her empty hands and proud song. She made a caught harsh sound in her throat. I picked up the rock and threw it at her skull again. The blood began to run into the ground, staining the papers, her sweater, the earth. I bent and smoothed the hair above her forehead. I saw that her chest had stopped rising and falling. I drew back my hand, and of course it was bloody. I looked all around to see if anyone was there. The sky was still dim, and I saw no one. I walked up and back, toward her and away, several times. I thought to drag her to the river and throw her in, but I could not touch her any-more, ever again, she was filthy and covered with blood. I felt all the strength rushing out of my legs, my legs shaking. I tried to run along the path, then stopped for breath. I noticed my gloves, and how they were soiled. I pulled them off and pushed them deep into my pockets. The air bit my fingers. I found the nearest exit from the park and headed home. I stopped to get a newspaper at the candystore. I put the gloves into a trash can a couple of blocks from my building. When I got inside, I lay on the couch with the newspaper and fell asleep.

In my sleep I was deaf. People spoke to me and to each other but I heard nothing. My dreams were like film sped up, vivid colors and rushing motions like water, but no sound. Sometimes in the nights that followed I could hear everything: the moans of love and of illness in the building across the street, the keys in the pocket of a girl, the saliva dripping in the throat of a dog who has just found something to gnaw in the trash, the old woman upstairs slicing an onion, her tear falling. At those times, though, I couldn't see very well. I could only distinguish outlines and a shifting of light and shadow in front of me.

25   After a week or so, my whole body went numb. I moved through the streets by will, not wanting to collapse with everyone rushing around me. I could not feel my arms, nor especially my legs. It was as if I were leaving, dying. Then smells began to assail me, sicken me. The most expensive perfumes left me gasping, my fist between my breasts, trying to break away from the crowd and its elegant suffocation. The neighbors' dinner cooking,

which usually prompted me to get up and begin preparing my own, now drove me gagging into the bathroom. My own smells affected me the worst. I took long showers and tried to imagine floating on my back in the ocean. In the park the vegetation made the air sweet and fresh, but there my vision became too sharp. I saw the veined surface of each leaf and the tiny insects that walked across, so I had to get out. I wandered through the streets until my vision calmed.

Down in the station it seemed almost the same. People paid less attention to the homeless ones because they had quieted down some, I supposed. The woman wasn't there anymore, singing and staring right into people's faces. I wondered whether people were already forgetting her.

I wondered whether she could vanish, clean of flesh, in traces of cloth, skeletal, into the earth and rocks, beneath the sky that permits anything. Would she vanish, or would she be found? Perhaps by a child who would be changed forever, who would not sleep well for a long time but would lay in the rocking of its closeness to birth and ask why, or perhaps by another of her own kind, one who could not tell the police for fear of being blamed, but sat on a rock by the body and stared at it, and drank. Perhaps others came near the body and picnicked or made love, or sat homeless and shaking with fever above her vanished bold lip and the quiet song of her bones mixing with earth.

It would have been better that way, but her remains brought the dogs whose masters let them run the park freely, and she was wrenched, in the middle of her vanishing, out of the earth and its drop of true air into a plastic body bag, into the morgue, into the end of herself.

I thought about confessing, but I knew I could never explain it. It wasn't my freedom I would miss so much; I would have liked someone to tell me what to do each day. But I could not bear to have people think whatever they wanted to about my crime. I could not speak about it, and reading the small article I clipped from the newspaper made my head spin because it wasn't about either of us. It was a lie, and someday, I knew, one of us must rise up and tell the truth.

———

30 SOME WEEKS HAD PASSED. Nothing more had appeared in the newspapers. I had figured that would be the case. Christmas was ten days away and I found those days more unbearable than usual, the world around me swelling like a balloon with activity and with objects to be bought and exchanged. Up and down Broadway, people were selling Christmas trees. I'd slow up as I approached these concessions and make a few inquiries about price so that I could breathe in the fragrance. With that hint of oxygen and pine, I began to yearn for the sky and the water, but I knew I could find them only at the edge of the city.

I walked through the middle of the buying and selling, with its rash of holiday purse snatchings and pickpocketing. I had never stolen anything, but all I could think about was the one thing I had taken away from the world and could never replace. Then the bells and the lights and the heavy scent of pine, the long lines of people having their presents wrapped, the last minute shoppers frantic to fill their sacks, and all those with their lists of family and friends drove me back into my apartment.

On Christmas Eve I went to Mass and tried to listen to the priest's voice as if he were talking to me, but I knew he was not. I listened to the voices of the singers rise to the free air in the highest points of the vaults, and watched the faces—believers, spectators, tourists, witnesses—swelling with the sounds they consumed, and I felt small and thin, as if nothing could enter my body ever again, as if I could hear and see nothing but only move toward the one voice I sensed singing by the water.

I REMEMBER LOOKING AT THE PHOTO in the newspapers of three white men with their jackets pulled over their heads as they were escorted into a police van. Along with ten or fifteen others, they had beaten up three black men whose car had broken down when they were passing through the white neighborhood. They had struck them with bats, then chased one of them onto the highway, where they beat him again and left him. From the side of the road they saw a car run over and kill him.

They hadn't wanted to be photographed, but they shared their guilt with each other. They had shared the hatred that led them to their crime. They beat him and chased him and beat him again, all three of them. Perhaps a long time before it happened they talked about doing just what they did. They might be punished, or they might get off. They could be beaten up in jail, or even killed.

35 But no one knew what I had done, none but the earth I had delivered the body to. No one would ever punish me for my crime. I would live, walk freely through the streets, make money and spend it and die, I supposed, only at the natural end of my life. I would speak everyday in someone else's voice, the voice of one who has not killed. I stopped my late walks and every night remained in my room, soundless and still, until the pain started in my head, and with both fists I beat on the floor until I fell, very far perhaps, and then slept, without joy, like an animal that doesn't know it is sleeping.

Susan Straight

Susan Straight is a fiction writer who has
published stories in several magazines.
Aquaboogie is her first book.

Two Days Gone

DARNELL AND ME WERE DRIVING TO HIS
HOUSE LIKE ALWAYS, but *nobody* out on they lawn, not even the
Thibodeaux boys and they *live* on the grass. This supposed to be a
Friday night, it's summer, and people should be washing cars,
breathing some air, getting ready to go out. When we got to
Picasso Street, I saw the record player wasn't out on the front
porch at Darnell's. Mr. Tucker, Darnell's father, play records on
Friday evening, put the old beige stereo facing out to the street so
you can hear it for a couple of houses. He play Billie Holiday, sad
Billie, and some scratchy records by Earl Grant. I wanted to hear
them, the organ real husky and low swinging in the background,
because nobody play music on my street, in my neighborhood,
but I knew tonight me and Darnell wouldn't be sitting on his car
in the driveway. No Tiny or KC coming by to say, "What up,
homes?" Darnell always say, "The Lakers, man, they up by ten
games." Tiny answer, "I heard *that,*" and always looking down the
street to see who's at Jackson Park. He usually start singing, "In the
Westside, the cool Westside, where the people gon party all night."

Tonight it wouldn't be kids walking by to yell, "Take that old stuff off the stereo, man. Play some Ice T, some Tone Loc. Bust a rhyme out them ancient speakers." None of Mr. Tucker's friends, Roscoe Wiley and Floyd, standing around to laugh at the kids. "Red Man ain't hardly playin none a that rap mess. Listen. These people *singin,* not hollerin. World a difference, boy." Darnell's arms wouldn't be around me at my waist and his father working on a old battery or motor. The street was empty all the way down to the park. Nobody out in they yard or in the street because the cops looking for Ricky Ronrico, and they been searching one night and one day. Longer than it sound.

Everybody in the front room, near the swamp cooler. Darnell's little sisters, Sophia and Paula, making those string bracelets all the kids are wearing. Darnell tell his father, "I heard it on the radio comin back."

"Where was y'all workin this week?" his mother ask. Darnell with the firefighter crew the county runs in the summer, out in the dry mountains all over the county, from the desert to near L.A. I only see him on the weekends, and he pick me up straight from work.

5   "We was over by Chino Hills. Rattlesnakes everywhere. I heard the two cops got shot on the south end, over on Eddy Avenue past the mall. That ain't no black neighborhood."

"So? Ricky Ronrico shot them and he black for a fact. Bout as no good as that sickly stuff he name after," his father say.

Mr. Lanier standing there with a big shopping bag full of plums. "And you know they figure he somewhere on the Westside." He live on the next street, always musty because he got a bunch of pigs out somewhere. My mother use to buy chitlins and pig knuckles from him every New Year's, before we moved away from the Westside.

Mr. Lanier say, "That why I *walk* over here, ain't takin no chances with my brake lights. Rio Seco finest in the streets tonight, lookin hard."

It's only the TV talking then, and I know everybody thinking about 1973. I was eight, and the only thing I remember was all the red lights flashing on my bedroom walls cause the cops came and took Mr. Wiley from next door. He was gone all weekend.

Somebody had ambushed two white cops at Jackson Park, but I just knew the lights looked like Hawaiian Punch spilling over my bed, and I thought they were so pretty then.

10   "What they lookin for this time?" Mr. Lanier say.

"It was white tennis shoes back in '73," Mr. Tucker say. "That's what they said the fellas did it was wearin. What was them two cops name?"

"I don't rightly remember," Mr. Lanier say.

"Please and Christensen." Darnell talk real quiet. He never forget anything. "Kelvin and every other Westside brother between 16 and 30 went down to the station, all weekend."

His mother looking at her catalogs, don't say anything. Her oldest son, Kelvin, live in L.A. now. Darnell's father light another cigarette. "White tennis shoes," he say. "But they got Roscoe Wiley and that other poet, the one use to teach in your school, Brenda."

15   "Brother Lobo," I say.

"Kept his ass for a week." For a second between the commercials, we could hear the drip of water from the cooler, the fan going around over our heads. Mrs. Tucker put in a beautiful one, with wood and lamps, this summer.

"So who they want this time?" Mr. Lanier say again, getting up to go.

"They want Ricky Ronrico," Mr. Tucker say. "And they talkin about somebody hidin him, wantin to harbor him. Huh." His face pull itself together while I watch, like his eyebrows and that big nose and mouth get in a line straight up and down as a totem pole, piled on top of each other. Like he's Indian all the way through. That's why they call him Red Man. "Damn sure wouldn't hide no Ricky Ronrico he came to me."

Nobody on Picasso Street liked Ricky because he always raced his van up and down by the park. But that wasn't what Mr. Tucker was thinking about, I know. Hearing that name remind him of the time Darnell spent two nights in jail, in the same cell with Ricky. Thinking about that still make Mr. Tucker hot.

20   "Go on and take Brenda home, now," he say, real loud, to Darnell. "This ain't no time to be out. And bring your ass right back."

"Huh," Darnell start to say, but then his father cut him off.

"You know you gotta drive her up to the Ville, and I ain't playin."

When we close the front door, I hear Mrs. Tucker say, "He 20, he ain't a boy no more," and Darnell's father quick to stop her, too.

"You know that's the point."

25   AT FIRST, I THINK HE'S MAD ABOUT THE WAY HIS FATHER TALK TO HIM. He don't say anything going down Picasso, waiting a long time at every stop sign. "Good enough?" he whisper real strange at the last two, looking out his window. I look out on mine, and I see the chainlink fences around yards like they lit up, electric, because the sun just now going down. The folding chairs on somebody's lawn seem like fire, glowing metal. I can smell the cooking meat, the way it drift through the streets when we get closer to Canales' plant.

Only railroad tracks to pass now, on Third Avenue, and then the plant and The Pit. After you leave the Westside, you smell nothing but orange groves for a few miles. My cousins from L.A. always laugh at me when they come out to visit Rio Seco. "Man, y'all niggers *country.* Only a hour away and might as well be in Mi-sippi. Y'all ain't got no clubs, no disco, nothin live. You got Jackson Park and The Pit."

Nobody's even parked down there at the Pit now, that dirt bare as the playground. My mother use to work at the plant—they cook the meat for Mexican food, frozen burritos and tamales, and when the shift is going, the whole Westside full of a smell so rich, so warm and spicy, ain't nothing better. Mama said the meat itself was real poor, but when I was small, I'd walk down there to meet her getting off work, sit in the heat next to the fence and breathe that smell, sometimes mixed with the barbecue smoke coming from the chimney at The Pit. I wasn't allowed anywhere near even the parking lot of that place; people drank and played cards and ate ribs there, and fought each other, too.

Darnell look over there, laugh a little. "Them country dudes hang out at The Pit know better than to come out tonight. They scared of they own shadow cause it got a Mi-sippi accent."

I've known Darnell since we were five, when I lived on Picasso. Three times I've seen him like this: when Max got shot at our graduation party, when Darnell got out of jail that time last summer, and now. It feel strange not knowing what to say to him, and we almost up Third Avenue to the Ville already.

30 Everybody from the Westside call it the Ville cause only white people lived up here on the slope. Honkyville. We left the Westside and moved up here when I was nine. Some Japanese people, three or four Mexican families around by then, and after we came, the Orlandos and Tyners move here from DaVinci Street. But everybody still call it the Ville, laugh at my father and say does our grass grow greener and our mail come earlier? When the Santa Ana wind blow the power out, do the city come and fix things a hell of lot faster than they do on the Westside?

All the orange groves thin out now, and we pass by the little park just off Third. About five cars there, stoner white boys drinking beer, smoking at the picnic tables. Darnell say, "Can I get a swig, *homes? Can we chill in the park with you?"*

"Getting mad ain't likely to change the situation, Darnell," I say. "Don't you go driving crazy on the way back to the Westside."

"What do you suggest I do?" He finally look at me, and the scar push out mad and jagged on his forehead, just heading into his hair. Even when he got that, it turned into something else. He and his father were looking for a radiator at the junkyard, and he ran into a pole, split his head open. I took him to the emergency and they made us wait. Blood all in his hair, his pants got mud at the hems, and I was trying to clean him up when the doctor take him into a room. Darnell came busting out a few minutes later, said, "We *gone*. Now." He told me the doctor didn't believe the pole, kept laughing, "Your woman must have hit you over the head with something awfully heavy. What did you do to deserve this?"

While I laugh about stuff like that, Darnell get blind mad. I say, "I suggest you come inside when we get to my house. Cool you down."

35   "I gotta be up at six to help Daddy fix the big truck. He's supposed to pick up a load of brush somebody cleared off for fire season." When we stop at the last four-way before my street, a boy pull up beside us, gunning his engine like firecrackers. Darnell look over and wait til he drive off. "I suggest white boy racin around fast as he want. Probably got a open container of Jack Daniel's on the seat and shit. Hair *streamin* in the wind." He don't even bring his lips close to mine when he pull into the driveway. I thought he would walk me to the porch so I could stand on the steps above him, like always, and look into his eyes, touch his eyebrows, straighten them with my fingers.

POP COME UP BEHIND WHEN I LOOK THROUGH THE WINDOW to see Darnell's car go down the street. "What the hell were you doin? You never even came after work to eat."

"John, she never come home on Fridays, I been told you that." Mama's sitting at the dining room table picking through a bowl of beans, finding the rocks. "Darnell always get her, ever since he been working for the Forest Service."

"You didn't have any business on the Westside tonight, Brenda," Pop go on. "When this Forest Service foolishness over?"

"At the end of fire season," I answer. "Was it on the news, even in L.A.?" Rio Seco's close enough to get on TV sometimes, but not usually.

40   Pop sit back on the couch. "Bad stuff always play on the news." He turn to the nine o'clock early broadcast. "Jackson Park was on TV back in '73."

The blond lady get her serious face on. "Police are following several leads in Rio Seco tonight searching for murder suspect Ricardo Ronrico, who is believed to have shot and killed two police officers late last night. Officers Terry Kimball and Gregory LaDonna were attempting to serve Ronrico with a warrant to appear in court for sentencing on a parole violation when he allegedly shot them in this residence on Eddy Avenue."

They show the house, the neighbors standing around, cop cars everywhere.

"Bastard get us all in trouble," Pop say. "How in the hell he get a name like that? He about your age, Brenda."

"No, older than us. About 25. Darnell say his brother name Falstaff after some beer and his sister Virginia Dare."

"How in the hell Darnell know him, if he older than you?"

45   Mama say, "Why you always assume the worst about Darnell, John?"

"Cause she don't need to be with him and him only. He musta done something to get in all that trouble last summer," Pop say, and I'm tired of hearing this to-the-curb attitude. It's lame.

"He was just sitting in the driver's seat, playing the radio, I *been* told you," I yell. "Him and Londale were taking down the election posters for Mack Ellison. Someone *you* didn't vote for cause you said a black man couldn't win for county supervisor."

"Then why the cops take him in? Cause he didn't have no driver's license and no business bein there in that rich neighborhood." Pop's voice echoing.

"At least they was takin *down* the signs," Mama say. "You always complainin about them being up for months after an election."

50   "Darnell don't have a license because of that insurance shit, cause the white dude hit him and Darnell didn't have insurance. Yeah, they had warned him, gave him tickets, offa *that.* You know how high insurance is on the Westside. You were laughing when you bought it last time, too, because of your *address.*" I feel that water pushing behind my eyes, starting to come up my throat, so I go in my bedroom and shut the door.

Mama come in a while later. "Did you eat at Darnell's house?"

"I wasn't hungry. I had a big lunch at work."

"You sit outside in that nice plaza they got in front of the county building?" Mama lean against the edge of the bed. "I always think about you sittin out there with all the other secretaries, and them cute little cafes and boutiques they got now. Look like L.A." Every time she even mention the county building, I hear how proud she is about my job. I had to stop telling her not to call me a secretary, I'm only a clerk, because she won't listen.

"Yeah, Mama, I sat in the sun. I'm going to sleep now." After she close the door, I look outside my window, listen for the helicopter. It takes off from the top of the county building, where they get a helipad, or whatever it's called. Sometimes when I'm at Darnell's, in the front yard in the dark, the police shine the spotlight from it and cut over us jagged as lightning. Circle loud and angry as a wasp, making the whole street silver. Mama always asking me what new flowers they planted in the county plaza this month. I sat out there today, next to the fountain look pale blue like glass. People popping open their soda cans loud, little rifle shots. I couldn't stop thinking about Ricky Ronrico, about what those red flashing lights in my bedroom would look like now, me in Darnell's blankets on the couch. I lay in the bed for a long time, hearing the helicopter then, humming distance, hoping Darnell went straight home and didn't run into Tiny or someone else who loved to instigate, just stand on the corner and talk smack.

55   When I wake up, I know they still haven't caught him. I could feel it somehow, almost see Ricky Ronrico's face, and I call Darnell right away. He say the Westside still steppin light and drivin slow, but not too slow, and I can hear a smile in his voice, know he thinking about last night.

"You suggesting you still pick me up at the usual time?" I say, and he laugh. He always come about two o'clock, so we can go by the park. I clean house for Mama; Pop already at work, doing an extra shift. He already talking about property taxes due pretty soon, even though it's not til December. Me and Mama make a peach cobbler since we had all these peaches from my Aintie Mae out in Perris. Mama sew up a hole in Pop's other work pants, and I fix the rip in my white blouse. When Darnell come over, Mama's done. "How are things on Picasso?"

"Quiet. People doing a lot of talking, but mostly it's nothin but a long wait."

We tell her we'll just stay at Darnell's and play cards, and won't go cruising or looking for parties.

"Well, why you don't stay here and play cards then?" She turn her head at me like she does when I know she know why we don't stay here. We sit around at Darnell's and people come over to watch the basketball game or wrestling, and everybody's laughing and talking about everybody else. Nobody comes up here. Nobody borrows an egg or bring over some extra greens, and the phone might ring, but the doorbell doesn't. "I won't be late," I say, and she shake her head.

60   But when we on the Westside, it's not Saturday any more than the day before was Friday. Nothing seem natural at all. The sky was tinged all brown, like usual, but even the smog seem angry, and the palm trees hanging dusty, sorry-looking. The streets gray and glittery, rising in the heat almost, and everything faded, like the color been drained out. The houses and cars pale, people's lawns sand-color; we in one of those old-time photos Mr. Tucker has from Oklahoma, from where he grew up.

The heavy chains are up blocking the parking lot by Jackson Park, and not a brother in sight. "Daddy didn't want me to come and get you," Darnell is saying, but he put his hand on my arm. "I'm tellin you, I had to think twice about it." He smiles at me careful, touch a knuckle to my neck. "Good enough?" he whisper.

His father's inside watching TV, talking on the phone. Darnell and me play dominoes in the back, and Tiny come in after a while. "Man, it's definitely cooler back here than in the front room with your old man, *homes*. He so pissed, put you in *a world* of hurt you say the wrong thing."

"I know. And everything wrong. You in the streets, hot as it is?"

"Just kickin it." Tiny anything but tiny. Six-two, got a big natural even though nobody wearing naturals anymore. He just love his own hair, and everything else about himself. "Man, when Johnny Law pull you over," he say, "You put your hands like *this*." Spread his fingers out wide. "You put them hands on top of the wheel and pray with em apart." He was driving his mother's car an hour ago, got stopped on the way back from the liquor store on Third.

65   "The wheel ain't good enough for me," Darnell say. "Remember when I was at that gas station last year, six in the morning and the cashier trip the silent alarm by accident? Shoot, seven black and whites and I hadn't even seen picked my pump. I had my hands *outside* the window, man." He slam down a domino. "Least you

wasn't wearin that nasty John Shaft leather piece you call a coat. Lucky it's summer. You usually look so bad cops stop you on G.P."

"My middle name, homey. General Principle."

"You ain't marked down my fifteen, baby. Oh, I know it hurts." He look up at me. "We ain't goin nowhere today, I can see that." I give him the points and Tiny go into the kitchen for some Kool-Aid. No air is moving at all.

MISS RALPHINE FROM ACROSS THE STREET IS SIT-TING at the table with Darnell's mama when we come out the bedroom to walk Tiny to the front yard. Her face is small like a baby's under her wig, and even though she must be seventy, the only wrinkles are on her forehead where she raise her eyebrows all the time. I know what she fixing to say. "Brenda! How you and this boy? When y'all gettin married? I needs to go to a weddin soon."

She been asking for two years now, since we graduated together. I smile and tell her I don't know, while Darnell and Tiny pass under the fan and look up for some air.

"Where you think you goin?" Mr. Tucker say. Him and Mr. Lanier just outside the front door, looking at a battery recharger.

"Damn, give me a break," Darnell say, and then he lift up his hands. "Sorry. The feet stops here." I see Jane Jones walking down the sidewalk, wearing her uniform. She works at Church's Fried Chicken on Sixth Avenue. "Tiny, Darnell. And Bren-da," she call out, saying my name all slow. She still won't forgive me.

We went to work experience at school together, for a year. Bank of America took us for clerk/tellers, and we figured out how to talk different, talk white, dress right. Like I do at work now.

But Jane was twice my size, her shoulders big as Darnell's, and dark. Brother Lobo, the poet, used to call her "the real thing." Ebony. I was always jealous of her face and skin when we were little; her jaw was so smooth, her neck so long, and she never had marks on her skin like I did. Mine was light enough to show nicks and scratches for months. When it came time for the

county and the banks to check all the work experience girls out
for jobs, though, I saw how they looked at Jane when we showed
up together for the interviews. We were both talking right, but
her hair, her shoulders. She could relax her hair every day and
it would still be African; she wear a short fade, and it make her
neck even longer.

She never asked me about the job at the county. I didn't see
her for a long time, and Darnell told me her mother had gotten
sprung, started smoking that rock cocaine. Jane took care of her,
and then she got a job at Church's.

75 "You gon walk with me, Tiny," she say over her shoulder,
"or Brenda gotta have a harem?"

"Don't be opening your mouth tonight to see if your tongue
work, boy," Mr. Tucker holler at Tiny's back.

WE STAY IN THE BACK ROOM THEN, and Darnell mess
with my hair, tease me about my neck. "What if I give you a most
embarrassing souvenir of my love?" He try to pinch my neck,
and then he's kissing me, but Sophia and Paula keep running in
and out to get something. We give up and go in the front to help
Darnell's mama cook, because everybody who barely knows the
Tuckers could come by and eat on a Saturday. We make chicken,
fry up with pepper and onions, string beans, macaroni and
cheese, neckbones and blackeye peas for Mr. Tucker. Yellow cake
with chocolate icing. That's how she cook every Saturday.

All the kids eat, and Mr. Tucker, Mr. Lanier, and then
Roscoe Wiley come from down the street. They all sit in the living room and watch TV, Sophia and Paula and they friend
Takima go singing out the back door, and Darnell take me out to
the side steps by the kitchen. The night got hotter instead of
cooling off, it seems, and we can smell the greens tree tangled up
the chainlink like it's cooking in the air. Pop told me about time
going fast but in circles, in a storm he sat through once in Tulsa.

Nobody walk by, and then we hear the helicopter again for a
long time, over near Seventh Avenue where all the hotels and
restaurants are. Miss Ralphine come over to say they got a SWAT
team at the Holiday Inn; they plan to find Ricky Ronrico

tonight, and that's headquarters, she heard on her police radio. They must think he in the Westside for sure.

80 Only Mr. Tucker left in the living room now, and Darnell and me sit to watch "Invasion of the Body Snatchers" with him. "Not a dark face on the screen," Darnell say, and he keep getting up to drink something, sit down careful so he don't touch my leg. "This shit getting old," he say, "and we out of soda." The helicopter circle around like a race car on a track in the sky. When I wake up, the phone ringing and the movie been off. The police just raided Mr. Wiley's house on the corner, and he talked big trouble when they tried to take his son for questioning. Said they heard he had evidence in the house, and went through all the rooms. Darnell's mama tap her foot on the linoleum fast as a cricket, and when Tiny come in the screen door everybody jump. "Boy, what in hell you doin out?" Mr. Tucker say, his whole face pomegranate red. Red Man. "Get your ass on the couch where it belong on a night like this."

"Man, this ain't Alabama," Tiny say, but then he smile. "I couldn't miss the food, now." He don't even eat, though, just sit on the floor far away from Mr. Tucker. "Lester and Timmy and them say blood cool and they hope he get away with it. He probably in L.A. anyway. Ain't no place to hang in this country-ass . . ."

"Shut up, boy, fore I shut you up," Mr. Tucker holler; I feel tight in the chest. If we say Ricky Ronrico's name, they'll come busting in for us.

"You call your mother, Brenda. You won't be home for awhile."

On the phone, Mama sound mad, but she say he's right. Another TV show is gone, and I think Darnell asleep, but he stare at the wall. The old beige stereo sit quiet next to the fireplace, under the picture of the African queen. She's even darker from all the years of smoke settled on her.

85 Mr. Tucker asleep in his leather chair, and Mrs. Tucker go into their bedroom. Tiny still on the floor, and me and Darnell the only ones awake. He doesn't have a bedroom; he's slept on the couch since I've known him. He put his arm around my neck for a minute, and I rest my chin on that soft part by his elbow, but then he shift away again. "Too hot," he say. Huh.

Two Days Gone | 275

On the eleven o'clock news, the blond lady start out with, "Rio Seco police have captured murder suspect Ricardo Ronrico, the object of an intense manhunt since Friday." He was in a house on Gate Street, way back on the south side where he shot the two police. On the screen, his hair is all nappy, his eyes flat and red, lips with a gray ring around them. "My man sprung, seriously sprung. Rock daddy," Tiny say, and I didn't even know he was awake.

"Clues as to his whereabouts were found in a raid of a house earlier in the evening," she go on, and Darnell say, "Yeah, *tell* me. Treasure hunt time. How many stolen TV's and shit you think they found?"

"Blood knew better than to hang out on the Westside," Tiny say. "Nothin but a anthill. Stompin easy." He look at me. "Unless you want to move to the Ville like Brenda."

"Shut up, Tiny," I say. "Don't start on me."

90

"Wasn't nobody bangin on your daddy's door, huh?" he keep on, and the blond lady smiles. "In our next story, children learn about the great outdoors in some of the Southland's many summer camps." The little white kids race around, building fires, hiking in the woods, and Darnell say, "Please."

He pull me up from the couch. "I be back soon, Tiny. Brenda's daddy gon be breathin fire, so it ain't like I'll be lingerin." I'm about to say something and I hear Mr. Tucker's chair creak.

"They got him," Tiny say to Darnell's father, and I'm pushed out the door.

The car seat's warm as the couch was. I kiss Darnell's neck, give him problems driving. I won't see him again for another week. I look out at the streets, see Lester and Timmy walking, and Darnell honk but he doesn't slow down. It feel strange driving, like we still in a bottle even through the car windows are open. I unbutton Darnell's shirt, and when we getting ready to pass Canales' plant, I pull on the wheel. "Stop for a minute," I tell him, and he let me turn into the parking lot.

I feel like things should be all messed up, tumbleweeds and palm fronds and boxes thrown around like after the winds come in winter. I want to tell him I'm afraid for him every day, but he won't listen, I know. "Go close to the building," I whisper, and it's the weekend, so I can't smell the spicy breeze I want. I pull Darnell down onto the seat, and he say, soft, "You know I don't have no protection. I didn't think about it."

95   "I know," I say, and kiss his eyelids, put my hands like fans on his back. I think if the helicopter flew over now, shone the floodlight on us, they see my arms covering the back of Darnell's neck, where the skin so soft and blind.

Allen Wier

Allen Wier is the author of several novels, including *Blanco, Departing as Air, A Place for Outlaws,* and *A Cloud of Witnesses,* and *Things about to Disappear,* a book of stories.

Texas Wedding Party

(*from* A Cloud of Witnesses)

THE ONLY DOOR OPENS INTO THE WINDOWLESS ROOM, lets in the noise of rain splattering the street, light slanting across bottles and glasses. A man comes in wearing a long oil cloth slicker that slaps against his legs. He tips his head as if in momentary prayer and water runs off the wide brim of his hat.

Goddamn Galveston weather, the man says to no one. Pouring down and the sun still shining. He pauses at a table by the door where a whore sits between two men, both her hands busy, one in each man's lap.

Devil's beatin' his wife, the whore says.

Water drips from the man's slicker and pools on the packed earthen floor; his boots are huge with mud. His left eye is fixed and unmoving, the other jumpy as a flea. A scar runs like a thin white mustache above his upper lip. He reaches beneath the slicker and a long-barreled military pistol clatters down onto the bar. His right hand rests on the pistol handle, his left hand beside it. Both

hands are brown as the plank bar except for the darker whorl of a
scar that looks like a knothole on the back of his left hand. The
forefinger of that hand ends at the knuckle—his remaining finger-
tips are splayed, a curve of dirt black as pitch under each horn-
thick nail. With a motion as natural as scratching an itch, the
scarred hand reaches back down behind the bar and comes up with
a full bottle of rum. The man bites hold of the cork with small yellow teeth and pulls the bottle off, spits the cork into a spittoon at
his feet. With his fixed eye on nothing, he tilts the bottle and splat-
ters the bar for the seconds it takes the barkeep to position an
empty glass under the fall of rum. The man's fingers open to take
the drink. His right hand has not moved from atop the pistol. He
stoppers the bottle with the pink stub of his forefinger and tips
glass and bottle back, downing the drink, spilling nothing.

5   The man smells like a wet dog. His name is Portis Goar, but
he is called Eye. He's in Galveston to meet a shipload of German
immigrants and lead them to one of Beale's Colonies. As usual,
Eye's in the mud while someone else's in the money. Before the
war, Eye worked a wrecker's boat scavenging the coast for ship-
wrecks from Galveston to Aransas Inlet. Threat of the Union
blockade cut down on shipping, then a spell of calm weather cut
down on storms so he took a job of work as an enforcer for a
broker in land grants. A dispute over property rights nearly cost
him his life, but he only paid half a finger—his upper lip surprised him and grew back. After Texas seceded, he became a
drover to avoid conscription. Texas beeves was drove to New
Orleans to be shipped to hungry Confederate troops.

Now, Eye says, there is so many cattle over all of Texas, gone
on the wild while men was off fighting, they isn't worth more'n
a dollar or two a head. You can have all the mavericks you can
round up and brand, but at them prices, who cares.

It's a fact that money is a problem, the whore says.

Not havin' any makes me, Eye says, feel downright mean.

The whore looks up from her seat between the two men.
Both her hands still moving, she asks, How mean?

10   Mean enough, Eye says.

Mean enough to do what he does.

The barkeep tops off Eye's drink.

You think red Indians is hard-assed, you ain't rode the immigrant trail. I have—the way I got this job. Took a steamer last fall thirty-six hours to the mouth of the Mississippi. At Pass a L'Outre a longboat ferried me off the steamer to the *Assurance* for her return voyage to Bremerhaven. That was bad enough, with just me and the crew and no shortage of supplies. But the ride on that immigrant ship was worse than bad dreams, and nightmares is the only way I'll ever ride a buckin' sea horse again.

The *Assurance*, a brigantine owned by Radeleff and Company, is an old tramp cargo ship, converted to haul immigrants. She was well-built but leaks a bit now. Solid, but slow.

15 Two masts, see—the foremast is square rigged, and she's got a fore and aft mainsail with square maintopsails.

The whore rolls her eyes; she refuses to be impressed with this man's sailor lingo.

In Bremerhaven she had her anchor lines out for four days and nights, taking on stores and victuals. Four days Eye walked around that place and the sun never once come out. At least it's wet and green over there. On board, caulkers at work, smell of pitch and tar burns your eyes and nose, settles in your throat. Ship's carpenter replacing rotted boards near the stern. Stern end of the hold empty except for huge ballast stones and salt-shit smelling bilge water that coats trousers black from the knees down. The carpenter's hammer echoes down in that wet dark emptiness. He stops hammering to wipe his cheek with his sleeve. Don't worry, he tells Eye, most of her is good oak, well seasoned. If she takes on water it's the caulkers coming up short. Then we'll join the poor settlers with a turn on the pumps.

Four days. Repairs complete. Revictualing complete. Immigrants show on covered river boats from Bremen. Wooden crates packed with their necessaries are swung into the hold, aside the ship's store of salt pork, corned beef, peas, beans, rice, sauerkraut, potatoes, flour, and plums. Also, casks of drinking water, kegs of pickled herring for the seasickness, and a poke of doctorin' needs—quinine and Glauber's Salt.

May 8. Haul up anchor. Heave-ho. Hoist a sheet. Yessir, head 'em out. She rides low, heavy with the weight of so much longing, so much fear. Eye's slept on the desert and on the prairie, but at sea was the darkest nights he ever knowed. Down in them dark cabins, air stale and smelly around you, straw whispering tales ever' move you make, and under ever'thing, the roll and the sway to remind you how far you be from solid ground.

20   Babes cry. Men long for a shot of wine or a smoke, but wine is doled out small and no smokes allowed below deck. (Fire at sea—there's a hellish thought.) Peas and beans bloat up your stomach. Ever' other one gets the seasicknesses. Slop jars fill and spill. Men, women, and children lie in the smells their bodies make and pray for sleep. Water is short; nobody washes until it rains.

June 7. Boatswain's whistle—like some ole bird squawkin' out. Except for long lists of necessaries to bring over, the immigrant advice books start off in Texas. Don't mention storms that stir up the bottom of the ocean till the ship sails straight up and down. Strike topmasts. Can't know sky from sea—both gray-green, icy and salt-stinging, both howling mad. Sails down, but the wind's after the masts. Vomit, sea spray and rain soak the upper deck. Not in them guide books is the look on Captain Henry's face, of purdee piss-your-pants terror.

June 12. Storm battered. Repairs at sea. Not mentioned in the immigrant advice books, bilging—the godawful endless sound of water coming in through the hull; not mentioned is blood rushing to your brain and pounding with the pounding of the pumps, blisters on top of blisters from the pump handle, the fearful pumping of your heart and sucking of your lungs.

Eye breathes slow and deep, holds to the bar with his gun hand and empties his glass of rum.

June 14. Days off course after the storm. Low on drinking water, all portions halved. Not mentioned in the immigrant books are rancid pork, weevils in the flour, tongue-swelling thirst, and surly sailors.

25   June 16. The *Assurance* hails a five-masted clipper, the *Emma,* biggest immigrant ship afloat. She was out of Antwerp a full three weeks behind the *Assurance.* The *Emma* sends over one full barrel of water, half a keg of wine, a little corned beef, and enough bad news from Germany to worry all the settlers on the accounts of ones they left behind. Riots and maybe war behind them; the wide ocean and maybe Texas ahead.

July 6. The bilious fever—not mentioned in them books. Men, women, and children packed into little plank rooms in steerage. No portholes, just the spitting light of a whale-oil lamp, and air to breathe has to come down the stairs from the upper deck.

The fever-struck are stacked tight, four bunks on top of one another, locked in the smells of their own sweat and shit, them stinky sausages they brung, and the black vomit—not mentioned in no immigrant book. Some recover, plenty don't.

July 23. Five putrefying corpses sacked in sailcloth on the fore deck, weighted at the feet with ballast rocks. A sailor called Little Joe holds the end of a board stuck out over the gunwale, a sixth body on that board, stuck out over the ocean. A face white as that winding cloth—a girl nineteen or twenty—sticks out of the burial bag. Her man bawls and holds the hand of a silent little girl, two or three. Captain Henry nods to a immigrant preacher who starts up a funeral song, *In dem Himmel ist's wunderschon*, about how wonderful heaven is ... the husband gets to the rail and vomits overboard. Captain Henry stops the preacher quick. Captain Henry reaches into his coat and brings out a poke and tosses a fistful of tobacco over the body. Dust to dust. The Quartermaster, Mr. Keene, brings out a big, curved needle and sews the bag closed. They lift the board with a hard jerk and the rocks inside slide, pulling the bag off and into the sea with hardly no splash. *Vater Unser*, Little Joe calls out, as if he were relaying an order from the mate. The little girl dabs at the vomit on her daddy's shirt. Little Joe and Mr. Keene are already lifting another body onto the plank.

Eye clinks his empty glass against the bottle and the barkeep pours him another.

30   August 7. North of Hispanola. Watling's Island where Columbus landed, off to the Northwest. Caulkers and pumps at work in the hold. Eye unties and reties knots up in the rigging on the mizzenmast to avoid a turn on the pumps, to avoid standing thigh-deep in choler and black bile—the humors of despair, to avoid breathing the foul-smelling darkness.

August 9. Becalmed on the tip of Haiti. Worse, even, than the unmentioned storms, seven days and nights of dead calm.

The sea tightens like a corpse, the sky harder'n rock. A week of nights so dark and still you bite your arm to know you ain't already buried deep in your grave. Captain Henry drops a longboat to the island for firewood.

August 18. At anchor off the island of Cuba, loading the water barrels into a longboat. Not mentioned in them hand books, how heavy the empty wooden barrels are, heavier still when the longboat returns. Not mentioned, clouds of mosquitoes. The men bring back a little coffee, plenty of sugar cane. The boatswain cuts a section of the cane and sucks the sweet juice, a stub of cane constantly in his mouth like some fat, green cigar.

August 19. A sudden wailing down in the hold. Frau Lindheimer delivers a smidge of a baby girl. Herr Lindheimer and Herr Schleuning take the first dipper of that Cuban water and name the baby . . .

Eye raises his glass in a toast.

. . . Johanna Galveston Lindheimer.

Eye turns the glass up and his adam's apple bobs three times and the glass is empty again.

Some men of a *Gebirgssanger-bund,* a singing society, sing, *Gott ist die Liebe,* about how loving God is, bless our children, keep us safe, bear us all to Texas. *Hin nach Texas!* Everyone sucks sticks of sugar cane. They talk about birds and flowers, they hug, they smile. Even that fellow whose woman got buried in the ocean, even he sings along. That was more'n Eye could take.

I took me a good stob and went down below decks to find me some rats to kill.

Eye holds out his glass and the barkeep fills it again.

Eye keeps wondering how bad can it be over there that they keep coming, full of questions as children. Load after load, he meets them at the dock with Mexican hand carts. They pile the carts high with trunks of Sunday clothes, as if ther'll be anyplace fit to wear them, and farm tools, as if anthing'd grow in the wild-horse desert he's leadin' them to.

They get a labor of land and a sixty by ninety foot town lot—a red square of dirt. Other colonies, Austin's, Dewitt's, Burnet's, give a league of land and two acre town lot. Eye gets his pay all the same.

Eye turns and faces the whore, the shadow of his hat brim hides his expression, but she feels his jumpy eye moving all over her.

But I'm not so mean I don't hate my part. What's that fellow's expression in the book, *an exercise in futility*.

Sure, he tells them about the country. Land on fire. It burns. Wind rises with the sun and blows hot all day. Locusts buzz the noise of blood rushing in your ear. Land as far as you can see, red and crusty as a scab. Ever'thing that grows has thorns—mesquite, prickly pear, Spanish dagger. Ever'thing that breathes stings—ants, tarantulas, centipedes, scorpions, and snakes—ever' kinda snake from ever' kinda nightmare, 'cept there won't be no water moccasins like you seen near the Gulf. No more mosquitoes neither, 'cause there's not enough water. Prairie snakes fast as a horse at trot, rattlers slower and more deadly. Eye tells them all about it. It's a country of parasites you're walking a month to. Bot-flies lay eggs on horses, bore into stomachs and turn into worms. Gad-flies lay eggs in old tick wounds and in a day and a half hatch maggots. What grows? Besides hardship and misery? Well, there's corn. You'll have cornbread for breakfast and coffee made from roasted corn; for lunch, corn mush with your cornbread; supper's the same, another cup of corn coffee, sometimes a jackrabbit all bone and muscle, sometimes prairie dog, and when you're hungry enough, prickly pear. Sure, you'll scatter them seeds you brung, you'll plant corn, melons, beans, peas—and ever'thing 'cept some of the corn will burn up and you'll wish it would too. Set out orange and apple trees, they wither and die.

45   He tells them, but you think it does any good? Listen, he tells them, cattle die of thirst. You'll share alkali water with your plow horse or mule til ever'thing burns up in the fields and you start thinking about horsemeat, mule steak.

The widow Krueger—Indians kilt her man, run off with her daughter, left her one son. Son went off his head in the heat, wandered around and fell into a den of rattlers coily as a nigger's hair. Eye was at the burying. Hot gust of wind come up and blew Widow Krueger's hat in the boy's grave. It plopped down on his blanket—no trees, no wood for a box. Now she goes hatless in the sun and hopes for her brains to fry.

Think on that, Eye says to nobody in particular.

But these people persist in their foolishness. The Lord's supposed to watch over idiots and children. Add immigrants. They cut loose the only nigger slaves in the colony. They make up to Meskins and talk about irrigation. Herr Lindheimer shoots a tough old deer and they invite the niggers and Meskins and a couple of starving old Indians. Thanksgiving—like them other pilgrims.

A crazy idea—coulda been anyone's, they all been too long in the sun—they gonna have a wedding party, marry ever' one to this new life. Eye reminds them married life's hell.

No flour or sugar for a wedding cake, the women get three of their round hatboxes. Biggest box on bottom, middle-sized box next, then that air little one atop. For icing, they spread corn meal mush over all and set him out in the sun to bake hard as adobe. Old man Waldeck produces a jar of powdered arsenic carried all the way from Germany to kill weeds and rats. Ain't no weeds and rats surviving here in the new land, so they put that poison to different use, mixing a spit-paste to whiten up the icing. Nobody better lick that bowl nor stick his finger in for a taste. Way they all waste most of the day on that cake, puts Eye in mind of them people in the Bible melting down all their gold to make a cow idol.

Finally, a reason to open them trunks for fancy duds and keepsakes they toted across the ocean. Late afternoon and hot as the hinges of Hell; they set the wedding cake out in the dusty street and promenade in embroidered shirts with stand up collars, wool frock coats, round felt hats that come outta them cake-shaped boxes. Their faces, red as the desert, stick out of white collars above black coats. They look like buzzards circling. Indians see that cake sitting out in the road, war dance all around it. Niggers laugh. Meskins call it a *fandango*.

Sun goes down sudden into the barren land, heat underfoot all night. Hot winds die down like a burned out fire. Meskin guitars and Indian drums stir the still night air and it throbs with heat like coals.

All night they grin to beat the band, niggers and Meskins dancing and Indians doing pantomimes and ever' dutchman singing a German beer hall song to the fiery taste of mescal.

Them people, they hang on to their foolishness like a comet to its tail. Eye shakes his head and polishes off the last dregs of rum in his glass.

55   And what for? Tomorrow, the wedding party's over and the sun hot as ever. No honeymoon out there. Next day, wool coats and felt hats packed back in trunks, put away with all their shivaree. Next day, that hollow wedding cake still be baking in the sun, so many layers of hot air, a graven image of sweetness poison to eat.

Lisa K. Buchanan

Lisa K. Buchanan has published two stories in *Mademoiselle*.

The Mother Who Never Was

SHE HAS NEVER SPOKEN, but I'm sure that it must be my daughter who is calling. I imagine her coming home from school, throwing her red sneakers in the corner, shoving a chocolate brownie into her mouth, sitting down at the phone in her sister's room and dialing my number. She must wonder who I am and how I could have given her up; she must dream of the person I might be. She longs to hear my voice—then hangs up when I answer. It's her turn to reject.

The ring seems to get longer each time, 11, 12, 13 rings. I try to resist, but finally I give in, jump up from where I'm working in the garden, bolt into the house and lunge for the phone. Hello, hello! Silence, click, the dreaded dial tone. I think of her like me: curious, persistent, terrified, hopeful; trying to make sense out of the strange arrangement by which she, my only child, is being raised by a couple I met the day before she was born.

AFTER I HANG UP, I stand on the deck for a moment, descend the cedar stairs back to the garden. It is February and I've switched to working evening shifts at Porter's Nursery so I can spend the days landscaping the yard that the previous tenants used for a trash burial. My husband thinks I'm pleasantly insane to build a garden here in the gritty, forgotten dirt between urban houses. I find plastic bags of dirty dishes that someone couldn't face, piles of rotten newspaper along with plastic take-out containers that will never decompose, old scuffed shoes, an unopened bag of kitty litter, some wadded-up T-shirts. But amid the mess, I like the shaping of a landscape over months of hard labor. I like the sifting of soil with manure and the exhilaration of unearthing discarded elements all morning. I'm mud-caked and sweaty, and today is one of the many in which I can't stop thinking about my daughter.

When the calls come, I use tricks to try to get her to speak. I say, "Hello, this is Anna," so she'll know she has the right person. I say, "Hello, Baskin-Robbins," so she'll stammer and maybe ask if we have Bananamellow today. This, to hear her precious voice, know some small detail about her, such as the ice cream she likes. Once I tried pretending I was an answering machine: "Hello, you've reached Anna Pasciano and I can't come to the phone right now but please leave a message." I was sure I heard her soft, third-grade breathing. I begged silently for the sound of her voice, but the phone had been hung up.

5   Once I even picked up the phone and answered, "Hello. Kathleen?" That's what they said they were going to name her and I thought that if I could just catch her off guard. . . . But it was my husband calling home from work. "Anna," he said, "you need to let go."

Ross is patient and loving, but he can't feel my pain. I used to recite him my series of if-onlys: If only there had been money or a place to go; if only they could have predicted that she would be the only child I would conceive; if only they had let me hold her just once. But Ross and I exhausted the topic of children years ago, during long afternoons of working in each other's yards, digging, potting, talking, making love outside and contemplating a life together.

In our eight years of marriage we have acquired nieces and nephews, numerous godchildren and countless neighbor kids. And I rarely speak of Kathleen.

According to the social worker who handled the adoption, I would have other children. I would forget the pain. I should be proud to have provided a childless couple with the gift of a daughter. But I find little satisfaction in these noble sentiments. There is no resolve to having relinquished my only child. I think I will mourn her forever.

I HAVE STARTED MANY GARDENS IN MANY BACK-YARDS and it's a different process each time. Here the soil is grainy and full of tiny pebbles. The bay fog is moist and salty. The sun warms the ground in the morning, then once again by late afternoon in our yard sunken among the tall Victorian houses. Impatiens will flourish in the shade near the house, and basil will go to seed with summer's last gasp. White lilies abound, but the delphiniums that towered over me in my childhood will not grow here.

I remember summer mornings helping my mother water her garden. I remember lying in bed at night, while the loud Montana winds ripped through the yard. I remember waking up one November morning to a frost that had crushed every delphinium in the garden. My mother laughed gently at my tear-streaked face and explained that frost and wind are as much a part of the earth as the sunshine and delphiniums, and that each has its season. But Mom, I moaned, we made them grow. They grew from seeds, she said, we only nourish their environment. I stared at my mother. She and God had conspired, casually, in the sad fate of the delphiniums. They'll be back in the spring, she promised, then lit the wood stove and started breakfast.

SOMETIMES I THINK OF KATHLEEN WHEN I READ THE NEWSPAPER: New Jersey Youths Carry Out Suicide Pact in Garage. Man Picks Up Hitchhiker, Age 11, Hacks Off Her Left Leg Below the Knee. Adopted Child Found Alive, Parents Murdered by Housekeeper. Mother Kills Porn-Star Daughter. I grab at the small things I remember: the Irish surname, the father's optometry practice in Pleasant Creek. I sift out the parts that can't be my daughter. Asian facial features, the November birthday, the identical twin. Hideous as it is—the momentary thought, that any of these victims could be Kathleen—the morbidity comforts me somehow, as if imagining the worst prevents it from occurring. Or because the fantasy is something and the void is nothing.

IT WILL BE NICE IN APRIL TO PAINT the trellises and flower boxes, to have hoed and sifted and planted seeds. I will water twice a day, nourishing life I can't see. I will worry that the seeds may be poor, the soil too sandy or that the neighbor kids will play war games in the yard while I'm at work. I will worry that the beauty shop downstairs may dump strange chemicals by the fence. Where I see fertility and the potential for life, others see dirt.

But my affair with life underground will pass, and by March, my daffodils will sprout, the first sign of life poking quietly through the dirt in the northeast corner of our yard. I will water them, talk to them, play music on the patio for them and everyone will think I am insane. The tiny, dark leaves will be pliable and vulnerable in this harsh environment, but they will survive. Other sprouts will follow; it will be a triumph.

I NEVER SAW KATHLEEN IN THE HOSPITAL, but I did see her once when she was about five, in a restaurant in San Francisco. I had ordered a sandwich to go and was standing by the cash register when I felt someone staring at me from a booth. It was my daughter's adoptive mother and I knew her immediately, though she looked older and not so glamorous as when I had met her at the hospital. Her lips had been bright red then, she had been a proud, beautiful woman of 38, with an Anne Bancroft-ness about her. She had sat next to my bed and shown me pictures of the little girl she and her husband had adopted the year before, pictures of toys and rooms and the backyard of the house my daughter would live in. The husband had paced nervously around the room while his wife held my pale hand and massaged my swollen knuckles.

15   But in the restaurant the woman was alone in her terror, being the only one who recognized me. She went white and damp, and her mouth fell open. When our eyes met, she turned quickly to her older daughter, helped her with the complicated task of getting the bite of rhubarb from plate to mouth. The woman was hoping she had imagined me, that the next time she looked up I would be gone forever, as planned from the beginning. My daughter sat next to her, slurping soup from a big spoon, her hair dark and unruly like mine, her skin fair and Irish like her father's. She looked like I had at five, dressed dorkish and square, in clothes chosen by her mother, who is 20 years older than me, the same age as my own mother.

Kathleen's father laid his finger gently on my daughter's fat elbow and gave her a quiet-the-slurping look. I left the sandwich on the counter and ran, sprinted across the parking lot, threw the car in gear and barreled through the back driveway into the alley. I didn't stop till I got home, the blades having dutifully wiped the dry windshield for six miles. All I could think of was that I wouldn't have dressed her that way.

I consider the horrors Kathleen must have about me: that I died from giving her birth. That I didn't want her or try very hard to keep her. That there was something about the way she felt inside my body that made me decide to relinquish her or that I was stupid or careless or promiscuous, and that those traits are genetically ingrained in her character. Or that I never think of her now. Her parents said they planned to tell her from the beginning that she was adopted and that they would answer her questions but encourage her not to dwell on it. What if she's too shy to ask? Did they tell her the truth, or that I had been killed in a car wreck along with her father?

THE SOCIAL WORKER FROM THE COUNTY said that when Kathleen is 18, she can request background information based on interviews with me when I was pregnant. The social workers will tell her that I made my unselfish choice with her best interests in mind, that her adoptive parents wanted her more than anything in the entire world and could give her a better home. They might tell her that musical talent and hay fever run in the family, that I am of Italian descent, that I sew, garden and sing in a choir. They will tell her that by now I probably have children of my own, that to contact me could disrupt my family, that I have probably put my painful past behind me and that they have no current address for me. They will probably not tell her that tetracycline may give her a throat rash. Nor that tailbones run long in the Pasciano line and, though surgery is possible, the bone grows back after a few years. And they probably will not tell her that her mother and one of her aunts have endometriosis, and that losing a child is not a pain you forget.

IT WOULD BE EASY ENOUGH FOR ME TO FIND MY DAUGHTER and I may try when she is older, though I have promised in writing and in spirit to stay away. I want to know that she has a good life; I want her to know she was loved. I want us both to have the peace of mind that could come only from looking into each other's faces.

20   But for now, I imagine her sitting by her sister's teal-colored phone, her long legs in some gawky position, brownie consumed. I see her living in a big house at the end of a cul-de-sac in the suburban hills. She has her own room, full of pretty things, clothes and books, maybe a flute.

She has a peach tree outside her window. She is physically stunning with thick Italian curls and liquid, dark eyes like mine; she has the narrow family feet and a tailbone just long enough to make one hour of math in a wooden chair impossible. She has her father's milky skin and his fine neck and jawbone. She is immune to the Pasciano double chin.

There are times when my garden is a burden: mornings when I don't feel like watering, afternoons when I get tired of screaming at the neighbor kids every time they hop the fence and land on my begonias. Sometimes the worms get the tomatoes before I do, and when the beets I have grown, picked and washed go moldy in the refrigerator, I bemoan the waste of my efforts, swear off forever this need to cultivate botanical life.

Then I will pinch back the fuchsias and make pesto sauce from the basil, plant spinach, carrots and brussels sprouts for fall. In the spring we'll serve fresh strawberries and drink wine with friends and neighbors and people from work. The garden will be lush with petunias and foxgloves; my husband will take his annual snapshot of me among them. And some afternoon when I'm sitting on the patio with a cup of tea, my daughter will call. I will answer; her heart will pound as she speaks. She will not hang up.

Alberto Alvaro Ríos

Alberto Alvaro Ríos is the author of *The Lime Orchard Woman, Teodoro Luna's Two Kisses, The Iguana Killer: Twelve Stories of the Heart,* and several books of poetry. He has received the Walt Whitman Award, the Western States Book Award for Fiction, and three Pushcart Prizes.

Trains at Night

MR. LEE, AS HE TRANSFERRED CHICKEN FEED FROM THE LARGE BIN to his everyday pitcher, noticed how the dust rose from the seeds, how steam rises from a landscape, cold, or hot from a white cup of *café con leche,* how smoke rises from a casual backyard fire, how a soul is given up from a sick man. He did not take meaning from this, it was not instruction to him. He simply saw it.

However, when the soldiers came, he had wished possession of that capability, of effecting a rising beyond his own body, of leaving it for them to take, and thereby not feeling what they would do to him, which was unimaginable.

He saw the moment of his imagined escape everywhere, in everything, in the rising of smoke from a cigarette, in a flock of sparrows taking flight. Even, he thought, in the sound of a song let go from the mouth, a whistled aria. That a note of music should take its rightful place with the birds.

He wished it equally for all of them, but his wish did not work very well. The soldiers rounded up all the Chinese they could find, in a day and a night, without warning or manners, without explanation, by neighbor's direction and by rumor and by store sign. Who could have thought this is what would happen, said the townspeople afterward.

5   But a soldier is a soldier, and who could say *no* to a soldier's voice. A brown suit like that takes a man, and turns him into his parts. He is nobody's son anymore.

They are always there, without birth and without death, these soldiers. Nobody could say where a soldier comes from. Or who his teachers are, or what they must look like. Where are manners such that a loud step, a stiff neck, a salute in place of the rightful shaking of a hand, are marks of grace. Without the hand offered, where is the chance of agreement. Where is the chance of understanding what another has been through by the feeling of roughness in his palm.

MR. LEE WAS MARRIED WITH HIS BODY AND IN HIS HEART for a thousand years to Jesusita, married because of, he would shrug his shoulders, who can say. It was like the workings, the intestines, of an opera, he would suggest, and were they not, the two of them, worthy singers in the plot. She would shake her head at him and say she did not understand.

But she did. Not in the way he said it, but she understood in some other way, in the words spoken by his face, clearly what he said.

Mr. Lee was glad that she herself was not Chinese, today. He was glad that she did not look like she needed to be taken away to the trains. He was glad that she did not look like she could profit from a stay in the place where the train would go. Wherever that was, and whatever it meant. To the landscape at the end of the tracks.

10   And Mr. Lee was glad that his daughters looked like their mother. That he had not given them on their faces a ticket for the train, had not attached it to them so that they would not lose

it, the way one might pin a child's mitten to his jacket. In that way, he was happy not to have been able to provide for them. To have been an unfit father, only in this way. Only today.

The Twenties were over now and things had seemed to be getting better, the Revolution, the Depression: it was all over. But to climb out of something like that a country has to grab a hold of something else, some foothold to lift itself, something to step on. That is what this new decade was for, and that is what the Chinese were for, said the president.

Like Mr. Lee, he had said this not in regular words, but with some other part of himself. Something equally understandable, equally forceful.

These kinds of nights happen as one would imagine: the president gets indigestion after a meal of bad fish and spoiled butter, a suspect wheel of cheese. He tries to do something, he tries the carbonating powders.

And more. In pain he orders the arrest of all Chinese in the country and their deportation back to China. Who would complain, after all, or who would complain any louder than anyone else, since there were so many voices of complaint for so many things.

15 It could have been someone else, the Germans, or the Americans, but what was the use. People thought the Chinese were beginning to own everything, and there were just enough of them. In truth, it was that their store signs stood out so much, and their faces. In truth, which everybody knew, there were many other choices, but this one was the quickest.

There were the people in Alamos, for example, who lived next to the great silver mine. The ones who ran the operation, at home they had silver everything, silver broom covers, brooms themselves made of silver, and silver on the pillars holding up their houses. Anything to which silver might be added was fashionable there.

But to get them to give it up, well, it was a different thing.

HIS FOUR DAUGHTERS CRIED WHEN THEY HEARD what was happening, and cried when they heard the soldiers getting closer. But Jesusita did what she could.

In those days the family lived in *Los Apóstoles,* twelve row houses, or rather, twelve row rooms, owned by Don Lázaro, who did not worry about things very much, and who when asked said that he most certainly did not rent to the Chinese. With what he charged, he said, one could hardly call it rent.

20   That there were twelve apartments gave rise to both the humor of the name and the mathematics of a problem. Since they were all built at once and were identical, if one problem arose, there were as if by magic twelve. It was a simple and devastating equation for Don Lázaro, who did not always put much stock in the laws of multiplication.

Through the years, each of these quarters began to take on an individual aspect, as Don Lázaro approached each problem as something different from the one before and the one after. He did not, after all, want to insult anyone by not giving them the consideration of listening to their particular problem. Nor, for that matter, did he wish to offend them by turning down a *café con leche* as he listened. He was a good listener, and sometimes he would offer to boil the milk for the second cup of coffee. And he gave each problem its own solution.

But at very least, twelve similar-looking yards occupied the space behind these apartments, each with a small fence, or some such barrier. And those who knew their own yard knew their neighbor's.

IT WAS NIGHT BY NOW, and as the soldiers came and knocked at the first house, Jesusita took her husband into the next yard, and so on down as the soldiers knocked in sequence, as only soldiers with their peculiar efficiency would do.

There were enough garbage cans and compost heaps, enough odd noises by dogs disturbed and grizzled cats, that Jesusita was able to move her husband with some ease. Not the least reason was the irregular rule of geometry, which stated that a small garbage heap was a large mountain to a lazy man. These soldiers were tired already from so much work in the afternoon, and without respite.

25   The seven soldiers in the vicinity did not equal one mother calling her child to dinner here. A mother knows how to find a child.

When the soldiers reached the last apartment, Jesusita, who had said she was bringing in laundry, brought her husband back to their rooms, and in through the back door.

His four daughters had said when the soldiers knocked that he was not there, and had not been there for some time, and that they did not know where he was or when he would return, and then shrugged their shoulders.

It figures, the lieutenant, or the captain, or whatever he was, had said, these Chinese, after all. He had a deep voice, too loud.

The daughters said nothing and went about their business, and at that cue the soldier harrumphed and did the same, saying something vague. If you see him, well, you know then, call us, and the daughters replied also with something vague. Of course, all right, then.

30   When they left, Jesusita brought her husband in and they all helped to hide him inside the cabinet of the radio, a Ward's "Airline" model, with the word *Heterodyne* underneath. It was a brown piece of furniture, part Greek columns and part lyre in decoration. Before they moved the radio back against the wall, they all looked at him, with the radio tubes and wires all above his head.

He looked like something from the movies, something from a Saturday morning, and they wanted to laugh and cry at the same time. And they heard him say, This cannot be happening. And as they looked at him, they saw that he was right. This was not like doing the laundry or preparing the evening meal. This was nothing they knew. This was after all something from the movies. But it was as if the manager had locked the doors of the theater, and they had to live with this beast.

NO ONE SAW MR. LEE FOR MANY YEARS. He did not live here anymore, his family said. But they were not sad. He lived in between the bed sheets and in the bathroom. He fit into the small spaces of the house, and did not eat much.

The soldiers never came back to look for him, but then again there was nothing to look for. Everyone in the town knew that he had disappeared. A pity, they would say, *qué lástima*. He was such a smart man.

But times changed, and every now and then people saw him, slowly.

35   They were not surprised. They understood something of how a thing could happen and not happen. There had been nothing in the newspapers or on the radio about that singular night. They understood how Mr. Lee could be gone and still be here. There was no mystery in seeing something that did not exist. The government had taught them well, and they were good citizens. There were, they knew, many kinds of ghosts.

The rounding up of the Chinese lasted only the one night, as long as the president's heartburn. They loaded them, as people later told one another even in public, into boxcars and open cattle and cotton cars. All over the country the soldiers looked, but especially along the border, where they might have been heard, so many voices, such a different language.

Many of the wives who had grown up in this town went with their men, to live in China. They took their children, too, and something or other in their arms. Some of them later came back, and some did not. They were not treated well. But such a thing was not a new life, and they were used to it. Being treated well was not much of a measure for anything anymore.

Not all of the Chinese left, however, and Mr. Lee was not the only one to be hidden. Some men had been dressed like women, and like animals, which was a gypsy trick. And none of them was seen for many years. There was a yipping at the moon some nights during this time, recognizable as coyotes in any other decade, but some townspeople said it was the Chinese. By this they did not mean that they were still in the animal disguises they had worn, but, rather, it was a remark about the quality of voice they heard.

It was a sound reminiscent of the German man, Mr. Luder, whose wife Margarita had died in childbirth along with the child. In the daytime he had a business in clocks, something regular, but every night he slept on the grave of his wife and child, and he wept.

40   The business later failed, and all he could do was to sleep on that stone and dirt, or walk around the town getting ready to sleep. This walking toward sleep became his job. People, in fact, had sometimes heard Mr. Luder's sobbing, and thought it was coyotes, and later the sounds of the Chinese. It was a sound many animals shared.

Some time later, as many Chinese had made their way up into Arizona, some of them would be mistaken again, this time for Japanese, and taken away once more. But they were returned. Again without the courtesy of manners.

When the government later rounded up the Yaqui Indians, they did it the other way around. They could not capture the men. But the women and children who came down from the mountains to trade goods were easy enough to take.

This time they put the women in trains, the old trick of how to catch the men, and sent them to the Yucatán just like that. Traveling was dangerous then, as the Yaquis took up the attacking of all the trains in the region. The Yaquis, many people said, were vicious.

MR. LEE, THE TOWNSPEOPLE REMARKED REGULARLY, was very smart, but by smart they meant a great deal more, which they could not say. He was rumored not so much to be Chinese, but to have had a gypsy father himself, who had shown him the ways of other worlds, who had given him the singular ability to live well in a radio. By now they had heard the story of that night from Jesusita. In our radio, she to them, looking like a Martian.

45   Everyone had laughed when Jesusita told the story, but not too hard. Of course, they thought, with a look each to the other. Of course. He was not, after all, of this place.

When he walked along the path between the black walnut trees lining the streets, it was clear now that he had made his place. That the government had not been able to take him, no matter what the law. That he, because of his head that lit up with tubes, knew something more than the law.

They laughed, but not too hard, and they called on him for advice when they were in trouble, because he would understand.

They were a little scared of him, of course, because he knew something about things. He knew the underbelly and the tomorrow and yesterday of things, he knew their opposites and their half-turns. He knew the radio, after all, from the inside out.

He was like Mr. Luder, they sometimes said. He knew about life. He knew about it as if he had walked the perimeter of a park, and thereby gauged something of the dimensions of neat lawn and the heights of the eucalyptus trees.

And his pronunciation of words, unlike the laws of the presidents, never changed, a little stilted even after so many years, a little wrong: it showed that he understood their language better than they did, that he spoke correctly. There was something wrong in this place and in these days, and they heard it in Mr. Lee's accent. He would talk, strangelike, and they knew he was right, about anything, about the weather.

50   The *wedder*, he would say, and they would understand. And when he smoked, they would think they sometimes saw him in the cloud.

Margaret Atwood

Margaret Atwood published two stories in *The New Yorker* in 1990. Among her books of stories are *Dancing Girls, Encounters with the Enemy,* and *Bluebeard's Egg.* Among her many novels are *The Edible Woman, Surfacing, Lady Oracle, Life Before Man, The Handmaid's Tale,* and *Cat's Eye.* She has also published several books of poems and nonfiction.

Kat

ON THE THIRTEENTH OF NOVEMBER, DAY OF UNLUCK, month of the dead, Kat went into the Toronto General Hospital for an operation. It was for an ovarian cyst, a large one.

Many women had them, the doctor told Kat. Nobody knew why. There wasn't any way of finding out whether the thing was malignant, whether it contained, already, the spores of her death. Not before they went in. He spoke of "going in" the way she'd heard old veterans in TV documentaries speak of assaults on enemy territory. There was the same tensing of the jaw, the same fierce gritting of the teeth, the same grim enjoyment. Except that what he would be going into was her body. Counting down, waiting for the anesthetic, Kat, too, gritted her teeth fiercely. She was terrified, but she was also curious. Curiosity has got her through a lot.

She'd made the doctor promise to save the thing for her, whatever it was, so she could have a look. She was intensely interested in her own body, in anything it might choose to do or produce; although when flaky Dania, who did layout at the magazine, told her this growth was a message to her from her body, and she ought to sleep with an amethyst under the pillow to calm her vibrations, Kat told her to stuff it.

The cyst turned out to be a benign tumor. Kat liked that use of "benign," as if the thing had a soul and wished her well. It was big as a grapefruit, the doctor said. "Big as a coconut," said Kat. Other people had grapefruits. "Coconut" was better. It conveyed the hardness of it, and the hairiness, too.

5   The hair in it was red—long strands of it wound round and round inside, like a ball of wet wool gone berserk or like the guck you pull out of a clogged bathroom-sink drain. There were little bones in it, too, or fragments of bone—bird bones, the bones of a sparrow crushed by a car. There was a scattering of nails, toe or finger. There were five perfectly formed teeth.

"Is this abnormal?" Kat asked the doctor, who smiled. Now that he had gone in and come out again, unscathed, he was less clenched.

"Abnormal? No," he said carefully, as if breaking the news to a mother about a freakish accident to her newborn. "Let's just say it's fairly common." Kat was a little disappointed. She would have preferred uniqueness.

She asked for a bottle of formaldehyde, and put the cut-open tumor into it. It was hers, it was benign, it did not deserve to be thrown away. She took it back to her apartment and stuck it on the mantelpiece. She named it Hairball. It isn't that different from having a stuffed bear's head or a preserved ex-pet or anything else with fur and teeth looming over your fireplace; or she pretends it isn't. Anyway, it certainly makes an impression.

Ger doesn't like it. Despite his supposed yen for the new and outré, he is a squeamish man. The first time he comes around (sneaks around, creeps around) after the operation, he tells Kat to throw Hairball out. He calls it "disgusting." Kat refuses point-blank, and says she'd rather have Hairball in a bottle on her mantelpiece than the soppy dead flowers he's brought her, which will anyway rot a lot sooner than Hairball will. As a mantelpiece ornament, Hairball is far superior. Ger says Kat has a tendency to push things to extremes, to go over the edge, merely from a juvenile desire to shock, which is hardly a substitute for wit. One of these days, he says, she will go way too far. Too far for him is what he means.

10   "That's why you hired me, isn't it?" she says. "Because I go way too far." But he's in one of his analyzing moods. He can see these tendencies of hers reflected in her work on the magazine, he says. All that leather and those grotesque and tortured-looking poses are heading down a track he and others are not at all sure they should continue to follow. Does she see what he means, does she take his point? It's a point that's been made before. She shakes her head slightly, says nothing. She knows how that translates: there have been complaints from the advertisers. *Too bizarre, too kinky.* Tough.

"Want to see my scar?" she says. "Don't make me laugh, though, you'll crack it open." Stuff like that makes him dizzy: anything with a hint of blood, anything gynecological. He almost threw up in the delivery room, when his wife had a baby two years ago. He'd told her that with pride. Kat thinks about sticking a cigarette into the side of her mouth, as in a black-and-white movie of the forties. She thinks about blowing the smoke into his face.

Her insolence used to excite him during their arguments. Then there would be a grab of her upper arms, a smoldering, violent kiss. He kisses her as if he thinks someone else is watching him and judging the image they make together. Kissing the latest thing, hard and shiny, purple-mouthed, crop-headed; kissing a girl, a woman, a girl in a little crotch-hugger skirt and skintight leggings. He likes mirrors.

But he isn't excited now. And she can't decoy him into bed; she isn't ready for that yet, she isn't healed. He has a drink, which he doesn't finish, holds her hand as an afterthought, gives her a couple of avuncular pats on the off-white outsized alpaca shoulder, leaves too quickly.

"Goodbye, Gerald," she says. She pronounces the name with mockery. It's a negation of him, an abolishment of him, like ripping a medal off his chest. It's a warning.

15   He'd been Gerald when they first met. It was she who transformed him, first to Gerry, then to Ger. (Rhymed with "flair," rhymed with "dare.") She made him get rid of those sucky pursed-mouth ties, told him what shoes to wear, got him to buy a loose-cut Italian suit, redid his hair. A lot of his current tastes—in food, in drink, in recreational drugs, in women's entertainment underwear—were once hers. In his new phase, with his new, hard, stripped-down name ending on the sharpened note of "r," he is her creation.

As she is her own. During her childhood, she was a romanticized Katherine, dressed by her misty-eyed, fussy mother in dresses that looked like ruffled pillowcases. By high school, she'd shed the frills and emerged as a bouncy, round-faced Kathy, with gleaming freshly washed hair and enviable teeth, eager to please and no more interesting than a health-food ad. At university she was Kath, blunt and no-bullshit in her Take-Back-the-Night jeans and checked shirt and her bricklayer-style striped denim peaked hat. When she ran away to England, she sliced herself down to Kat. It was economical, street-feline, and pointed as a nail. It was also unusual. In England you had to do something to get their attention, especially if you weren't English. Safe in this incarnation, she Ramboed through the eighties.

It was the name, she still thinks, that got her the interview, and then the job. The job was with an avant-garde magazine, the kind that was printed on matte stock in black and white, with overexposed closeups of women with hair blowing over their eyes, one nostril prominent: *the razor's edge*, it was called. Haircuts as art, some real art, film reviews, a little stardust, wardrobes of ideas that were clothes and of clothes that were ideas—the metaphysical shoulder pad. She learned her trade well, hands-on. She learned what worked.

She made her way up the ladder, from layout to design, then to the supervision of whole spreads, and then whole issues. It wasn't easy, but it was worth it. She had become a creator; she created total looks. After a while, she could walk down the street in Soho or stand in the lobby at openings and witness her handi-work incarnate, strolling around in outfits she'd put together, spouting her warmed-over pronouncements. It was like being God, only God had never got around to off-the-rack lines.

By that time her face had lost its roundness, though the teeth, of course, remained: there was something to be said for North American dentistry. She'd shaved off most of the hair, worked on the drop-dead stare, perfected a certain turn of the neck that conveyed an aloof inner authority. What you had to make them believe was that you knew something they didn't know yet. What you also had to make them believe was that they, too, could know this thing, this thing that would give them eminence and power and sexual allure, would attract envy to them—but for a price. The price of the magazine. What they could never get through their heads was that it was done entirely with cameras. Frozen light, frozen time. Given the angle, she could make any woman look ugly. Any man, as well. She could make anyone look beautiful, or at least interesting. It was all photography, it was all iconography. It was all in the choosing eye. This was the thing that could never be bought, no matter how much of your pitiful monthly wage you blew on snakeskin.

20   Despite the status, *the razor's edge* was fairly low-paying. Kat herself could not afford many of the things she contextualized so well. The grottiness and expense of London began to get to her; she got tired of gorging on the canapés at literary launches in order to scrimp on groceries, tired of the fuggy smell of ciga-rettes ground into the red-and-maroon carpeting of pubs, tired of the pipes bursting every time it froze in winter, and of the Clarissas and Melissas and Penelopes at the magazine rabbiting on about how they had been literally, absolutely, totally freezing all night, and how it lit-erally, absolutely, totally, usually never got that cold. It always got that cold. The pipes always burst. Nobody thought of putting in real pipes, ones that would not burst next time. Burst pipes were an English tradition, like so many others.

Like, for instance, English men. Charm the knickers off you with their mellow vowels and frivolous verbiage, and then, once

they'd got them off, panic and run. Or else stay and whinge. The
English called it "whinging" instead of whining. It was better,
really. Like a creaking hinge. It was a traditional compliment to
be whinged at by an Englishman. It was his way of saying he
trusted you, he was conferring upon you the priviledge of getting to know the real him. The inner, whinging him. That was
how they thought of women, really: whinge receptacles. Kat
could play it, but that didn't mean she liked it.

She had an advantage over the English women, though: she
was of no class. She had no class. She was in a class of her own.
She could roll around among the English men, all different
kinds of them, secure in the knowledge that she was not being
measured against the class yardsticks and accent detectors they
carried around in their back pockets, was not subject to the petty
snobberies and resentments which lent such richness to their
inner lives. The flip side of this freedom was that she was beyond
the pale. She was a colonial—how fresh, how vital, how anonymous, how finally of no consequence. Like a hole in the wall, she
could be told all secrets and then abandoned with no guilt.

She was too smart, of course. The English men were very
competitive; they liked to win. Several times it hurt. Twice she
had abortions, because the men in question were not up for
the alternative. She learned to say that she didn't want children
anyway, that if she longed for a rug rat she would buy a gerbil.
Her life began to seem long. Her adrenaline was running out.
Soon she would be thirty, and all she could see ahead was more
of the same.

THIS WAS HOW THINGS WERE WHEN GERALD TURNED
UP. "You're terrific," he said, and she was ready to hear it, even
from him, even though "terrific" was a word that had probably
gone out with fifties crewcuts. She was ready for his voice by that
time, too: the flat, metallic, nasal tone of the Great Lakes, with its
clear hard "r"s and its absence of theatricality. Dull normal. The
speech of her people. It came to her suddenly that she was an exile.

25   Gerald was scouting, Gerald was recruiting. He'd heard
about her, looked at her work, sought her out. One of the big

companies back in Toronto was launching a new fashion-oriented magazine, he said: up-market, international in its coverage, of course, but with some Canadian fashion in it, too, and with lists of stores where the items portrayed could actually be bought. In that respect, they felt they'd have it all over the competition, those American magazines that assumed you could only get Gucci in New York or Los Angeles. Heck, times had changed, you could get it in Edmonton! You could get it in Winnipeg!

Kat had been away too long. There was Canadian fashion now? The English quip would be to say that "Canadian fashion" was an oxymoron. She refrained from making it, lit a cigarette with her cyanide-green Covent Garden-boutique leather-covered lighter (as featured in the May issue of *the razor's edge*), looked Gerald in the eye. "London is a lot to give up," she said levelly. She glanced around the see-me-here Mayfair restaurant where they were finishing lunch, a restaurant she'd chosen because she'd known he was paying. She'd never spend that kind of money on food otherwise. "Where would I eat?"

Gerald assured her that Toronto was now the restaurant capital of Canada. He himself would be happy to be her guide. There was a great Chinatown, there was world-class Italian. Then he paused, took a breath. "I've been meaning to ask you," he said. "About the name. Is that Kat as in Krazy?" He thought this was suggestive. She'd heard it before.

"No," she said. "It's Kat as in KitKat. That's a chocolate bar. Melts in your mouth." She gave him her stare, quirked her mouth, just a twitch.

Gerald became flustered, but he pushed on. They wanted her, they needed her, they loved her, he said in essence. Someone with her fresh, innovative approach and her experience would be worth a lot of money to them, relatively speaking. But there were rewards other than the money. She would be in on the initial concept, she would have a formative influence, she would have a free hand. He named a sum that made her gasp, inaudibly of course. By now she knew better than to betray desire.

30   SO SHE MADE THE JOURNEY BACK, did her three months
of culture shock, tried the world-class Italian and the great
Chinese, and seduced Gerald at the first opportunity, right in his
junior vice-presidential office. It was the first time Gerald had
been seduced in such a location, or perhaps ever. Even though it
was after hours, the danger frenzied him. It was the idea of it.
The daring. The image of Kat kneeling on the broadloom in a
legendary bra that until now he'd seen only in the lingerie ads of
the Sunday *New York Times,* unzipping him in full view of the silver-
framed engagement portrait of his wife that complemented the
impossible ballpoint-pen set on his desk. At that time he was so
straight he felt compelled to take off his wedding ring and place
it carefully in the ashtray first. The next day he brought her a box
of David Wood Food Shop chocolate truffles. They were the best,
he told her, anxious that she should recognize their quality. She
found the gesture banal, but also sweet. The banality, the sweetness, the hunger to impress: that was Gerald.

Gerald was the kind of man she wouldn't have bothered with
in London. He was not funny, he was not knowledgeable, he had
little verbal charm. But he was eager, he was tractable, he was
blank paper. Although he was eight years older than she was, he
seemed much younger. She took pleasure in his furtive, boyish
delight in his own wickedness. And he was so grateful. "I can
hardly believe this is happening," he said, more frequently than
was necessary and usually in bed.

His wife, whom Kat encountered (and still encounters) at
many tedious company events, helped to explain his gratitude.
The wife was a priss. Her name was Cheryl. Her hair looked as
if she still used big rollers and embalm-your-hairdo spray.
Her mind was room-by-room Laura Ashley wallpaper: tiny,
unopened pastel buds arranged in straight rows. She probably
put on rubber gloves to make love, and checked it off on a list
afterwards. One more messy household chore. She looked at Kat
as if she'd like to spritz her with air deodorizer. Kat revenged
herself by picturing Cheryl's bathrooms; hand towels embroidered with lilies, fuzzy covers on the toilet seats.

The magazine itself got off to a rocky start. Although Kat
had lots of lovely money to play with, and although it was a chal-

lenge to be working in color, she did not have the free hand Gerald had promised her. She had to contend with the company board of directors, who were all men, who were all accountants or indistinguishable from them, who were cautious and slow as moles.

"It's simple," Kat told them. "You bombard them with images of what they ought to be, and you make them feel grotty for being the way they are. You're working with the gap between reality and perception. That's why you have to hit them with something new, something they've never seen before, something they aren't. Nothing sells like anxiety."

35   The board, on the other hand, felt that their readership should simply be offered more of what they already had. More fur, more sumptuous leather, more cashmere. More established names. The board had no sense of improvisation, no wish to take risks, no sporting instincts, no desire to put one over on the readers just for the hell of it. "Fashion is like hunting," Kat told them, hoping to appeal to their male hormones, if any. "It's playful, it's intense, it's predatory. It's blood and guts. It's erotic." But to them it was about good taste. They wanted Dress-for-Success. Kat wanted scattergun ambush.

Everything became a compromise. Kat had wanted to call the magazine *All the Rage,* but the board was put off by the vibrations of anger in the word "rage." They thought it was too feminist, of all things. "It's a *forties* sound," Kat said. "Forties is *back*. Don't you get it?" But they didn't. They wanted to call it *Or.* French for "gold" and blatant enough in its values, but without any base note, as Kat told them. They sawed off at *Felice,* which had qualities each side wanted. It was vaguely French-sounding, it meant "happy" (so much less threatening than "rage"), and, although you couldn't expect the others to notice, for Kat it had a feline bouquet that counteracted the laciness. She had it done in hot pink lipstick-scrawl, which helped some. She could live with it, but it had not been her first love.

This battle has been fought and refought over every innovation in design, every new angle Kat's tried to bring in, every innocuous bit of semi-kink. There was a big row over a spread that did lingerie, half pulled off and with broken glass perfume bottles strewn on the floor. There was an uproar over the two nouveau-stockinged legs, one tied to the leg of a chair with a third, different-colored stocking. They had not understood the man's three-hundred-dollar leather gloves positioned ambiguously around a neck.

And so it has gone on, for five years.

AFTER GERALD HAS LEFT, Kat paces her living room. Pace, pace. Her stitches pull. She's not looking forward to her solitary dinner of microwaved leftovers. She's not sure now why she came back here, to this flat burg beside the polluted inland sea. Was it Ger? Ludicrous thought, but no longer out of the question. Is he the reason she stays, despite her growing impatience with him?

40   He's no longer fully rewarding. They've learned each other too well, they take shortcuts now; their time together has shrunk from whole stolen, rolling, and sensuous afternoons to a few hours snatched between work and dinnertime. She no longer knows what she wants from him. She tells herself she's worth more, she should branch out; but she doesn't see other men, she can't, somehow. She's tried once or twice, but it didn't work. Sometimes she goes out to dinner or a flick with one of the gay designers. She likes the gossip.

Maybe she misses London. She feels caged, in this country, in this city, in this room. She could start with the room, she could open a window. It's too stuffy in here. There's an undertone of formaldehyde, from Hairball's bottle. The flowers she got for the operation are mostly wilted, all except Gerald's from today. Come to think of it, why didn't he send her any at the hospital? Did he forget, or was it a message?

"Hairball," she says, "I wish you could talk. I could have a more intelligent conversation with you than with most of the losers in this turkey farm." Hairball's baby teeth glint in the light; it looks as if it's about to speak.

Kat feels her own forehead. She wonders if she's running a temperature. Something ominous is going on behind her back. There haven't been enough phone calls from the magazine; they've been able to muddle on without her, which is bad news.

Reigning queens should never go on vacation, or have operations, either. Uneasy lies the head. She has a sixth sense about these things, she's been involved in enough palace coups to know the signs, she has sensitive antennae for the footfalls of impending treachery.

The next morning she pulls herself together, downs an espresso from her mini-machine, picks out an aggressive touch-me-if-you-dare suède outfit in armor gray, and drags herself to the office, although she isn't due in till next week. Surprise, surprise. Whispering knots break up in the corridors, greet her with false welcome as she limps past. She settles herself at her minimalist desk, checks her mail. Her head is pounding, her stitches hurt. Ger gets wind of her arrival; he wants to see her A.S.A.P., and not for lunch.

45 He awaits her in his newly done wheat-on-white office, with the eighteenth-century desk they chose together, the Victorian inkstand, the framed blowups from the magazine, the hands in maroon leather, wrists manacled with pearls, the Hermès scarf twisted into a blindfold, the model's mouth blossoming lusciously beneath it. Some of her best stuff. He's beautifully done up, in a lick-my-neck silk shirt open at the throat, an eat-your-heart-out Italian silk-and-wool loose knit sweater. Oh, cool insouciance. Oh, eyebrow language. He's a money man who lusted after art, and now he's got some, now he is some. Body art. Her art. She's done her job well; he's finally sexy.

He's smooth as lacquer. "I didn't want to break this to you until next week," he says. He breaks it to her. It's the board of directors. They think she's too bizarre, they think she goes way too far. Nothing he could do about it, although naturally he tried.

Naturally. Betrayal. The monster has turned on its own mad scientist. "I gave you life!" she wants to scream at him.

She isn't in good shape. She can hardly stand. She stands, despite his offer of a chair. She sees now what she's wanted, what she's been missing. Gerald is what she's been missing: the stable, unfashionable, previous, tight-assed Gerald. Not Ger, not the one she's made in her own image. The other one, before he got ruined. The Gerald with a house and a small child and a picture of his wife in a silver frame on his desk. She wants to be in that silver frame. She wants the child. She's been robbed.

"And who is my lucky replacement?" she says. She needs a cigarette, but does not want to reveal her shaking hands.

50   "Actually, it's me," he says, trying for modesty.

This is too absurd. Gerald couldn't edit a phone book. "You?" she says faintly. She has the good sense not to laugh.

"I've always wanted to get out of the money end of things here," he says, "into the creative area. I knew you'd understand, since it can't be you at any rate. I knew you'd prefer someone who could, well, sort of build on your foundations." Pompous asshole. She looks at his neck. She longs for him, hates herself for it, and is powerless.

The room wavers. He slides toward her across the wheat-colored broadloom, takes her by the gray suède upper arms. "I'll write you a good reference," he says. "Don't worry about that. Of course, we can still see one another. I'd miss our afternoons."

"Of course," she says. He kisses her, a voluptuous kiss, or it would look like one to a third party, and she lets him. *In a pig's ear.*

55   She makes it home in a taxi. The driver is rude to her and gets away with it; she doesn't have the energy. In her mailbox is an engraved invitation: Ger and Cheryl are having a drinks party, tomorrow evening. Postmarked five days ago. Cheryl is behind the times.

Kat undresses, runs a shallow bath. There's not much to drink around here, there's nothing to sniff or smoke. What an oversight; she's stuck with herself. There are other jobs. There are other men, or that's the theory. Still, something's been ripped out of her. How could this have happened—to her? When knives have been slated for backs, she's always done the stabbing. Any headed her way she's seen coming in time, and thwarted. Maybe she's losing her edge.

She stares into the bathroom mirror, assesses her face in the misted glass. A face of the eighties, a mask face, a bottom-line face; push the weak to the wall and grab what you can. But now it's the nineties. Is she out of style, so soon? She's only thirty-five, and she's already losing track of what people ten years younger are thinking. That could be fatal. As times goes by, she'll have to race faster and faster to keep up, and for what? Part of the life she should have had is just a gap, it isn't there, it's nothing. What can be salvaged from it, what can be redone, what can be done at all?

When she climbs out of the tub after her sponge bath, she almost falls. She has a fever, no doubt about it. Inside her something is leaking, or else festering; she can hear it, like a dripping tap. A running sore, a sore from running so hard. She should go to the emergency ward at some hospital, get herself shot up with antibiotics. Instead, she lurches into the living room, takes Hairball down from the mantelpiece in its bottle, places it on the coffee table. She sits cross-legged, listens. Filaments wave. She can hear a kind of buzz, like bees at work.

She'd asked the doctor if it could have started as a child, a fertilized egg that escaped somehow and got into the wrong place. No, said the doctor. Some people thought this kind of tumor was present in seedling form from birth, or before it. It might be the woman's undeveloped twin. What *they* really were was unknown. They had many kinds of tissue, though. Even brain tissue. Though of course all of these tissues lack structure.

60   Still, sitting here on the rug looking in at it, she pictures it as a child. It has come out of her, after all. It is flesh of her flesh. Her child with Gerald, her thwarted child, not allowed to grow normally. Her warped child, taking its revenge.

"Hairball," she says. "You're so ugly. Only a mother could love you." She feels sorry for it. She feels loss. Tears run down her face. Crying is not something she does, not normally, not lately.

Hairball speaks to her, without words. It is irreducible, it has the texture of reality, it is not an image. What it tells her is everything she's never wanted to hear about herself. This is new knowledge, dark and precious and necessary. It cuts.

She shakes her head. What are you doing, sitting on the floor and talking to a hairball? You are sick, she tells herself. Take a Tylenol and go to bed.

THE NEXT DAY SHE FEELS A LITTLE BETTER. Dania from layout calls her and makes dovelike, sympathetic coos at her, and wants to drop by during lunch hour to take a look at her aura. Kat tells her to come off it. Dania gets huffy, and says that Kat's losing her job is a price for immoral behavior in a previous life. Kat tells her to stuff it; anyway, she'd done enough immoral behavior in this life to account for the whole thing. "Why are you so full of hate?" asks Dania. She doesn't say it like a point she's making, she sounds truly baffled.

65   "I don't know," says Kat. It's a straight answer.

After she hangs up she paces the floor. She's crackling inside, like hot fat under the broiler. What she's thinking about is Cheryl, bustling about her cozy house, preparing for the party. Cheryl fiddles with her freeze-framed hair, positions an overloaded vase of flowers, fusses about the caterers. Gerald comes in, kisses her lightly on the cheek. A connubial scene. His con-science is nicely washed. The witch is dead, his foot is on the body, the trophy; he's had his dirty fling, he's ready now for the rest of his life.

Kat takes a taxi to the David Wood Food Shop and buys two dozen chocolate truffles. She has them put into an oversized box, then into an oversized bag with the store logo on it. Then she goes home and takes Hairball out of its bottle. She drains it in the kitchen strainer and pats it damp-dry, tenderly, with paper towels. She sprinkles it with powdered cocoa, which forms a brown pasty crust. It still smells like formaldehyde, so she wraps it in Saran Wrap and then in tinfoil, and then in pink tissue paper, which she ties with a mauve bow. She places it in the David Wood Box in a bed of shredded tissue, with the truffles nestled around. She closes the box, tapes it, puts it into the bag, stuffs several sheets of pink paper on top. It's her gift, valuable and dangerous. It's her messenger, but the message it will deliver is its own. It will tell the truth, to whoever asks. It's right that Gerald should have it; after all, it's his child, too.

She prints on the card, "Gerald, Sorry I couldn't be with you. This is all the rage. Love, K."

When evening has fallen and the party must be in full swing, she calls a delivery taxi. Cheryl will not distrust anything that arrives in such an expensive bag. She will open it in public, in front of everyone. There will be distress, there will be questions. Secrets will be unearthed. There will be pain. After that, everything will go way too far.

70   She is not well; her heart is pounding, space is wavering once more. But outside the window it's snowing—the soft, damp, windless flakes of her childhood. She puts on her coat and goes out, foolishly. She intends to walk just to the corner, but when she reaches the corner she goes on. The snow melts against her face like small fingers touching. She has done an outrageous thing, but she doesn't feel guilty. She feels light and peaceful and filled with charity, and temporarily without a name.

Kazuo Ishiguro

Kazuo Ishiguro has published several novels including, *The Remains of the Day. When We Were Orphans,* and *The Unconsoled.*

A Family Supper

FUGU IS A FISH CAUGHT OFF THE PACIFIC SHORES OF JAPAN. The fish has held a special significance for me ever since my mother died after eating one. The poison resides in the sex glands of the fish, inside two fragile bags. These bags must be removed with caution when preparing the fish, for any clumsiness will result in the poison leaking into the veins. Regrettably, it is not easy to tell whether or not this operation has been carried out successfully. The proof is, as it were, in the eating.

Fugu poisoning is hideously painful and almost always fatal. If the fish has been eaten during the evening, the victim is usually overtaken by pain during his sleep. He rolls about in agony for a few hours and is dead by morning. The fish became extremely popular in Japan after the war. Until stricter regulations were imposed, it was all the rage to perform the hazardous gutting operation in one's own kitchen, then to invite neighbors and friends round for the feast.

At the time of my mother's death, I was living in California. My relationship with my parents had become somewhat strained

around that period and consequently I did not learn of the circumstances of her death until I returned to Tokyo two years
later. Apparently, my mother had always refused to eat fugu, but
on this particular occasion she had made an exception, having
been invited by an old school friend whom she was anxious not
to offend. It was my father who supplied me with the details as we
drove from the airport to his house in the Kamakura district.
When we finally arrived, it was nearing the end of a sunny
autumn day.

"Did you eat on the plane?" my father asked. We were sitting
on the tatami floor of his tearoom.

5   "They gave me a light snack."

"You must be hungry. We'll eat as soon as Kikuko arrives."

My father was a formidable-looking man with a large stony
jaw and furious black eyebrows. I think now, in retrospect, that
he much resembled Chou En-lai, although he would not have
cherished such a comparison, being particularly proud of the
pure samurai blood that ran in the family. His general presence
was not one that encouraged relaxed conversation; neither were
things helped much by his odd way of stating each remark as if it
were the concluding one. In fact, as I sat opposite him that afternoon, a boyhood memory came back to me of the time he had
struck me several times around the head for "chattering like an
old woman." Inevitably, our conversation since my arrival at the
airport had been punctuated by long pauses.

"I'm sorry to hear about the firm," I said when neither of us
had spoken for some time. He nodded gravely.

"In fact, the story didn't end there," he said. "After the
firm's collapse, Watanabe killed himself. He didn't wish to live
with the disgrace."

10   "I see."

"We were partners for seventeen years. A man of principle
and honor. I respected him very much."

"Will you go into business again?" I asked.

"I am . . . in retirement. I'm too old to involve myself in new
ventures now. Business these days has become so different.

Dealing with foreigners. Doing things their way. I don't understand how we've come to this. Neither did Watanabe." He
sighed. "A fine man. A man of principle."

The tearoom looked out over the garden. From where I sat
I could make out the ancient well that as a child I had believed to
be haunted. It was just visible now through the thick foliage. The
sun had sunk low and much of the garden had fallen into
shadow.

15   "I'm glad in any case that you've decided to come back," my
father said. "More than a short visit, I hope."

"I'm not sure what my plans will be."

"I, for one, am prepared to forget the past. Your mother,
too, was always ready to welcome you back—upset as she was by
your behavior."

"I appreciate your sympathy. As I say, I'm not sure what my
plans are."

"I've come to believe now that there were no evil intentions
in your mind," my father continued. "You were swayed by certain . . . influences. Like so many others."

20   "Perhaps we should forget it, as you suggest."

"As you will. More tea?"

Just then a girl's voice came echoing through the house.

"At last." My father rose to his feet. "Kikuko has arrived."

Despite our difference in years, my sister and I had always
been close. Seeing me again seemed to make her excessively
excited, and for a while she did nothing but giggle nervously.
But she calmed down somewhat when my father started to question her about Osaka and her university. She answered him with
short, formal replies. She in turn asked me a few questions, but
she seemed inhibited by the fear that her questions might lead to
awkward topics. After a while, the conversation had become even
sparser than prior to Kikuko's arrival. Then my father stood up,
saying: "I must attend to the supper. Please excuse me for being
burdened by such matters. Kikuko will look after you."

25   My sister relaxed quite visibly once he had left the room.
Within a few minutes, she was chatting freely about her friends

in Osaka and about her classes at university. Then quite
suddenly she decided we should walk in the garden and went
striding out onto the veranda. We put on some straw sandals that
had been left along the veranda rail and stepped out into the
garden. The light in the garden had grown very dim.

"I've been dying for a smoke for the last half hour," she said,
lighting a cigarette.

"Then why didn't you smoke?"

She made a furtive gesture back toward the house, then
grinned mischievously.

"Oh, I see," I said.

"Guess what? I've got a boyfriend now."

"Oh, yes?"

"Except I'm wondering what to do. I haven't made up my
mind yet."

"Quite understandable."

"You see, he's making plans to go to America. He wants me
to go with him as soon as I finish studying."

"I see. And you want to go to America?"

"If we go, we're going to hitchhike." Kikuko waved a thumb
in front of my face. "People say it's dangerous, but I've done it
in Osaka and it's fine."

"I see. So what is it you're unsure about?"

We were following a narrow path that wound through the
shrubs and finished by the old well. As we walked, Kikuko persisted in taking unnecessarily theatrical puffs on her cigarette.

"Well, I've got lots of friends now in Osaka. I like it there. I'm
not sure I want to leave them all behind just yet. And Suichi . . .
I like him, but I'm not sure I want to spend so much time with
him. Do you understand?"

"Oh, perfectly."

She grinned again, then skipped on ahead of me until she
had reached the well. "Do you remember," she said as I came
walking up to her, "how you used to say this well was haunted?"

"Yes, I remember."

We both peered over the side.

"Mother always told me it was the old woman from the vegetable store you'd seen that night," she said. "But I never
believed her and never came out here alone."

45   "Mother used to tell me that too. She even told me once the old woman had confessed to being the ghost. Apparently, she'd been taking a shortcut through our garden. I imagine she had some trouble clambering over these walls."

Kikuko gave a giggle. She then turned her back to the well, casting her gaze about the garden.

"Mother never really blamed you, you know," she said, in a new voice. I remained silent. "She always used to say to me how it was their fault, hers and Father's, for not bringing you up correctly. She used to tell me how much more careful they'd been with me, and that's why I was so good." She looked up and the mischievous grin had returned to her face. "Poor Mother," she said.

"Yes. Poor Mother."

"Are you going back to California?"

50   "I don't know. I'll have to see."

"What happened to . . . to her? To Vicki?"

"That's all finished with," I said. "There's nothing much left for me now in California."

"Do you think I ought to go there?"

"Why not? I don't know. You'll probably like it." I glanced toward the house. "Perhaps we'd better go in soon. Father might need a hand with the supper."

55   But my sister was once more peering down into the well. "I can't see any ghosts," she said. Her voice echoed a little.

"Is Father very upset about his firm collapsing?"

"Don't know. You never can tell with Father." Then suddenly she straightened up and turned to me. "Did he tell you about old Watanabe? What he did?"

"I heard he committed suicide."

"Well, that wasn't all. He took his whole family with him. His wife and his two little girls."

60   "Oh, yes?"

"Those two beautiful little girls. He turned on the gas while they were all asleep. Then he cut his stomach with a meat knife."

"Yes, Father was just telling me how Watanabe was a man of principle."

"Sick." My sister turned back to the well.

"Careful. You'll fall right in."

65 "I can't see any ghost," she said. "You were lying to me all that time."

"But I never said it lived down the well."

"Where is it then?"

We both looked around at the trees and shrubs. The daylight had almost gone. Eventually I pointed to a small clearing some ten yards away.

"Just there I saw it. Just there."

70 We stared at the spot.

"What did it look like?"

"I couldn't see very well. It was dark."

"But you must have seen something."

"It was an old woman. She was just standing there, watching me."

75 We kept staring at the spot as if mesmerized.

"She was wearing a white kimono," I said. "Some of her hair had come undone. It was blowing around a little."

Kikuko pushed her elbow against my arm. "Oh, be quiet. You're trying to frighten me all over again." She trod on the remains of her cigarette, then for a brief moment stood regarding it with a perplexed expression. She kicked some pine needles over it, then once more displayed her grin. "Let's see if supper's ready," she said.

We found my father in the kitchen. He gave us a quick glance, then carried on with what he was doing.

"Father's become quite a chef since he's had to manage on his own," Kikuko said with a laugh.

80 He turned and looked at my sister coldly. "Hardly a skill I'm proud of," he said. "Kikuko, come here and help."

For some moments my sister did not move. Then she stepped forward and took an apron hanging from a drawer.

"Just these vegetables need cooking now," he said to her. "The rest just needs watching." Then he looked up and regarded me strangely for some seconds. "I expect you want to look around the house," he said eventually. He put down the chopsticks he had been holding. "It's a long time since you've seen it."

As we left the kitchen I glanced toward Kikuko, but her back was turned.

"She's a good girl," my father said.

85   I followed my father from room to room. I had forgotten how large the house was. A panel would slide open and another room would appear. But the rooms were all startlingly empty. In one of the rooms the lights did not come on, and we stared at the stark walls and tatami in the pale light that came from the windows.

"This house is too large for a man to live in alone," my father said. "I don't have much use for most of these rooms now."

But eventually my father opened the door to a room packed full of books and papers. There were flowers in vases and pictures on the walls. Then I noticed something on a low table in the corner of the room. I came nearer and saw it was a plastic model of a battleship, the kind constructed by children. It had been placed on some newspaper; scattered around it were assorted pieces of gray plastic.

My father gave a laugh. He came up to the table and picked up the model.

"Since the firm folded," he said, "I have a little more time on my hands." He laughed again, rather strangely. For a moment his face looked almost gentle. "A little more time."

90   "That seems odd," I said. "You were always so busy."

"Too busy, perhaps." He looked at me with a small smile. "Perhaps I should have been a more attentive father."

I laughed. He went on contemplating his battleship. Then he looked up. "I hadn't meant to tell you this, but perhaps it's best that I do. It's my belief that your mother's death was no accident. She had many worries. And some disappointments."

We both gazed at the plastic battleship.

"Surely," I said eventually, "my mother didn't expect me to live here forever."

95   "Obviously you don't see. You don't see how it is for some parents. Not only must they lose their children, they must lose them to things they don't understand." He spun the battleship in his fingers. "These little gunboats here could have been better glued, don't you think?"

"Perhaps. I think it looks fine."

"During the war I spent some time on a ship rather like this. But my ambition was always the air force. I figured it like this: If your ship was struck by the enemy, all you could do was struggle

326 | Kazuo Ishiguro

in the water hoping for a lifeline. But in an airplane—well, there was always the final weapon." He put the model back onto the table. "I don't suppose you believe in war."

"Not particularly."

He cast an eye around the room. "Supper should be ready by now," he said. "You must be hungry."

100   Supper was waiting in a dimly lit room next to the kitchen. The only source of light was a big lantern that hung over the table, casting the rest of the room in shadow. We bowed to each other before starting the meal.

There was little conversation. When I made some polite comment about the food, Kikuko giggled a little. Her earlier nervousness seemed to have returned to her. My father did not speak for several minutes. Finally he said:

"It must feel strange for you, being back in Japan."

"Yes, it is a little strange."

"Already, perhaps, you regret leaving America."

105   "A little. Not so much. I didn't leave behind much. Just some empty rooms."

"I see."

I glanced across the table. My father's face looked stony and forbidding in the half-light. We ate on in silence.

Then my eye caught something at the back of the room. At first I continued eating, then my hands became still. The others noticed and looked at me. I went on gazing into the darkness past my father's shoulder.

"Who is that? In that photograph there?"

110   "Which photograph?" My father turned slightly, trying to follow my gaze.

"The lowest one. The old woman in the white kimono."

My father put down his chopsticks. He looked first at the photograph, then at me.

"Your mother." His voice had become very hard. "Can't you recognize your own mother?"

"My mother. You see, it's dark. I can't see it very well."

115   No one spoke for a few seconds, then Kikuko rose to her feet. She took the photograph down from the wall, came back to the table, and gave it to me.

"She looks a lot older," I said.

"It was taken shortly before her death," said my father.

"It was the dark. I couldn't see very well."

I looked up and noticed my father holding out a hand. I gave him the photograph. He looked at it intently, then held it toward Kikuko. Obediently, my sister rose to her feet once more and returned the picture to the wall.

120   There was a large pot left unopened at the center of the table. When Kikuko had seated herself again, my father reached forward and lifted the lid. A cloud of steam rose up and curled toward the lantern. He pushed the pot a little toward me.

"You must be hungry," he said. One side of his face had fallen into shadow.

"Thank you." I reached forward with my chopsticks. The steam was almost scalding. "What is it?"

"Fish."

"It smells very good."

125   In the soup were strips of fish that had curled almost into balls. I picked one out and brought it to my bowl.

"Help yourself. There's plenty."

"Thank you." I took a little more, then pushed the pot toward my father. I watched him take several pieces to his bowl. Then we both watched as Kikuko served herself.

My father bowed slightly. "You must be hungry," he said again. He took some fish to his mouth and started to eat. Then I, too, chose a piece and put it in my mouth. It felt soft, quite fleshy against my tongue.

The three of us ate in silence. Several minutes went by. My father lifted the lid and once more steam rose up. We all reached forward and helped ourselves.

130   "Here," I said to my father, "you have this last piece."

"Thank you."

When we had finished the meal, my father stretched out his arms and yawned with an air of satisfaction. "Kikuko," he said, "prepare a pot of tea, please."

My sister looked at him, then left the room without comment. My father stood up.

"Let's retire to the other room. It's rather warm in here."

135   I got to my feet and followed him into the tearoom. The large sliding windows had been left open, bringing in a breeze from the garden. For a while we sat in silence.

"Father," I said, finally.

"Yes?"

"Kikuko tells me Watanabe-san took his whole family with him."

My father lowered his eyes and nodded. For some moments he seemed deep in thought. "Watanabe was very devoted to his work," he said at last. "The collapse of the firm was a great blow to him. I fear it must have weakened his judgment."

140   "You think what he did . . . it was a mistake?"

"Why, of course. Do you see it otherwise?"

"No, no. Of course not."

"There are other things besides work," my father said.

"Yes."

145   We fell silent again. The sound of locusts came in from the garden. I looked out into the darkness. The well was no longer visible.

"What do you think you will do now?" my father asked. "Will you stay in Japan for a while?"

"To be honest, I hadn't thought that far ahead."

"If you wish to stay here, I mean here in this house, you would be very welcome. That is, if you don't mind living with an old man."

"Thank you. I'll have to think about it."

150   I gazed out once more into the darkness.

"But of course," said my father, "this house is so dreary now. You'll no doubt return to America before long."

"Perhaps. I don't know yet."

"No doubt you will."

For some time my father seemed to be studying the back of his hands. Then he looked up and sighed.

155   "Kikuko is due to complete her studies next spring," he said. "Perhaps she will want to come home then. She's a good girl."

"Perhaps she will."

"Things will improve then."

"Yes, I'm sure they will."

We fell silent once more, waiting for Kikuko to bring the tea.

Ann Beattie

Ann Beattie is a frequent contributor to *The New Yorker*. Her books of stories include *Distortions, Secrets and Surprises, Jacklighting,* and *The Burning House*. Among her novels are *Chilly Scenes of Winter, Falling in Place,* and *Picturing Will*.

Such Occasions

LET ME TELL YOU WHAT HAPPENED TO ME WHEN MY HUSBAND DIED and my husband's brother came to help me pack for my move to Toronto. Actually, he came not once but three times. The first time he kept excusing himself from the task of packing clothes to go into the bathroon and cry. The second time it was an unusually sunny day, so we took a walk. During the walk he told me about all the women he had jilted in the past ten years. The third time he came with a woman he had not yet provoked into hating him. She was a woman in her early forties, though I thought she looked younger and said so when she told me her age. Her name was Sandy, but he called her Spud because when they first met, she had just returned from a Bermuda vacation and was as brown as a potato. She had some money. You could tell from the little details. For example, an extremely nice keychain, instead of a metal ring. A keychain with a little gold dog that dangled from it, and a collar that sparkled with blue and green stones. Her nails were painted a very nice shade of pink. Her eyeglasses had sidepieces attached almost at the bottom of the frame. She drove to the house, with George in the passenger seat. The car was a black Lincoln.

"I never know what to say in situations like this, so I'm going to make you feel my heart, so you'll know how upset your position makes me," she said.

Before I could say anything, she put my hand over her heart and pressed lightly. That was when I saw her manicured nails. Underneath our hands, her heart was beating hard.

"Aaaah," George said, walking past us. "If her heart's going haywire it's because she almost creamed a cat that ran in front of the car."

5   She looked after him. "That didn't happen," she said to me. "There was no cat. Though he may not know it, there was a period of my life when my cat Cleopatra was my best friend, and she *was* killed on a highway in Sarasota. She was only a cat—well: she wasn't only a cat, because I loved her—but after I saw her run over I had to take anti-depressants for a year. I had to go to a doctor and get medication. So I can only imagine what you're going through."

She put her car keys on the hall table. About a dozen collapsible cartons were leaning against the table. They were for dishes, but for some reason I'd decided to dismantle the kitchen last. I hadn't even taken the dish boxes in there.

"I appreciate your concern," I said. "People have been very kind. I've never known what to say in such situations myself."

"How many situations have there been?" George called from the living room. He'd put on the t.v. to see what the score was in the football game. He knew I hated sports, so after he heard the score he switched off the t.v.

"What are you asking?" I said, when George re-appeared in the hallway. "How many people I've known who've died?"

10   "No. How many times you've had to say something to the relatives."

I thought. "More times than I can count."

"This is a cruel line of questioning," Sandy said.

"Let me make my point," George said. "People always want to rush in before the point's even made. My point is that if there have been that many such occasions when you've been on the spot having to offer sympathy, then doing that is just a part of life. Death is just a part of life. Somebody dies, and you find that you're saying again and again that you're sorry. Life goes on."

"Well," Sandy said, "I was trying to relate it to my own experience."

15   George looked at me. "I heard what you were saying from the other room, Spuds. You might be off the drugs, but that cat creeps into conversation every day."

The phone rang. I went to the kitchen to answer it. The kitchen looked cozy, compared to the other rooms. Only cartons stacked beside the stove gave the impression that anyone was moving.

It was the real estate lady, Marsha Feinberg, on the phone. She had a couple she wanted to bring by. They were in the neighborhood, and she hadn't been able to reach me earlier. That was because I had been out buying more packing supplies.

"Well," I said, "my brother-in-law and his friend. . . ."

"Intended!" George hollered from the hallway.

20   I did a double-take. His intended? He had told me a few days before that his new strategy was to drive women away on the third date, if it hadn't happened before. He had not mentioned Sandy to me until the night before, when he said he would bring a friend. Frankly, I had expected a man—someone strong, to help us pack.

"All right?" Marsha said. A little edge crept into her voice. "I'm calling from a pay phone at a gas station."

"It's fine," I said, "but I'd rather not leave, if you don't mind. We can all sit in the kitchen while you go through the house."

"Tie up the dog," Marsha said.

"I don't have a dog," I said.

25   "Of course you don't," she said. "It's awful that I just say that reflexively. It's because I, myself, am afraid of dogs."

There was a popping sound, and the dial tone began to hum. It was exactly the sound a cork made when it popped out of a wooden gun. My husband had had one of those toys, which he often brought out at parties. I suddenly realized that in going through his things, I had not found the gun.

George and Sandy came into the kitchen. She pulled out a chair and sat down, while he drew a kettle of water and turned on the electric stove.

"That was the real estate lady," I said. "She's bringing some people by who want to look at the house." I looked at George, who was lifting the kettle to make sure the burner was heating up. He was addicted to coffee, and always waited impatiently for the water to boil.

"I'll tell them I'm the man of the house, and any dickering that needs to be done should be brought to my attention."

30   "Honey," Sandy said quietly. "That's a little insensitive."

"Please don't say anything at all when they're going through the house," I said.

George poured some water out of the kettle and put it back on the burner. He muttered something I didn't catch.

Sandy looked at me. Her eyes darted to George and then back again. "I guess he's not the most romantic person in the world," Sandy said. "That wouldn't have been my ideal way to announce our engagement."

"She's not the newspaper, she's my sister-in-law," George said.

35   I was taken aback. I was partly taken aback that after I hung up, I had put what George said about Sandy being his intended out of my mind. I looked at her hand. There was no ring. There was only a watch on her wrist, and those pretty pink nails.

"Congratulations," I said. "I must admit, I wasn't expecting to hear news like that today."

At the stove, George said something that I couldn't hear.

"Instead of having an engagement party, I'll be packing your dishes," Sandy said. "I guess as we get older, there's only the reality of our everyday lives to deal with."

"That's not why I'm marrying you," George said. "I'm marrying you because you don't believe any such thing. You think there's a whole world out there to explore, and that people who adhere to routines are fools."

40   Sandy looked at me. "That's not exactly the way I'd sum up my philosophy," she said.

The kettle whistled as there was a knock on the door. I got up, missing both what Sandy said and what George said.

Marsha Feinberg shook my hand enthusiastically. It seemed like she might lose herself in the handshake. As if once she gripped my hand, that became the day's business, instead of showing the house. She gave my hand a final squeeze and dropped it so I could shake hands with the man and woman who stood just inside the doorway. As he shook my hand, the man reached behind him and closed the door. They were the Merchants—Bud and Nancy Merchant.

"If you have any questions, we'll be in the kitchen," I said. "I hope you can see the house all right, in spite of all the boxes."

"Our house is all boxes, too," Nancy Merchant said. "We're packing to move. We sold our house and we have to be out by the first of next month. There's no reason to hide our desperation, I suppose."

45 "Oh, darling," Bud Merchant said. "I'd hardly say we were desperate."

"A previous housing inspection revealed that a boa constrictor was living under the porch of a house the Merchants had previously considered," Marsha Feinberg said.

"Brrrrr," Nancy Merchant said. "I could never live in a house after an inspection turned up something like that."

"Someone's pet that crawled away," Marsha Feinberg said.

"Enough to make you wonder if alligators really are crawling around in the sewer system," Bud Merchant said.

50 Nancy Merchant put her hands to her lips."I love to razz her," Bud Merchant said. "She's a great one to kid with."

"Shall we?" Marsha Feinberg said, handing each of them a photocopy of the listing with a picture on top. It looked more like the mark left by a muddy foot on a doormat than a photograph of the house.

"Would you like to put your coats on the sofa?" I said.

When I looked at the sofa, I saw for the first time a small box wrapped in shiny paper and tied with a bow on the seat cushion. The volume had been turned off the t.v., but the picture was still on. Football players with enormous shoulders huddled, helmet to helmet.

"What's the score?" Bud Merchant said.

55   "23/16," George hollered from the kitchen.

Marsha Feinberg looked startled.

"My brother-in-law is visiting," I said. "I believe I mentioned that on the phone."

"Somebody who was backing up toward the air hose almost
ran over me," Marsha Feinberg said. "I had to jump out of the
way. I'm afraid I wasn't listening to what you said. It scared the
wits out of me when that man almost backed into my legs. You
did say it was an opportune time to stop by, didn't you?"

"Yes," I said.

60   "The house is on the market because the occupant is moving
to Canada," Marsha Feinberg said. "Did I mention that on the
way over?"

Nancy and Bud Merchant nodded.

"This is a very desirable location," Marsha Feinberg said.
She swept her arm toward the staircase. "Shall we ascend and
work our way down?" she said. As she started to climb, she said,
"There are thermal panes in the upstairs bedroom windows."

I could remember my husband cursing as he installed them.
He always cursed when he worked around the house. He was
most obscene when the use of a drill was required.

In the kitchen, George and Sandy were sipping Maxwell
House. There was powder in my cup, but he had not yet poured
the water.

65   "Ah, God," George said. "Last month he was alive and sitting at the table, sitting right where I'm sitting now. What do you
think of that bro of mine? Wouldn't put his back to a doorway.
Wouldn't face any way in a room but straight out. It was bad for
you," he said, twirling his finger through the powder in my cup.
"But hey: just because he wouldn't sit in a movie house doesn't
mean we can't all go to the movies today. Start you in on years of
catching up. What do you say we go to an early movie when the
vultures stop swirling?"

"George!" Sandy said. "They're perfectly nice people looking for a house to buy. *You* didn't want to rent the house. I was
there when she called and asked if you wanted to rent the house,
and you encouraged her to put it right on the market. Now she's
in the position of moving to Toronto with no safety net. If she

doesn't like Toronto, it's not as if she can ever come back to her lovely house."

George slammed his fist on the table. "What are you *talking* about?" he said. "I work thirty miles from where this house is located. I can *walk* to work from where I live. I wonder if you don't just have big ideas about living in an expensive, fancy house like your Sugar Daddy had down there in Sarasota. But I'm not him. I'm a hard-working man who's got no time to commute. It's not my fault my brother up and walked in front of a truck."

Sandy burst into tears. "I resent that!" she said. "I resent the implication that I've ever told anyone what to do with his life. You just want to drive me off. With your outspokenness, you just want to drive me off."

Over my head, something went thud-thud-thud. It didn't take long to realize it was Marsha Feinberg, jumping on the floor, telling us to keep it down. I didn't know whether to laugh or cry. Whatever I did, I'd either be joining Sandy, who was crying, or George, who had thrown his head back and had started to laugh loudly, letting the laughter shake his body until his head lolled sideways and he began to hiccough. He put his hand over his eyes and shook his head from side to side.

70   "We could have used your real estate lady when everybody was weeping and wailing at the funeral," George said. "I said at the time somebody was needed to keep order." He hiccoughed again. Then he sat up straight and looked at Sandy.

Through her tears, she looked at him coldly. "Apologize to me for what you said," she said. "Apologize to me, and apologize to her."

"What?" he said. He shrugged. "Her husband did walk in front of a truck."

Then Sandy turned to me. "I don't know how you can stand this," she said. "I know you must be very upset, but a woman has got to stand up for herself in the world. He's trying to trivialize your husband's death."

"If a woman has to stand up, stand up," George said.

75   I looked at the little pile of instant coffee in the bottom of my cup. "Could you get me some water, George?" I said.

"You're both crazy!" Sandy screeched, getting out of her chair so fast she stumbled. "Let me tell you, you are not the people I want to associate with for the rest of my life. No indeed, I do not. I'm going to walk right out the front door and thank the Lord that I drove my own car here today, so I don't even have to sit beside you, George, on my way home."

"There's cabs," George said. "If the good Lord—or probably your Sugar Daddy—hadn't provided you with your Lincoln Continental, you could always have called a cab."

She threw the cold coffee that remained in the cup at George. Then she ran in a wobbly way out of the kitchen. She slammed the front door behind her.

Upstairs, all was quiet. Then an eerie wailing began. At first I thought it was Sandy, out on the front lawn, but then I realized it had to be either Marsha Feinberg or Nancy Merchant, upstairs. When I heard Marsha Feinberg's voice, I knew it was Nancy.

"What is it?" Nancy cried. "What is it that every time we walk into a house something terrible happens. Are we cursed?" There was more crying. Then she repeated the question: "Are we cursed?"

Bud Merchant began to talk, but his voice was just a dull hum; it was constant, like an undertow, but no more distinct.

I went out into the hallway. I turned on the table light. I cleared my throat. Eventually Marsha Feinberg came down the stairs, but Bud Merchant's talk continued its ebb and flow.

"They weren't going to buy this house anyway," Marsha Feinberg said quietly. She stepped off the last step. We stood in the hallway together. "Do you know what it's like to constantly be subjected to other people's trouble?" she said. "If the sellers don't confide in you, then the buyers do. Mrs. Merchant is a very unstable woman. He wants an old house—and that's what he'll buy, and what she'll live in—but I had to show them your house because Mrs. Merchant wants a newer house. She's phobic about dirt. Everything has to be clean. And it was just my luck that she was standing on the front lawn of that other house when the inspector came out of the crawl space, running for his life. He ran into me with such force I almost fell backwards.

Mrs. Merchant was so frightened, before she even knew what he was frightened about, that she jumped and I had to steady her or she would have toppled to the ground. Something like that might be funny in a movie, but in real life it's only depressing. Everyone is so desperate and out of control. It was a very bad idea to show this house when you and your . . ."

"Brother-in-law," I said.

85 "Brother-in-law," she said. "When you and your brother-in-law were present."

From the way she said the words, I could tell she did not think that George was my brother-in-law. But he certainly was. He was the same brother-in-law who always ruined holiday dinners by arriving late, who let all the houseplants die the one time we had him house-sit when we had a two-week vacation. It was the only two-week vacation my husband ever had. They always lied to him and said he'd get two weeks, but in the end the most he ever got was ten days. On the two-week vacation there was no phone, so they couldn't call and ask him to come back. The pressure was too much for him, and they were bringing in younger people and not making them rotate onto the night shift, and I knew he was terribly depressed. He never drank except when things seemed hopeless. He wouldn't have stepped into the path of a delivery van if he hadn't been drunk, and he wouldn't have been drunk if he'd been treated better.

That was why I was happy to see Bud Merchant had his arm around his wife's shoulders when they descended the stairs. There is always too little human kindness. What good is kindness if it's only expressed at funerals, or maybe when someone is hospitalized, or forced into retirement? The value of a hand on the shoulder is much underestimated. Seeing them that way even seemed to quiet down Marsha Feinberg.

"Another day," Bud Merchant said, extending his free hand. His wife wept against his biceps. "Another day we hope to return so we can consider buying your lovely house."

"I'm sorry about the noise," I said, shaking his hand. "Emotions always run high after a funeral."

90 "Her brother-in-law is upset," Marsha Feinberg said. She seemed to be saying it as much to herself as to Bud Merchant.

I opened the front door, switching on the outdoor light so they could find their way down the path to the car.

"Did I hear her mention the movies?" George hollered from the kitchen. "What say we go to the movies?"

I closed the door. The package on the sofa looked quite beautiful. I went a little closer and saw that it had been professionally wrapped.

George came up behind me. "Open it," he said.

95   I said, "This is for me?"

"It was for her," he said. "It was a fail-safe, in case I didn't manage to drive her off some other way."

"Then what would I want with it?"

"Go on," he said. "Open it." He nodded yes. He kept looking from the package to me. "I told her it was a token of our engagement. You were going to watch while the box was opened." He shifted from one foot to the other. In the dim light, he looked like my husband. The same height. The same doggedness about getting something done, if he wanted it done.

I opened the box. Naturally, I was expecting a ring, but instead there was a miniature ball and chain. That, too, was like my husband: their childish enthusiasm for toys. Toys that would be used to play pranks.

100   But who knew why George wanted to drive women away? Who could explain to me why my own husband hadn't stood up for his rights? Who was there—floating up in the sky, or anywhere else—looking down on all this and about to stomp his foot, requesting order?

I got my coat, and George put on his jacket, and the two of us set out, on foot, for the movies.

Outside, it was dark. If there hadn't been so many houses on either side of my house, and lined up across the street facing us, there would not have been enough illumination to walk without moving very gingerly, looking down each time we took a step. But the houses were there: all in a line, as far as we could see. And, as my husband had done with our house, in recent years many people had added shutters to spruce them up. Shutters, and aluminum siding.

Credits

pg. 251 Anya Achtenberg. "Cold Ground" by Anya Achtenberg. Copyright © 1990 by New Letters. Reprinted by permission of the author and *New Letters*. "Cold Ground" was first published in *New Letters*.

pg. 263 Susan Straight. "Two Days Gone" by Susan Straight. Copyright © 1990 by Milkweed Editions. Reprinted by permission of Milkweed Editions. Published in *The North American Review*.

pg. 277 Allen Wier. Broadcast on "The Sound of Writing," a production of the PEN Syndicated Fiction Project and National Public Radio, Fall 1991. Published by permission of the PEN Syndicated Fiction Project. Copyright © 1990 by Allen Wier.

pg. 287 Lisa K. Buchanan. "The Mother Who Never Was" by Lisa K. Buchanan. Copyright © 1990 by Lisa K. Buchanan. Reprinted by permission of the author. "The Mother Who Never Was" first appeared in *Mademoiselle*.

pg. 295 Alberto Alvaro Ríos. First appeared in *Ploughshares*. Copyright © 1990 by Alberto Alvaro Ríos. Reprinted by permission of the author.

pg. 303 Margaret Atwood. Reprinted by permission of Margaret Atwood, first published in *The New Yorker Magazine* September 17, 1990.

pg. 319 Kazuo Ishiguro. First appeared in *Esquire*. Copyright © 1990 by Kazuo Ishiguro. Reprinted by permission of ICM.

pg. 329 Ann Beattie. "Such Occasions" first appeared in *New England Review*. Copyright © 1990 by Ann Beattie. Reprinted by permission.